Ulster Gay

Ulster Gay

Stephen Birkett

Copyright 2009 Stephen Birkett

ISBN 978-1-4452-0580-9

Background

I have been teaching biology in Strabane, in Northern Ireland since 1973. I came out the year I started teaching and soon got involved with Cara Friend, the gay help-line in Belfast. In 1979 I was one of the founder members of Derry Cara-Friend which eventually became Foyle Friend and I was involved with the group until it folded in 2000. Although our main function was as a gay help-line we also got involved in campaigning and education and I attended many 'Campaign for Homosexual Equality' conferences in England in the '70s and '80s. At present I am involved in Strabane and Lifford LGBT Group which works to improve the lives of Lesbian, Gay, Bisexual and Transgendered people in the Strabane Area.

Every gay person has had a battle to fight and all the more so here in conservative Northern Ireland. Working for all that time in the gay rights sphere I have heard many gay people's stories. Most are very personal and they can probably never be told so there's a whole gay history in Northern Ireland that remain unknown.

Thrice Alien was begun in 1988 at a time when the anti-gay hysteria in Britain was becoming very frightening. It was initially conceived as a fantasy, set in a future Britain that had descended into a police state where gay people were being rounded up and put into internment camps; an idea that was being mooted at the time. As I developed the character of Matt I began to realise that I could use his life to chronicle that hidden gay history, so the futuristic fantasy was dropped and the story developed into Matt's odyssey.

It was, perhaps, a mistake to make Matt a biology teacher because people assume he is me. Thank goodness he isn't, although I have evidently used what I know to pad out his character.

Thrice Alien refers to Matt's alienation from Ballycol, the fictional Nationalist town in which he finds himself. This is due to his Englishness, his Protestant background and his homosexuality.

Gay Men's Press published the first part of 'Thrice Alien' under the title 'Ulster Alien' in 1999. It tells of little Matthew Woodhead, the son of an English father and a Northern Irish mother. At primary school he is befriended by Danny, the only Catholic in the class, but the class bully, Alex, constantly tries to break up their friendship. Where Alex fails, the sectarian divide succeeds and the friends are torn apart in their secondary school years. However it's the middle class Willy-John and Aaron, not Alex, who become Matt's new friends at grammar school.

At university the friendship between Danny and Matt is rekindled but Matt is now coming to terms with the fact that he is gay. His only mentor is Piet, a gay Dutchman he meets on holiday. Piet guides him through the difficult process of coming out. His school friends all react differently to his sexuality; Willy-John takes it in his stride, Aaron condemns him with religious fury, Danny takes advantage of his vulnerability and big, rugby playing Alex first censures him, then becomes his lover.

'Ulster Gay' tells Matt's story through the 1980s. A third story, 'Ulster Queens' continues the story into the 1990s and I am currently working on a book to take them into the 2000s.

Stephen Birkett, November 2009
strabanelgb@btinternet.com

Acknowledgements

Patti Christie again proof-read the manuscript and corrected my appalling spelling and grammar. Thanks, Patti.

This book could not have been written if I hadn't had the fortune to know so many gay people in Northern Ireland. I owe a debt to all of them.

Contents

Background v

Acknowledgements vii

Chapter 1	Easter 1981, David Robinson	1
Chapter 2	June 1981, Rathlin Island	11
Chapter 3	November 1981, Alex's Nemesis	19
Chapter 4	November 1981, Feargal Collins	25
Chapter 5	November 1981, The Low Life	31
Chapter 6	1982, Rehabilitation	43
Chapter 7	Spring 1983, Forced Moves	49
Chapter 8	Spring 1983, Chris Mcdaid	55
Chapter 9	Summer 1983, Painful Realities	63
Chapter 10	Autumn 1983, Romance	73
Chapter 11	Spring 1984, Trouble Brewing	83
Chapter 12	Summer 1984, Friends In Turmoil	99
Chapter 13	Autumn 1984, Mary And David	109
Chapter 14	Spring 1985, Damian Kelly	115
Chapter 15	Spring 1985, Dangerous Liaisons	133
Chapter 16	Autumn 1985, Damian's Story	147
Chapter 17	Winter 1985, Oil And Water	161
Chapter 18	Autumn 1986, Storm Clouds	169
Chapter 19	Autumn 1986, Brutality	175
Chapter 20	Spring 1988, Disaster	187
Chapter 21	Winter 1988, The Beginning Of The End	193
Chapter 22	Spring 1989, Bozzy And Con	203

Errata – Chapters 2, 3, 4 & 5 take place in 1982, not 1981

Chapter 23	Summer 1989, Brief Respite	215
Chapter 24	Autumn 1989, Bigots Triumphant	225
Chapter 25	Spring 1990, Betrayal	241
Chapter 26	Spring 1990, Derrylaghan	249
Chapter 27	Summer 1990, Amsterdam	255
Chapter 28	Summer 1990, The End?	265

CHAPTER 1
EASTER 1981, DAVID ROBINSON

The rays of the climbing sun penetrated flimsy hotel curtains and warmed up the room. Shifting half consciously, the smaller of the two sleeping forms freed himself from the clinging sheets. Cooler now, he snuggled into the larger man and drifted back to his dreams. The contrast between them made their intimacy all the more touching. In his mid-twenties, Alexander was big with broad shoulders and an angular, muscular body, its contours accentuated by swathes of dense, black hair. Matt, on the other hand, was slight and fair and, other than a silky patch on his chest, the only sign of hair was a golden aura over his arms and legs in the morning light. A Greek scholar might fancy that they were a war-weary warrior and his youthful neophyte but appearances would be deceptive; they were neither age and youth nor experience and vulnerable innocence.

Matt and Alex had known each other for most of their lives but this friendship was relatively recent. Matt had actually hated Alex at primary school. He thought him a ruffian and a bully and Alex hadn't liked Matt's friendship with Danny; the only Catholic in the class. They hadn't much to do with each other at secondary school either as the terminally middle class Willy-John had occupied Matt's time. However, in sixth form, Matt's homosexuality was awakening and Alex's burgeoning, robust masculinity had drawn Matt to him. It was only after they had left school that their friendship had developed. Matt hadn't questioned the change in dynamic. He'd assumed that they had both changed with maturity and didn't suspect that mutual sexual attraction was drawing them together. But now Matt was irrefutably gay and he was beginning to take pride in being so.

Being a teacher, his first tentative steps to asserting his sexuality had caused him some anguish but, with the help of Piet, a gay Dutchman, his self-esteem had gone from strength to strength. Alex had no such confidence. Matt hadn't even suspected that the strapping lad was anything other than totally straight until they had ended up in bed together one drunken night. Alex had been appalled at what he'd done. Appalled by the implications for his own sexuality, appalled by using a friend and, most of all, appalled because he was a policeman and, in Northern Ireland, sex between men was a crime punishable by life imprisonment.

After that first crazy night of love, Alex had gone out of his way to display his interest in a procession of women. The implication was clear: his experience with Matt was an aberration and he was 'straight' from now on. Not long ago, Matt would have given up on him but Piet's influence was strong and Matt had engineered a quiet tête-a-tête at the Killyhevlin Hotel in Enniskillen. Once alone with his golden boy, all Alex's resolutions had evaporated and he had fallen on Matt like a thirsting man at a crystal fount.

Alex awoke to the gentle pressure of Matt on his chest. Luxuriating in his lover's warm body, he enveloped him in his massive arms and kissed his soft, fine hair. "Morning," Matt yawned.

"Morning," the policeman said sleepily.

"What time're you on duty?"

"Not until this afternoon."

"Good," he murmured snuggling further into Alex's ample torso. He could hear his big heart pounding like a steam hammer. I wonder how much more sleep I'll get this morning, he pondered happily.

Not much, was the answer, but not in the way he had hoped. Alex insisted on vacating the room by ten: "You're not paying for another night just so we can sleep late."

"It wasn't exactly sleeping that I was hoping for!" Matt said impishly.

"You slut!" Alex joked. "Where *did* you learn all these wicked ways?"

"Wouldn't you like to know?"

They drove out to Castle Archdale Forest Park and followed a track that wended its way through heavy summer trees towards Lough Erne. It was a glorious morning. The hum of insects and the quarking of mallard on the nearby lake lulled Matt into a serene happiness.

"When am I going to see you again?" Matt asked.

Alex looked sheepish. "I don't know. I'm still going out with Sandra, you know. I feel really bad about two-timing her... I can't just drop her. I really like her, you know. And I..."

"What?" Matt asked gently. He thought Alex was going out with the nurse for 'cover'.

"Oh! I don't know. I can't explain. You've confused me, Matt. I thought I had it all sorted out and now you've gone and screwed my head up for me."

"I know what I want," Matt said, feeling for his friend's hand.

Alex pulled it out of his grasp: "Not here," he whispered angrily. "Someone might see us."

Matt didn't care who saw them but he capitulated. "Well. When *will* I see you again?"

"I'll see," he said. "I'll see."

Alex drove Matt back to the Fermanagh border town where he taught. Being largely Nationalist, Ballycol wasn't considered safe for an R.U.C. officer so Matt was surprised that he didn't drop him at the bus station in Enniskillen. By nineteen eighty-one the violence had escalated with the hunger strikes and hardly a week went by without a policeman being murdered. That summer, the atmosphere in Ballycol was unbearably tense so Matt spent the rest of his holiday at his parents' farm near Londonderry.

Alex hadn't contacted him by the start of the autumn term, so he rang the barracks and left a message for him to ring back. He didn't phone but wrote a work of evasive literature. It started with a long, rambling account of how the hunger strikes were affecting life in the R.U.C. He told Matt about a colleague who had been shot dead, skillfully underscoring his need to avoid Ballycol. He also described David, a young recruit who had listened patiently as he unburdened his grief at losing a friend. It was the first time he had mentioned a fellow officer in such intimate terms and Matt found jealousy welling up inside him. This David was usurping Matt's role as Alex's confidant. Was he replacing Matt in Alex's bed? That fantasy was dispelled by the last few lines. Alex had thought long and hard about their 'conversation' at their 'last meeting' and he was going to 'make a go of it' with Sandra; a nurse in Belfast who had been part of their gang at school. Even through his distress, Matt smiled on noticing how careful his friend was to say nothing incriminating. During the R.U.C. anti-gay pogrom in seventy-six, prosecutions were prepared using letters as evidence that men had had sex together and Alex was always warning Matt not to put anything on paper that could be used in evidence.

The hunger strikes petered out in October but Alex still didn't appear in Ballycol. Just before Christmas, a letter came from Willy-John. He had decided to have a New Year's Eve party at his new house in Belfast.

"I should have known," Matt chuckled as he told his friend and colleague, Mary. "His father's Hogmanays were legendary and, once he was married and earning, it was inevitable that he would continue his daddy's tradition. Willy-John's nothing if not conventional! Last New Year Alex brought Sandra to make a point. I wonder if he'll try the same trick this year?"

Despite Sandra's not being there, it was well into nineteen eighty-two before Matt got Alex alone. He ambushed him coming out of the toilet and diverted him into Willy-John's bedroom.

"Why have you been avoiding me?"

"I haven't," he objected.

"Come on! This is the first time I've got you alone since August. What are you scared of? Me or you?"

Alex sounded aggressive: "You read far too much into things, young feller. I'm a busy man and you know it's not safe for me to come to Ballycol. Anyway," he ended guiltily, "I usually go and see Sandra when I get off."

"I don't figure in your plans at all, do I?" Matt asked mournfully.

"Of course you do," he insisted. "But Matt. You know I'm *not gay*. I really like you, but that's all."

"That's not what you said at the Killyhevlin."

Alex looked troubled: "I can't explain that. I was under a lot of stress, you know. It was pretty grim at work. We were all under a lot of pressure. I don't know..... I think I needed affection..... I needed to let go and you caught me in the right place at the right time. Don't get me wrong Matt. I don't regret what we did; it was great. But that was then and now it's Sandra that can give me what I need, not you!"

Matt seemed to shrink visibly and Alex put his arms round him and kissed the crown of his head: "I'm sorry Matt. Really; I am." He kissed him gently on his lips and left him to ponder his situation in the dark room.

A few weeks later, Alex invited Matt to go to Portstewart for the weekend. As he drove him up, Alex explained that David's folks were away and he thought that Matt would like a chance to get out of what he called 'That Fenian Hole' and meet David. Clever, Matt thought. David would act as a chaperone.

Alex's smart Honda sports car drew up at a nondescript bungalow in the sprawl of housing that crept towards Coleraine. The door was opened by a young man who wouldn't have looked out of place in bearskin outside Buckingham Palace. His height matched Alex's but he hadn't the same beef, which made him look taller. His military bearing was accentuated by his square jaw and high cheekbones and his hair was crew-cut; a style unfashionable for those days. Genetics had bequeathed David a permanent pout and his height forced him to peer down his long nose at mere mortals but, on seeing Alex, a smile cut through his haughty façade and lit up his face.

Directly they had unloaded the car, Alex took charge and they headed down to the Anchor Bar on the promenade. Only out of school a year or so, David was aloof and apparently uncommunicative. Matt tried to draw him into conversation but he didn't seem to have anything to say. When the Anchor closed, they moved on to the nightclub in the Strand Hotel. Matt fully expected to be left sitting as the other two went hunting women, but it was David who ended up alone at the table as Alex and Matt danced with a crowd of girls from Ballymena.

Back at David's Alex cracked open a bottle of whiskey.
"Oh!" Matt exclaimed, in mock surprise, "a bottle of Bushmills!"
"Yes," he grinned, "I thought that as we were so near the distillery I'd make an exception. Just in honour of that venerable Ulster institution, hey!"
David had one drink, then said that he was going to bed and would see them tomorrow. They were to sit up as long as they liked, as long as they made sure that all the lights were out and the doors were locked. With that he vanished with a formal "Good-Night".
Matt looked at Alex, wide-eyed.
"I know what you're thinkin'," said Alex with a slight toss of the head.
"Well. He *is* a bit of an odd-ball!"
"Listen to you! Mister normal thinks David's odd."

"You know what I mean," he whined. "He's not exactly a laugh a minute, is he? I'm sure he's very nice but... well... he isn't you, is he?"

"And you are, I suppose?"

"Aw, come on," Matt objected. "At least we have some craic together, don't we? He didn't even go out for a dance! And *I'm* supposed to be the one who doesn't like girls!"

"Yeah, yeah. He's a bit withdrawn sometimes but I thought you'd like him. I do.... 'cos he's like you."

"You mean he's........ ?"

"Fuck no! He's got a woman; we're meeting her tomorrow. No... he's the only guy on our station who I really *talk* to. He's not as cold as he seems. He's shy. Once you get to know him you'll find he's dead on. He's very gentle, you know. I reckon his reserve is a defence. It keeps people at a distance so they can't get through any chink in his armour."

"You know him quite well, then?"

"Aye. That's why I thought you'd like him."

"Alexander King, you really are a big softie!" Matt chided.

Alex smiled indulgently.

"That's why I feel the way I do about you," Matt continued, warily. "I wish......"

"What?" he demanded.

"Nothing."

"Come on. Tell me," Alex insisted.

"I wish I could make you understand how I feel about you."

"Try."

"Promise to listen?"

"Course."

"I've thought about it a lot. There's something odd about us."

Alex looked surprised: "Speak for yourself!"

"I thought you were going to listen!" Matt snapped.

Alex's eyes said sorry.

"There's something special between us. You know that as well as me."

He nodded but said nothing.

"Trouble is, we have different expectations of our relationship; different perceptions. I hadn't understood your true sexuality."

Alex scowled and Matt hurried on: "Oh! I know I *said* that I knew that you weren't gay, but in my heart I didn't believe; didn't *want* to believe it. I thought that one day you would come to your senses and realise you loved me. You see, I wanted you. I wanted *all* of you but I can't have that, can I? "

Matt glanced at Alex but he merely sat with his head bowed.

"You must have known that!"

Alex still didn't respond.

"I think you like what we '*do*' but I suspect that you're afraid I'm going to trap you, somehow."

Alex looked up and, pursing his lips, acknowledged Matt's supposition.

Matt continued cautiously: "I blew it by being too heavy. If I could have just been smart enough to accept that we were just two mates who happened to get pleasure out of each other's bodies, it might have been O.K." He laughed inwardly. "You know, I'm probably lucky you're not gay, actually. I would have lost you years ago to some gorgeous hunk. At least this way I've still got you as a friend!"

They sat in silence, then Matt said, "Sorry. Bit heavy that, wasn't it?"

Alex shook his head slowly: "Poor Matty. You do put yourself through it, don't you! You may be right. Every time I see you I wonder if we're going to end up in bed again; I just can't handle that, hey! I like you a lot, Matt, but not in the way you want. It never can be like that."

"What about Sandra? Do you love her in that way?"

He grinned: "I like her too but she's not the sort of woman that you have sex with!"

"Love's in the head not the groin."

Alex disagreed; the woman he ended up with would have to look good and have a great personality. "There must be women like that," he concluded sadly, "it's just that I haven't found one yet!" He stared at Matt: "Come here."

Matt looked up at him in surprise.

"Come on, then!"

Matt moved over to him on the settee and Alex slipped his arm round his shoulder but Matt was tense and awkward.

"Relax," Alex whispered, "I believe you."

Matt was in bed when Alex got back from brushing his teeth. He sat on Matt's bed and stroked his hair. Matt looked into his deep, brown eyes, which slowly drew him in until they were kissing passionately.

When Alex padded off to the bathroom to clean himself up, Matt assumed he would return to his own bed but he climbed back in with

Matt. There was no more sex that night, other than a kiss before falling to sleep in a warm huddle.

Next morning, Alex was careful to rumple the bedclothes on his bed but Matt knew the subterfuge was pointless. Early, as he dozed in Alex's strong arms, Matt heard the door open for a moment before being gently pulled closed again.

Saturday was a glorious day, so they decided to go to the Giant's Causeway. Matt hadn't been there since he was a kid and he'd forgotten how impressive a spot it was. They walked down the long track from the hotel on the cliff-top to where the tiers of hexagonal basalt columns marched out into the sea. There they sat, like a trio of leprechauns, on the convenient columns. As they watched the raucous gulls, the sea air purged the last vestiges of Bushmills from their lungs.

Matt spotted a pair of choughs reeling above them, calling like gulls and drew the others' attention to them as they settled in the short turf behind them to search for insects.

"You're interested in birds?"

Matt was so surprised that David had spoken, that he didn't take in what he had said.

"I beg your pardon?"

"Are you interested in birds?"

"Aye. Don't do much now but I was quite keen, once. Are you?"

David nodded: "I used to like to go off on my bike with a pair of binoculars. I must have spent hours bird-watching when I should have been stewing for my 'O' levels."

"What school were you at?"

"Inst." He was referring to Coleraine Academical Institution.

"You would be, wouldn't you, living round here. Did you ever play Alex at rugby?"

"Not very likely," Alex interjected, "he's a good bit younger than us."

"Didn't play anyway," David informed him.

"I'd've thought you were a dead cert for the firsts; big bloke like you!" Matt said.

"I was a hockey man. Played for the Ulster Schoolboys."

"Must've been good. Do you still play?"

"Yes. Not to be advertised around, you know. I'm on the Ulster Juniors."

"That's nothing to be ashamed of!" Matt objected.

"We play across the border."

Matt understood: "Ah! They let you go then?"

"Yes. I have to get special permission from headquarters and the Garda are kept informed. It's all a bit cloak and dagger but it isn't very often."

"Seems an awful hassle just to play hockey. Why bother?"

David adopted a determined look: "You can't let the fuckers wear you down, can you?"

"Suppose not. So you don't get bird watching these days?"

"No time really. Have you ever been to Rathlin Island?"

Matt shook his head.

"I'm surprised. It's beautiful: so peaceful. I've not been for ages though. It's a pity I've arranged to meet Alice tonight. We could have gone over this afternoon and come back tomorrow."

"That would have been nice. Another time, perhaps. What do you think, Alex?"

He had drifted off into a little world of his own: "What do I think of what?"

"How do you fancy us heading over to Rathlin for a weekend sometime?"

"What for? There's nothin' there!"

"Exactly: a bit of tranquillity," David enthused.

"Yeah, sure, but let's wait for the good weather. A storm could blow up and you'd be stuck there for a week. Your headmaster wouldn't like that and I'm damn sure we wouldn't be too popular either. Is it O.K. there anyway, David?"

"Safe as houses," David assured him, "It's all Roman Catholic but there's no trouble there at all. Actually the Reverend Ian's their M.P. and he's done a hell of a lot for the island. He's earned a lot of respect from the islanders."

"This country," Matt shrugged, "sometimes it completely baffles me!"

"Only sometimes, Matt?" Alex queried. "I don't think you English'll ever understand us."

It was all arranged; David, Alex and Matt would head over to Rathlin for half-term, providing that the security situation permitted it. Matt's initial enthusiasm waned when he thought about the implications. For a start, to be going on holiday with two policemen, even to such an idyllic island, seemed risky and he wasn't sure how things would be with Alex, with David there. He couldn't see them being able to sleep together even if Alex had wanted to.

CHAPTER 2

JUNE 1981, RATHLIN ISLAND

Alex picked Matt up from school on Thursday and drove him to Londonderry. They were at Matt's parents' getting the camping gear together but Alex was unusually quiet. Matt was dying to ask him what was wrong but hardly dared, in case he heard something to spoil the trip.

Suddenly, Alex broke the awkward silence: "His bird's coming."
"Sorry?"
"David's woman's coming."
"To Rathlin?"
"Aye."
"What's the problem?" Matt asked.
"What do mean?"
"You don't sound very happy about it."
"Why should it worry me? I don't care if he wants to bring her."
"You're not convincing me."
"Your head's away, young feller. I don't give a fuck... Just thought you might be a bit pissed off. You know? Having a woman along."
"Four's better than three. There's always someone left out when there's three," Matt reasoned. He was secretly pleased to hear the news. "Em. Where's she going to sleep?"
"With David, I suppose. He's bringing another tent."
Matt smiled inwardly: "There'll be more room for us in our tent then."
"Right enough," Alex said, but he still didn't sound too keen.

At David's they loaded a beat up Escort and the four of them headed for Ballycastle, in great spirits.
"Where did the car come from?" Matt wanted to know.
"It's Alice's brother's," David replied.
"Where's yours?"
"Her brother has it."

"I don't get it."

"This one holds more."

It was true, but Matt had a sinking feeling when it dawned on him that David couldn't leave his car at Ballycastle because it would be a terrorist target.

The crossing to Rathlin took nearly an hour and it was rough enough, despite being a nice day. The 'ferry' was a thirty-foot, open fishing boat piloted by a man who looked as if he could have heaved the boat onto his back and carried it. From the sea the island looked inaccessible: a streak of grey in the distance that slowly resolved itself into an apparently unbroken wall of cliffs. As the choppiness reached its worst, the boat slewed round and headed for a concealed bay. Ahead was a starkly white beach. The green fields beyond were dotted with houses and, to the left, in front of an impressive looking mansion, was the wall of a tiny harbour.

The campsite was perfectly situated in a field just behind the only pub on the island. It was less than a mile's walk along a rough white road that paralleled a beach of limestone shingle, brilliant in the noon sun. As they sauntered along, David pointed, delightedly, at ringed plovers, oystercatchers and eiders; Matt noticed that Alice wasn't in the least bit impressed. McQuaig's wasn't open but they found the back door through a yard. Matt was used to chaotic farmyards but this one was cluttered with beer kegs and crates. An elderly woman pointed to the campsite; a stony field beyond a decaying gate. A dilapidated shed by the gate was to be their toilet facilities for the next few days.

The island was an L-shape, three miles west to east and two north to south, with a rough road which ran from tip to tip. The island's cars were creatures of the M.O.T. man's worst nightmare but their intrusion onto the island's tranquility was minimal. It was all too easy to forget that they were in Northern Ireland. Walking down the winding lanes, Matt speculated that the rest of Ulster must have been like this in his mother's day; before the troubles and before the impact of technology. They wanted to find Bruce's cave where, legend has it, Robert the Bruce met the persistent spider. They clambered along the rocky shore towards the point marked on the map but cliffs and sea combined to defeat them. Deciding that you could only get to it by boat, they contented themselves with sunbathing in the rocky cove below the ruin known as Bruce's Castle.

Dinner that night wasn't a success and Alice was scathing about Alex's culinary expertise: "I'm not eating that! It's not food, it looks like dog's vomit!" she complained.

If Alex was offended he didn't show it: "Mon cheri!" he put on an abysmal Gallic accent, "I 'ave prepared for vous a dish of such," pinching his fingers and thumbs, raising his nose in delight, "frisson that you will nev-er want to eat of any other." He spooned the congealed, yellow mass from the pot and slopped a glob onto each plate. "Purdies a la Rathlin. A creation in Smash and Deeny's best saucissons seasoned with rare Rathlin grass and the tang of midget!"

Matt corrected him in his pedantic way: "They're midges Alex. Not midgets."

"Hush!" he whispered, "don't tell 'aer, it adds to ze mystery!"

"Come on," David entreated, "Have a go, it's all part of the pleasure of camping!" To prove his point he chomped at a spoonful of Alex's concoction.

What possessed Alex to mix chopped sausages in the instant mash, Matt didn't know. They weren't cooked, which was amazing, as they had been gently roasting in the heat of the tent all day.

She wasn't impressed: "There must be somewhere on this God forsaken island where you can get a decent meal!" she said, before stomping off to look for the improbable restaurant.

The three men sat in silence around the Trangia determinedly consuming their meal.

"You'd better go after her," Alex advised.

"Aye," David conceded and he got up, somewhat reluctantly, and wandered off towards the village.

"Why did she come?" Matt almost whined, "She obviously doesn't like camping."

Alex shrugged: "Don't ask me. I'm not privy to David's private life. Keep him occupied anyway."

Matt wondered what he meant by that.

They had cleaned up by the time Alice and David got back looking much happier.

"Found a chippy!" David grinned, as he waved a bundle of newspaper. "Want some?"

As they picked at the greasy chips they resolved to make more use of that particular amenity in future.

McQuaig's was very basic. A few benches and half beer barrels were all there were to sit on and the small bar was dominated by the obligatory pool table. The room was poorly lit and on the walls hung artifacts that bore witness to the pub's island situation. Pride of place was the horned head of a massive highland bull, which was reputed to have swum there from Scotland. There were also bits of ships that had come to grief on the treacherous coast and an aerial photograph of a huge freighter breaking up on the rocks. There wasn't a soul to be seen in the bar so they had to shout for service.

To their surprise the man that came was none other than their boatman.

"A man of many talents," Matt smiled, as he ordered the drinks.

"Everybody does what they can here," he told him. "The usual barman's over at Ballycastle."

"Do much trade here?"

"Quiet in winter but busy enough in the summer. The landlord has a farm to run too, of course. So we all help, so we do," he said as he handed Matt the last glass.

Coming up to midnight, customers started drifting in and the room buzzed with relaxed conversation. They soon got chatting with the locals, some of whom weren't local at all; there was even an English man working there. Alex and David played pool with a couple of burly farmers. Matt overheard Alex bemoaning the boredom of life as a civil servant. This was the line the policemen had agreed to take if anyone asked them what they did.

By the time they stumbled back to the campsite, more tents had appeared. From the racket coming from them, they were scouts or something equally unpleasant. David and Alice disappeared into their tent and Matt snuggled into his sleeping bag. Alex was ages coming in. In the inadequate light of their little torch, Matt watched his bulk struggling to undress then he slipped into his sleeping bag, turned his back on Matt and went to sleep. Matt lay in the dark, listening to his friend's regular breathing. He seemed to be asleep already. Matt wriggled across the tent until he was snuggled up to Alex's warm back but the pleasure was brief, for Alex shifted in his sleep and moved away.

They spent the Saturday wandering down to Rue Point; the southern tip of the island. Other than seeing a pair of buzzards at Doon Bay it was an uneventful day that ended, as before, in McQuaig's but at least Alex was being less distant with Matt. When they were in their sleeping bags he said, "I hope you're not going to try kicking me to death tonight."

"I wasn't trying to kick you," Matt said, indignantly. Then he whispered, "I was snuggling up to you."

"It felt like kicking to me."

"I need a cuddle," Matt said, in as low a voice as he could.

Alex didn't move, so Matt reached across Alex's chest and caressed his shoulder. To his relief, Alex gripped his wrist and returned the gesture. Matt kissed him on the shoulder and Alex's lips brushed his forehead. Matt slipped out of his sleeping bag and slithered into Alex's. The bag forced their bodies against each other and thus they caressed. They were in imminent danger of bursting Alex's sleeping bag so he found the zip and released their sweating bodies onto the cold ground-sheet. Matt was acutely aware of David and Alice in the next tent, let alone the scouts but, somehow, this made their lovemaking even more exciting. Alex must have been thinking the same thing because, when he came, he stifled his usually noisy gasps of pleasure.

"Time to sleep," Alex whispered.

"I've missed you," Matt replied.

"I know," he breathed.

Matt didn't want to let go but Alex gently prised him off and pulled his own sleeping bag around himself. This time, his good night was accompanied by an affectionate kiss and he allowed Matt to sleep snuggled up to his warm bulk.

Alex and Alice were finding the island boring and, on the third day, neither of them wanted to walk to the west light. It was only about four miles but they opted to stay around the bay. Alice said she had some letters to write, and Alex was engrossed in some awful Stephen King novel, so David and Matt headed off together along the narrow road that wound up past the ruined manor house and the pretty little chapel. On the seaward side of the lane an old wall was topped in grass and thyme, its heavy scent colouring the still air. There were strange yellow-brown flowers with no leaves. It was the first time Matt had seen anything like them and he decided that they had to be toothworts; flowers parasitic on the thyme. Beyond the wall, Church Bay swept out below them and, in the distance, they could just make out their tent with Alex and Alice sprawled on the grass next to each other.

It seemed to be far more than four miles to the west light, but that was because they kept stopping every few yards as they spotted another interesting bird. Here it was a snipe, there a chough and, at an area of marsh, they saw a pair of reed buntings. They must have spent half an hour trying to track a corn-crake down but it's curious, pepper-mill croak was impossible to locate; it seemed to be everywhere. David was keen to see the long-eared owl that was reputed to nest in the conifer plantation at the west end of the island but Matt was hardly surprised when they didn't.

The R.S.P.B. reserve at the west light was the highlight of the day. They descended steps down a vast sheet of concrete that sloped to the cliff edge. A lighthouse was perched on the cliff-top at the end of the steps where a balcony overlooked a natural amphitheatre. They heard the birds before they saw them. A sweeping arc of cliff-face ended in a sea-stack. A squawking seabird occupied every conceivable ledge and crevice. At university, Matt had learnt about the zonation of seabirds on sea cliffs and here it was, laid out in front of him like a textbook illustration. The rocky beach had a few oystercatchers and shags nesting. Above it a grassy bank was riddled with puffin burrows. Then there was the cliff itself: a birdie condominium; razorbills on the lower levels, then guillemots above them looking like so many penguins. Kittiwakes vied for space with the guillemots and above them were the fulmars. A couple of fulmars were within feet of them and they could clearly see their bulbous nostrils. David explained that, if you got too close to them they would spit an evil smelling oil at you that made you smell of rotting fish for days. At the top of this avian tenement was the grassy cliff-top where ordinary gulls nested.

The two of them were so engrossed that they completely lost track of time and, by the time they got back to the tents, Alex and Alice had eaten, so they headed to the chippy together. Matt was growing fond of the reserved young man. He didn't talk very much, except about birds, but Matt had the impression that he was thinking all the time. On their way to the chippy, he was so lost in thought that he missed a seal bobbing in the water just yards from the shore. Matt wondered if he had noticed how chummy Alex and Alice were becoming.

Being Sunday, the pub was shut but they had bought plenty of cans and made a fire on the beach. It was a glorious night and some of the other campers joined the party. The scouts weren't scouts, but a Catholic youth group from West Belfast. The youngsters quickly sussed that the four friends were Protestants, but they weren't hostile. In fact they went out of their way to be friendly; as if they wanted to show them that they weren't as bad as they were painted. Had they known that Alex and David were RUC men, they probably wouldn't have been so friendly but they were off guard, being on holiday, and they chatted to them with an innocent openness. That night was difficult for Matt as Alex had spent practically the whole night talking to Alice, hardly saying a word to him. When Alex couldn't talk to Alice, he would gaze, longingly at her and when he was talking to Matt he would lose concentration, glancing surreptitiously in her direction. Matt felt it was a bit unfair to go on holiday with him and then treat him like that. When they got back to the tent, Alex went straight to sleep without so much as a peck. Matt was so pissed off with Alex that he hardly noticed nor cared how David was taking the situation.

Monday was their last whole day on the island. David and Matt decided to walk round the west half of the island whereas Alex and Alice stayed in camp again. The bird watching contingent headed over to the north light and weaved their way westward. They made good progress and were well on their way back by lunchtime. According to the map, there was a harbour of some sort near Moylecrock but, search as they could, they couldn't see where it was. They eventually found a steep path down the cliff to a small, natural cove: hardly a harbour at all! Once down, they seriously doubted that they could get back up the same way. It gave them a feeling of splendid isolation. Like all beaches on Rathlin, this was strewn with great boulders and at the base of the cliff was a grassy bank that served them as a picnic spot. They relaxed in the sun and David lazily scanned the horizon with his binoculars as Matt drifted into a semi-snooze.

"You could do anything here and never be seen," Matt murmured.

"What're you planning to do then?"

"Dunno. Strip naked and leap into the sea?"

"I wouldn't if I was you. You would be smashed to bits on those rocks."

"Rape, perhaps?" Matt smirked to himself.

"Who were you thinking of?"

"I'd make do with what's available," he grinned.

"I hope you don't mean me. I'm definitely not available... Neither are you."

Matt hoisted himself up on his elbow and looked at David: "I was only kidding. What do you mean, anyway?"

"Well, I'm with Alice and you're... with Alex."

"Ah," Matt said. So he did know, he thought so. "It's not what you think you know. We're just good friends, as they say."

David looked at Matt solemnly: "You don't need to cover up. I don't mind you and Alex... you know... being friends."

"Look. I'd better explain."

David put a hand of reassurance on Matt's shoulder: "There's no need. I don't mind, honestly."

"There's nothing to mind, really. Alex isn't gay. We really are just good friends, nothing more. I am gay, though - you knew that, didn't you?"

"Aye.... You're sure he's not?" he asked, dubiously.

"Sure I'm sure. I wish he was. We have messed about a bit but it was nothing serious," he lied. "You can tell he isn't; look at the way he is with Alice?"

David shook his head in obvious distress.

Realising what he'd just said, Matt apologised profusely: "Oh fuck. I'm sorry. I shouldn't have said that."

"No, no. I don't mind, actually."

Matt was astonished: "You what?"

"If he likes her."

"What about you?"

David looked at him long and hard: "It's not been going that well, lately. That's why she wanted to come this week. She thought it might help."

"Alex hasn't exactly helped, has he?"

"Not at all!" David exclaimed, "He knows all about it. I told him everything. Alice thinks we're going to get married, I told Alex I wasn't sure about it. What has happened between them is to my advantage."

"So he's not doing the dirty on you, then?"

David shook his head: "He's doing me a favour."

"Boy!" Matt exclaimed, "I never will understand the heterosexual mind!"

David snorted a silent laugh through his nose and stared at the lapping waves.

David's revelations did nothing to settle Matt's feelings about Alex. He had tried to convince himself that he was annoyed with Alex because he was doing the dirty on David, but it was becoming increasingly obvious to Matt that, when it was a choice between him and a woman, the woman won every time and he resolved to write Alex off his list of potential lovers.

CHAPTER 3

NOVEMBER 1981, ALEX'S NEMESIS

Matt was transfixed by Anthony Andrews and Jeremy Irons mooning over each other in Brideshead Revisited, one Tuesday night, when his doorbell rang. His annoyance at being disturbed turned to delight when he saw Alex standing there.

Matt's pleasure soon soured as he caught Alex's mood: "What did you say to David?" he demanded.

Matt looked blank: "I haven't seen David. Why, what's happened?"

"It was on Rathlin."

"That's weeks ago!"

"Did you say anything about..." Alex looked embarrassed, "about us?"

Matt was relieved; he had been worried that he had said something out of place but, now Alex mentioned Rathlin, he felt more sure of himself: "NO! In fact I was commiserating with him because you seemed to be wiping his eye. Remember?" he said pointedly.

Alex looked deflated: "Well. You must have said something," he insisted half-heartedly.

Matt's heart went out to his friend: "Come along, Alexander," he said gently. "Sit down, have a beer, and tell your uncle Matthew what's happened."

Resignedly, he sat down and accepted a can of Smithwicks.

"What's David said to you?" Matt carefully asked.

Alex was acutely embarrassed: "He hasn't said anything, not really. It's what he's done."

"Go on."

"You know we spend a lot of time in my room at the Barracks, talking?"

Matt nodded, jealousy welling up again.

"Well, last night, we had a rake of cans and he was getting well on." Alex shifted uncomfortably. "And he starts getting a bit too friendly, doesn't he!"

Matt's heart leapt. The thought excited him and annoyed him at the same time: "You're sure? You might have just misinterpreted."

"You don't misinterpret a hand sliding towards your crotch!"

Matt tried to suppress a smirk: "Suppose not. What did you do?"

"Shifted out of the way."

"Did that work?"

"Aye. But then he said he was just being friendly, *like Matt is*, he said!"

Matt flushed with embarrassment then brightened: "Ah! I think I know what's happened."

"I know what's bloody happened," Alex exploded. "You've told him, haven't you?"

Matt shook his head sadly: "We both did, in a way. I didn't tell you at the time, but I'm pretty sure he came in on us that night we stayed at his place."

Alex looked appalled: "That's fucking great, that is! So he thinks I'm queer, now! He thinks he can screw me when he's feeling randy. Well he fucking can't!"

"Is that what you think about me? Someone to screw when you are feeling randy?" Matt demanded coldly?

Alex looked into Matt's eyes: "NO! It's different with us."

"Maybe he wants the same sort of relationship as we have."

"Jesus! I'm not getting into that game. I'm not gay, remember." He paused and grimaced at Matt. "Anyway, he's revolting. Have you ever seen him in the buff? He's as hairy as a teddy bear, yuck," he shivered.

Matt recalled David's hunky body with pleasure: "Actually, I think he's gorgeous. You aren't exactly silken skinned and look how much you turn me on!"

Alex shook his head despairingly: "I should never have got into this with you. I should have known it would end in disaster."

"You got involved because you wanted to. You enjoy having sex with me."

"I prefer it with a woman, but," he snarled. He indicated his cock, "I should put a bloody padlock on this. It would be far safer," he ended, miserably.

They drank beers and chatted about all and sundry. As one a.m. approached, Matt said that it was time to go to bed.

"O.K.," Alex smiled blearily, "I'll head now."

"Aren't you staying?" Matt suggested.

His voice hardened: "I've told you, Matt, I'm not like you. I am heterosexual and I'm going to start behaving like I am. You'll always be a good mate, Matt, but I'm afraid the special place in my bed's reserved for someone with tits and a fanny."

Next morning Matt was teaching a third form when a knock at the lab door heralded a first form girl. "Please, Mr. Woodhead. There's a telephone call for you. Mrs. Hammond says you should come up now."

In itself, this was odd. They never brought teachers out of class for phone calls. The fact that he was being called out was ominous.

In the office, Mrs. Hammond was looking serious. She looked at the phone, then left the room. A fragile voice came over the line: "Matthew?" It was Sandra.

"What's wrong?"

For an endless fraction of a second she didn't say anything, then she whispered, "It's Alex."

"Is he hurt," Matt asked, stupidly.

"Yes, seriously," she croaked.

"How?" Bombs, guns and all manner of terrorist devices ran through Matt's mind but the answer was so unexpected when it came.

"A crash, last night, outside Enniskillen."

"How is he?"

"Bad Matt. Severe head injuries and still unconscious."

"Where is he?"

"The Royal."

"Should I come up?"

"There's no need," she said, totally unconvincingly.

"I'll be on the next bus. I'll come straight to the hospital."

How he had the nerve to do it, Matt didn't know. He breezed into the head's study and announced that he *had* to go to Belfast, there and then. He was in a highly charged, emotional state and the headmaster must have realised that he couldn't be expected to teach any more that day. On the bus up he had time to think, and it didn't encourage him. There was a perfectly good hospital in Enniskillen so why was Alex in Belfast? The only possible reason for their moving him would be if he was so bad that the Erne couldn't treat him; that meant severe spinal or head injuries.

At the Royal's reception he was directed to intensive care but there they said that there was no way that he could see him. He sat down, not quite knowing what to do, then saw a nurse he recognised and asked her to find Sandra.

She was in a bad state. She must have been near breaking point when she rang him and, when she saw him, she finally cracked up. He took her in his arms and comforted her like a child. "There, there. It'll be O.K. You'll see. Alex's tough. He'll pull through, you wait and see."

Matt didn't convince her. He didn't even convince himself.

"His mum and dad're with him." She looked at him with big wet eyes, "Matt, he's going to die, I know he is. I've seen ones in, far less serious than him, and they've gone."

"Don't be daft. You can't say that. You've got to believe he'll be alright. There's no point, otherwise."

After a few sobs she straightened up, rearranged her tear stained face, and nodded.

"Is there any chance of me getting in to see him?"

"You're not supposed to, actually, and there is an RUC man on guard, too. But I could probably get you in. I'll have to ask his parents to O.K. it though, Matt. Wait."

There wasn't much to see as Alex was practically smothered in bandages. Obscene machines clicked, hissed and murmured around him. His Mum and Dad were so shocked that they didn't even think it odd that Matt was there when he should have been battling with 3V at the other side of the province. The Kings had been summoned to Enniskillen just after the accident but, by the time they got there, Alex had been whisked to Belfast by helicopter. They had been traipsed half way round the province by an obliging neighbour who had completed the trip by driving back to Londonderry before daybreak.

There really was no point hanging around in Belfast. Alex was showing no sign of life and Sandra had said she would contact him if he came round. He had missed the last bus back so he went round to Willy-John and Louise's.

Willy-John shuddered at Matt's account of the disaster: "The poor bastard! What're his chances?"

"Dunno," he replied. "Sandra really freaked out at first. Said he was going to die. Then she calmed down and said that people can be in a coma for days, then they can snap out of it just like that!"

"Yeah," Willy-John scowled, "And they can lie like a cabbage for years!"

Matt shook his head as if trying to shake away a bad dream: "I don't want to even consider that." Panic rose in his voice: "He's got to be alright."

Willy-John was uncharacteristically gentle: "You're not being very realistic, Matt. Alex would be the first one to face up to the facts."

"I don't have to be rational!" Matt snapped. "I have to believe he'll be O.K."

Something in his tone of voice alerted Willy-John: "You.... and Alex?" he said, incredulously.

At that moment, Matt knew he could have lived out a fantasy and claimed the helpless hunk for his own but he couldn't defile him like that: "Don't be daft. I care a lot for him. Like you, like Mum and Dad!"

Willy-John scrutinised his face for a long moment and said, "Aye," slowly. "You have to admit though, that he was asking for it," he continued.

Matt's gore rose: "What do you mean?"

Willy-John didn't flinch. "For as long as I've known him, he's been getting full and leaping into his car. He couldn't go on like that forever. It was bound to happen, some day."

"Who said he was drunk?" Matt challenged.

"You didn't have to. He prides himself on his driving. He reckons he's better with a few bevies inside him. He's looser, he says!" then he corrected himself, "Said!"

Matt scowled: "He might have been tired. He might have been on a double spell of duty. It happens a lot, you know."

"Possible, I suppose," Willy-John sneered. "And no doubt that's what the *official* story'll be."

"Official story?"

"Aye. They're not going to admit that one of their own was killed, driving under the influence of alcohol, are they?"

"He's not dead yet!" Matt shouted, "I mean, he's not dead at all!"

"I know, I know..... Just saying, that's all."

The subject was promptly dropped and studiously avoided for the rest of the evening. This proved easy, as Willy-John was full of his impending entry into his dad's law practice in Limavady.

The first bus got Matt to school just after ten. His colleagues commiserated with him at the gloomy prognosis. At every break he nipped into the office to see if there was any news and, by the end of the day, he was so impossibly restless that his colleague, Mary, advised him to ring the hospital. No change, was the noncommittal reply.

CHAPTER 4

NOVEMBER 1981, FEARGAL COLLINS

Back at the flat, he couldn't settle either. He found himself prowling from room to room and fidgeting with things that had remained undisturbed for months. Finally he grabbed his coat and headed for Micky's. The only familiar face amongst the sparse clientele was Feargal's. He'd met the art student when Danny had stayed with him. Danny was a serious drinker and he'd soon befriended Feargal as a kindred spirit. Matt had got quite friendly with Fergal by the time a horrible drunken mistake had driven Danny away.

Feargal was in earnest conversation with Micky himself. Matt loved Feargal's gravely voice which contrasted so markedly with his freckled, angelic face framed by a curly, strawberry-blonde mop. Despite his innocent appearance, Feargal was the most dissolute creature he had ever met. Conversations with Feargal were never dull; he spoke on every subject with a ferocious intensity.

Matt sidled up, said hello, ordered a drink and the two were soon engrossed in a most extraordinary discussion about the role of modern art in contemporary society. Feargal's contention was that contemporary art is never appreciated by the majority because they aren't properly educated. He was convinced that even the most revolutionary styles will become accepted and liked by the general public in time; provided that it was good quality art.

Matt disagreed: "Modern art will always be for an educated elite! It's essentially an onanistic activity!"

"You calling me a wanker?" Feargal grated in mock anger.

"Intellectually, yes!" Matt replied with a smirk.

"Well you're right," he roared, "I love wanking! Prefer screwing but love wanking!" Feargal finished with a serious nod of the head.

Matt was quite taken aback by such language but was determined not to show it. Feargal raved on for ages about the pleasures of sexual intercourse and Matt just hoped that no-one was listening.

When Micky's closed they ended up back at Matt's flat and the conversation continued in the same vein. Inevitably, Feargal wanted to know Matt's views on what was, evidently, his favourite subject. Matt was pretty sure Feargal knew he was gay but they had never discussed the issue. "I like it too... but with men, of course!" he said cautiously.

Feargal seemed delighted: "Every man should do what he wants with who he wants," he declared, "Man, woman or dog!"

Matt smiled, trying to look calm; the idea of accepting bestiality as equally valid as homosexuality hadn't occurred to him before.

"People aren't homosexual, heterosexual or hogosexual," Feargal went on. "They're just sexual. Last night I had a woman, tomorrow I hope I'll have another but who knows? Maybe it'll be a man. I can't tell."

The thought of having sex with Feargal intrigued Matt. "But that's not true!" he objected. "I am homosexual. I know that for certain. Women don't attract me at all. Just men."

"You're as trapped by convention as everyone else in this God-ridden country! How do you know you wouldn't go with a woman if you met the right one? Do you know what it's like to put it into a nice warm, wet pussy? It's the most delicious thing in the world; I love it," he chortled.

Matt hadn't the nerve to put the opposing point of view quite so graphically but he did insist that sex with another man could be just as wonderful.

Feargal didn't disagree: "I'm sure it is. But I haven't found the right man yet."

As they supped their tins the conversation ranged far and wide. Feargal was a Catholic but he hated his church with a rare intensity. He couldn't shake his conviction that there was a God up there somewhere but, as far as he was concerned, the church was a con; a power structure evolved to subjugate and oppress the ordinary Catholic people. He reserved his utmost vituperation for the priesthood: "Those fat, castrated, self-satisfied cats sit in their parochial houses. They try to tell the likes of you and me...."

"Not me!" Matt objected. "I'm not a Catholic, remember?"

"Don't be so sure," he warned. "Those bastards have more power than you think! They preach to us how we should conduct our sex lives, the sanctity of marriage, they say. How can they know what it's like living with a woman? How the fuck can they know how real, sexually fulfilled men really feel? All they want to do is keep a hold over you. They need families to produce more good Catholics and they need them to keep in business. They're parasites!"

Matt tended to agree with him but he had to play devil's advocate: "There's a hell of a lot of people who believe it all. The Pope is God's vicar on earth and the priest is his local agent in their parish."

"What a load of shit!" the dissident Catholic exploded.

Matt tried to keep a straight face: "It's not shit, it's true, they need their priest and the church. If they have any problems it's the church they turn to. And it doesn't matter what you say, the priests do help them!"

"That's a matter of opinion!"

"No. It's a fact. There's a hell of a lot of people need the church."

"Only because they've never been given the chance to think for themselves."

"Come on now! There's millions of intelligent, thinking people who keep their faith, and their integrity."

"Impossible!" Feargal spat. "I had a mate who was allergic to the host."

"Host?"

"You know, the wafers at communion. It has gluten in it; he was allergic to gluten. He used to have a special gluten free host made from rice flour."

"So?"

"Then those arrogant bastards in Rome decided that rice flour didn't count because it wasn't bread, which was what Christ used at the last supper, so it couldn't be the flesh of Christ."

"So what?" Matt queried.

"Well. 'Cos of that, the poor sod couldn't take communion, could he? If he did, he got sick. If he didn't, he felt spiritually deprived; incomplete, somehow. Fucking pathetic, isn't it?" he growled.

"Is that all true?"

"Fucking damn right it is!" he assured Matt.

"I'm sure he wasn't that bothered really. I wouldn't be. I'd be quite glad, really, if I didn't have to go to church."

"Shows you don't know how the bloody church works. It really freaked him. He was so brainwashed that he went through agonies until he got special permission to use the rice stuff. That's the hold mother church has on some of us. And what about yous?"

"Us?" Matt gulped.

"Aye, your lot, the gays. The Holy Roman Church hasn't much time for yous."

"None of the others exactly welcome us with open arms."

"Aye but they don't have policies specifically designed to repress you."

"Do the Catholics?"

"Do they! They have a wee booklet that lays out the churches position on gays. I've seen it, it reads like Mein fucking Kampf. It's full of stuff about preventing your point of view being put in any their schools or youth clubs. Then if they don't, by some miracle, stop you discovering that you're gay, they switch tactics and a completely different set of rules comes into play. Then it's all, we love you but not your sin. They tell you they love you but you mustn't, under any circumstances, be permitted to express your love to the very people you need to love 'cos that's evil. They've got you boys sewn up! The church actually encourages hatred of homosexuals by spreading the 'homos are evil' crap."

Until that night, Matt had neither known nor cared what the Catholic Church's views on homosexuality were. He had sort of assumed that they would be more or less like those of Aaron, his fundamentalist school-friend. Aaron was a Free Presbyterian, one of Ian Paisley's church, and he condemned anything to do with homosexuality, but that was easy enough to ignore. It came as quite a shock to discover that the Catholics had a more considered, insidious and, in its way, crueler approach.

"Does it actually work, though? How do Catholic gays manage?"

"Dunno. Most probably grow up with massive guilt complexes. They end up getting married to women they don't fancy; can't fancy. Fuck knows what sort of a married life they have. Likely as not they end up as child molesters or wife batterers."

"It's probably that sort who ends up going to the cottages."

"Cottages? Why should they go to cottages? I don't follow," Feargal puzzled.

"Cottages is gay slang for public lavatories. Cottaging is going into the loos looking for sex. That's how the police entrap gay men," Matt explained. Feargal snorted his disgust and Matt continued: "They send pretty policemen into the cottages so when some poor bastard propositions them, they're hauled in on indecent behaviour charges."

Despite a fascinating night's conversation, Alex still filled Matt's thoughts. He didn't know Feargal well enough to cry on his shoulder. In any case, Feargal might not have much sympathy for a policeman and, after Matt's damning revelation about police treatment of gays; Feargal probably wouldn't have much respect for his integrity if he said he was in love with a policeman.

Much, much later, Matt reluctantly packed Feargal off home and went to his bed almost wishing that he had a faith, then he could have prayed for Alex. Instead, the last thing he did before going to sleep was to hope, to wish, to think Alex well again.

The next evening, his desperate need to talk to someone brought him to Mary's door. He poured his heart out to her. He didn't mean to tell her about sleeping with Alex and didn't in so many words but he knew she knew, and she knew he knew she knew.

Mary never passed a value judgement and she never questioned his actions nor the validity of his emotions. She sat patiently, nodding and uttering little hums of encouragement. When he faltered she prompted by little probing questions and hints which unleashed great emotional cascades. He saw that there was little he could do at the present but she helped him extrapolate to the time when Alex would be on the road to recovery, and discussed how Matt could contribute to his eventual recuperation. An hour with Mary had drained him more than a night's boozing with Feargal. He left her digs on wobbly legs. As he bobbed down the hill, he realised that she had taken the wrinkled, sickbed sheets from his head. She had shaken them out, cooled, smoothed and dried them and tucked them in again.

CHAPTER 5

NOVEMBER 1981, THE LOW LIFE

A week after the accident Alex still hadn't regained consciousness, nor had he the week after that. On the third Wednesday Matt phoned Sandra.

"He's conscious," she revealed.

"When? Why didn't you ring me?" he demanded.

"Hold on Matt," she cautioned. "He came round on Monday. He's conscious, but only just. He hasn't shown any sign of communication yet. I was going to ring you at work on Thursday but I knew you would tear up here if you thought he was conscious and there's no point. It would be a waste of your time."

"I would have thought that was my choice," he replied huffily.

"I was only thinking of your job."

"If he's conscious but not communicating, what is he doing?"

She put on an official spokesperson voice, "He's taking liquids and we think he can see."

"And?"

"That's it. So far."

On Saturday he saw Alex for himself. He lay staring, unseeing at the ceiling. Plaster immobilised his body, but his eyes, too, were as still as glass beads. Matt stroked his face and leaned into his line of sight. He couldn't fail to see him, if he was able, but there wasn't a flicker of recognition.

"How do you know he can see?" he glanced at Sandra's face. Did he catch a fleeting look? Disgust? Jealousy? Or was it sorrow?

"We don't actually know he can. His iris reflex works. That means he is perceiving light and reacting to it."

"Can he hear?"

"We don't know. He could do."

Matt leaned close to Alex's ear and whispered, "It's me, Matt. You're going to get better, Alex. You're a fighter and you can do it." He glanced at Sandra and whispered in his ear, "I love you with all my heart. You've got to get better. If only for me, you've got to Alex, you hear that?" To drive the point home, he kissed his cold brow.

On the tedious journey home, Matt was lost in thought. What would happen if he didn't fully recover? He was Alex's only really close friend. Was it up to him to take whatever care of him that would be needed? He ran through scenarios. He might need round the clock supervision. Could he commit himself to that, did he love him enough to sacrifice himself to him? What about if he recovered enough to be at home but was crippled. It would be up to him to visit him whenever he could. He would be a real friend to him. How far would it go? Would he still be able to go drinking? Would he still want to have sex with him? Could he? What if he did dedicate his life to him and then he met the man of his dreams? How could he possibly develop any relationship, with Alex to look after? Alex would be like one of those house bound mothers who enmesh their gay sons into lives of unpaid nursing. Despite his contorted imaginings, he still slid into a cosy fantasy of catering for the crippled giant's every need. In return, Alex would devote his love to him.

He felt that he had a duty to make it up to Belfast at every opportunity. Mrs. King had moved up to Belfast but she wanted to get back to Derry every now and again because Alex's dad was still working. His duty, as he saw it, was to be with Alex at weekends so she could go home for a couple of days.

Gradually, Alex regained sentience. The first major development was when a nurse saw him crying. Sandra rushed to speak to him and the tears turned to sobs and great heaves.

Then Matt arrived, one weekend, to find Alex speaking but what he said couldn't be described as conversation. He spoke like a drunken infant who could only express his ideas in a few slurred words and his thoughts were as confused as his speech. It was as if it hurt him to think so he limited himself to bland and inane questions: "Is it raining? What time is it? Is it dinner time yet?" Worse still, he didn't seem to listen to what people were saying either. Matt would talk to him for great stretches and the only response he would get would be, "Is it dinner-time yet?" Even if he told him when dinner-time was, he was quite likely to ask again, ten minutes later.

Visiting Alex became a chore. Matt could see no improvement and he began to appreciate how much effort Sandra was putting in to assist his recovery. The hospital appreciated the work she was doing too. When Alex had recovered sufficiently for him to be moved to Londonderry, his mum wasn't so sure.

"What's the problem?" Matt asked her.

"The consultant told me that we have Sandra to thank," she explained.

"We have all the hospital staff to thank," he agreed.

"Yes, but he says that Sandra has been spending every spare minute she has with him, even when she's off duty. It's Sandra that's bringing him through this. If he comes to Londonderry, she won't be able to help any more. Mr. Heggarty says that he needs her."

"I'm sure he'll be better nearer home," he assured her. "He's well on his way to recovery. I doubt that she's as important now."

She wanted to believe Matt and concurred but, when Alex *was* moved, Sandra managed to get a transfer to Altnagelvin so she could continue her good work.

It was more convenient for Matt to visit Alex in Derry but visits didn't get any easier. He was physically better. He wasn't encased in plaster, but he wasn't the same. His muscles were flabby; totally lacking in tone. He lay propped against his pillows looking like a rag doll and about as interesting a conversationalist as one. Matt's visits became soliloquies on life in Ballycol. They invariably consisted of monotonous tales of drunken nights in Micky's or elsewhere with people whom Matt wouldn't even have admitted knowing before the accident.

Considering the extent of his injuries, he made remarkable progress but it was discovered that he was partially paralysed. The remarkable thing was that gradually, through physiotherapy, he seemed to be regaining some movement. Sandra really came into her own, here. She had infinite patience. She massaged him and moved his great flabby limbs back and forth, back and forth, every moment she had to spare.

When he returned home in a wheelchair, she was on hand to help whenever she was off duty. Her dedication could elicit nothing but admiration but she would get her reward. When he fully recovered, as Matt was sure he would, he would be bound to be influenced by her devotion to him. Matt couldn't see him forsaking her for him and he felt cheated out of a boyfriend that should have been his.

Matt began to accept that his emotional future didn't lie with Alex and his search for a boyfriend recommenced, but Ballycol was not the place to search for a gay partner and his social life degenerated as he found himself in situations which he couldn't have imagined a few years before. Patsy was a point in case. Indistinguishable from the majority of the town's youth, Patsy was invariably attired in a grubby white tee-shirt and worn denims. When he took his denim jacket off his slim, wiry body Matt couldn't keep his eyes off the self-inflicted tattoos on his sinewy arms. His slightly weasely face sported a weak moustache and the scars of subsiding acne. He wasn't particularly attractive but he was civil to Matt, and that interested him.

One night, Matt arrived in Micky's to find Feargal and Patsy sitting with Marie and Colette. Matt squeezed into a stall next to them and joined in the craic. Patsy was sitting opposite Matt, so their legs were interlaced. At first, Matt didn't take any notice of the contact, but as he downed more pints he began to interpret Patsy's leg movements as signals. That evening ended with them all going back to Matt's flat with a rake of tins. Feargal was all over Colette and hardly came up for breath. Patsy was, it seemed, happy chatting to Matt as he fondled Marie. Matt got the impression, possibly accentuated by alcohol, that Patsy would have been happier if Matt's personality was in Marie's body. Finally Matt gave up and went to bed, leaving the two couples to copulate in his living room.

Next time he saw Patsy, he was in the main street. The young man apologised for using the flat like that and asked him if he would be in Micky's that night. Stupid question! They spent the following evening stooped over the bar talking about all and sundry. Matt was painfully aware that Patsy had little of interest to say but there were hints that his attitudes weren't as limited as many of the other of the town's youths, and when Matt told him about his trips abroad he showed a keen interest; he was evidently intrigued by foreigners. Matt was interested enough to invite him to the flat when the pub shut and there the conversation took a different turn.

Matt was talking about hitching through Italy and he began to describe the beauty of Italian men, waxing lyrical about their smooth brown bodies and gorgeously groomed hairy chests. Far from being disgusted by Matt's narrative Patsy seemed fascinated. He asked Matt how he would match up to an Italian and before Matt knew it, Patsy had his tee-shirt off, displaying a surprisingly taught torso and a chest with a few wisps of hair. Matt reached over to touch and Patsy panicked, put his tee-shirt on and said he had to go. But all wasn't lost; as he left he mentioned that Declan was playing in a local pub the next night and did Matt fancy coming?

The Apostles was the old part of Ballycol around the tannery; an area into which Matt would not normally venture. According to Protestant conviction this was the haunt of the worst Republicans, and most of Matt's pupils would die before being dragged into that dreaded ghetto. The pub had a nondescript frontage in St. Peter Street, and as soon as he went through the door, he knew he shouldn't have been there. It was grubby in the extreme and smelt unpleasantly. All heads turned and silently observed Matt's progress into the lounge bar at the back. Patsy and Matt found an empty area of stained, cushioned seating not far from the little dais on which Declan was to perform.

At ten-thirty the place was still practically deserted. The few men at the bar were much of a muchness. Some were more or less Matt's age but, somehow, they looked older and they all looked as if they had seen better days. The older men wore threadbare suits, frayed shirts and grubby ties. Nearest Matt was a stocky bloke in his early twenties. He wore a battered leather jacket over the collar of which trailed ragged stands of greasy hair. When he turned, Matt saw the side of a bloated face with a fretwork of blood encrusted scores, recently stitched.

Matt tried to analyse his alienation. They're the other side, he reasoned, these are the "filthy Fenians" that Willy-John used to warn me about. He pulled himself up. No, I mustn't think like this, he thought. They are ordinary people. They just happen to be poor, that's all. They can't afford decent clothes and haircuts; these are the real people of Ballycol. He tried to rationalise his prejudices by persuading himself that they were a curious, ethnic folk and lulled himself into believing he was an impartial observer.

A group of women congregated on the next seat and they were even more exotic than the men. The younger ones wore mini-skirts, so thin and tight that no detail of their underwear remained concealed. Their blouses had the same effect and he had never seen so much make-up plastered over a face. Their dyed hair appeared to have the texture of coarse candy floss. Matt thought the older women, festooned with noisy jewellery, marginally worse. A smouldering cigarette drooped from each and every hand and from their mouths gushed the harsh, bronchitic Ballycol accent, liberally sprinkled with "fucks".

He worried about his attitude to the clientele; they must, he decided, be similar to those of most people towards gays. These people were so different from anything he knew that he couldn't be sure what they were thinking; what they might do next. In his subconscious they posed a threat and he didn't know how to handle them.

Some time later Declan had done his turn in what was a sort of talent competition called a back-to-back. Most of the competitors were middle aged women singing oldies out of key or very talented old men playing fiddles, tin whistles, et cetera but there had been a few youngsters like Declan doing more modern stuff. Matt was at the bar getting a round in. There was a young guy standing next to him and, at the time, Matt had thought he looked O.K. He said something to Matt but he didn't quite catch what was said so he smiled and said, "Beg your pardon?"

The man spat, "Jaffa bastard" and, the next thing Matt knew, there was a scuffle and a sickening jolt as the man's forehead connected with the bridge of his nose. Burly arms dragged the young man off Matt with calls of, "Come on now, Marty. Leave it." and "Cool it now, cool it," and then Patsy and Declan were helping him back to the table.

Marty, they explained, was an ignorant being at the best of times and these weren't the best of times. His best mate had just been put away for membership of the I.R.A. and Matt was a convenient object upon which to vent his anger. That was supposed to make Matt feel O.K. but he was feeling sick inside and knew he wouldn't feel safe until he got home. Patsy said he would walk him back to his flat, and they left together. They rounded the first corner and walked straight into Marty; this time without his friends' restraining arms. He lurched at Matt, uttering violent obscenities, but Patsy intercepted saying, "Stay out of this, Matt."

The two men connected and scuffled briefly but, being very drunk, Marty went down and soon Patsy was laying into the supine thug with his boot as he curled up to protect his face.

"For Christ's sake, Patsy!" Matt yelled, "That's enough! COME ON! Let's get out of here!"

Patsy turned, delivered a final kick to the back of Marty's head, and ran off with Matt in tow. For the second time that night, the adrenaline was churning his stomach.

They didn't stop running until they were well out of the way, along the Shore Road. Panting in the weak light of the street lamp, Matt saw a black trickle down Patsy's face. "Are you alright?" he asked, reaching to touch his saviour's brow.

"Aye, just a graze," he assured, retreating from Matt's touch.

"You're eye looks bad. You'll have a shiner tomorrow."

"Always bleeds bad there."

"We'll see, up in the flat," Matt said ominously, shifting into teacher mode.

In the flat, the damage was clearer. Patsy had bitten his tongue and the bloody mouth looked worse than it was but the nasty split above his eye really did look serious.

"I think he had a ring on," Patsy explained.

"It's going to need stitches, I reckon."

"No way! If the pigs find him they'll go to the surgery. See who's been fighting!"

"Was he that bad?"

"I hope I killed the fucker!" His tone was cold and sincere. It made Matt's skin creep.

Matt stuck the wound together as best he could with sticking plaster and removed Patsy's scarlet-stained tee-shirt for soaking.

Dabbing Patsy with damp cotton wool relaxed him and, then, Matt realised that Patsy was getting aroused. Matt was both excited and scared. Patsy was sexy but there was a very scary side to him and he didn't want to get involved. Patsy left the flat wearing one of Matt's tee-shirts and virgo intacta.

Some nights later, Matt bumped into Patsy in Micky's and, not a little concerned for his own reputation, he asked him if there had been any repercussions from the fight. No, he was informed, Matt wasn't Marty's first victim and he had 'been told'. Patsy's tone warned Matt not to pry any further; the Provos had stepped in. The Provisional I.R.A. acted as a sort of alternative police force, cum judge and jury in the Nationalist parts of the town. If anyone had a problem, it was to them they turned. Antisocial behaviour would not be tolerated and the punishment wasn't a ticking off by the resident magistrate!

At closing time Patsy bought what he called a Judas. He always explained this bizarre term by telling a joke: "How do you know that Jesus was a piss head?..... Because Judas' carry-out was worth six pieces of silver!"

Back at the flat, Patsy was not his usual self; he was edgy, unnecessarily talkative and sat slurping, jerkily at his can.

"How's your chest?" he suddenly asked.

Matt was puzzled: "It's O.K. thanks, I haven't been ill!"

"No. Your hair. You know?"

"Oh!" he expired, recalling the incident a couple of weeks back. "Not much different. How's yours?"

"Take a look," he offered, lifting his tee-shirt.

Matt would have been stupid not to have read the signals, but he was hesitant and not a little scared. He slipped his own shirt off and Patsy touched his chest hair: "It's soft," he said in a curiously baby-like tone. "I wish mine was like that."

Matt felt the sparse scattering of black hair on Patsy's well developed chest. "Yours is fine," he reassured. "Your eye's healed alright," he said, stroking the scar.

Patsy shifted his head so that Matt was caressing his cheek. He moved again and kissed Matt's hand. Matt risked a full kiss on the lips and Patsy responded greedily. They stumbled into the bedroom and stripped, falling onto the bed as they wrestled, trying to achieve as much flesh contact as they could, as they kissed. Matt tried his best but, once the initial rush of lust was satisfied, he realised that he was only going through the motions. Patsy's body, attractive only a week ago, was now a threat. What was worse, Patsy was evidently nervous and in need of a confident and controlling lover. He was waiting for Matt to do it all, and he didn't want to. Matt brought Patsy to a climax that satisfied him but then pulled away and left him lying spent and alone. They parted friends, but Matt was determined never to do it again with him.

Patsy was only one of a blur of various and nefarious young men who crossed Matt's path around that time. Some ended up having sex with him, some teased, but by far the majority were just friendly youngsters out for a good time. Having his own gaff made Matt a rare commodity in Ballycol; most would never have bothered to get to know him, otherwise. Matt's sexual adventures in the early eighties differed from his earlier Belfast exploits when he was experiencing what his contemporaries had gone through at university; discovering sex. Ballycol was a fruitless search for love. Life became an endless miasma of alcohol, talk and the occasional, unsatisfactory, sexual encounter. School, following interminable late nights became unreal. Staggering in, head swimming, he was hardly capable of delivering a particularly effective lesson and yet, other than Mary, no one made any comment. The only lasting friendship nurtured by this period of debauchery was Feargal's.

Matt's nadir arrived one evil evening in December. Against his better judgement, he had battled his way down the hill and along the lakeside to the pub. Bursting through the narrow door he struggled out of multiple layers, shaking the drops from coat, hat and scarf and leaving little cold pools on the ragged lino. Although warmer in the pub, it was hardly worth making the effort; there wasn't anyone there he knew well enough to chat to and so he spent most of the night lounging on the bar exchanging inconsequential pleasantries with Micky.

Evidently, anyone with any sense was curled up in front of a fire at home because no one had arrived in by eleven. He started preparations for the expedition home and was soon ploughing his way along the blustery lakeside road. A man had been watching him in Micky's. He looked like so many of Ballycol's men; about thirty, but with the careworn air of middle-age. Matt had caught his occasional glance but had no desire to speak to him; he looked rather sinister. The stranger lifted his coat, followed Matt and caught him up before he reached the Diamond. Matt's immediate fear was that he was some sort of psychopath.

"Matt," the stranger mumbled.

"Yes," he replied, tentatively.

"Can I have a word with you?"

"What about?" he asked cautiously.

"Can we go somewhere a bit more private?"

Matt wasn't happy with the idea. Quiet as it was on the street, there was at least a chance of someone coming along if he turned nasty, in 'somewhere a bit more private', he would be at this man's mercy

"Why? What do you want?"

"Are you gay?" he asked, putting a nasty slant on the last word making it sound more like gey.

He took a deep breath; he was ready to run if he made a swipe at him. His heart raced as he said, "Yes. Why do you want to know?"

Matt cowered, as the man moved closer to mumble, "I think I might be a little bit gay too. I need to talk to someone about it and you're the only person I could think of."

The man had won by appealing to Matt's ego. Here was the brave, bold Matt about to dispense a vital service; one that only he could perform.

Matt never really believed that talking was the man's prime motivation; his whole being was oozing tension, but Matt at least expected him to go through some sort of pre-coital formality. Not so. The man grabbed Matt from behind as soon as the flat door closed. There was no holding him. Strong, work-hardened arms coiled about the young teacher. The man clung to him like a great leech groping at his crotch. To Matt's eternal shame, he didn't resist. Carried along on a wave of sensuality, he let himself be drawn into his private fantasy but the eroticism soon faded to mechanism. Before long they were wrestling on the living room carpet, ridiculously naked but for crumpled trousers around their ankles. As if from above, Matt surveyed himself as the awful man pawed and slobbered over him. He winced inwardly at the thought of what the women in Auchinleck's shop below would think if they could see him now! He had to get out of this.

"Come on. It's time to go now," Matt said in a calm, calculating voice, shocking himself with its coldness; he even sounded like a prostitute.

"Fuck me," the horrible man begged.

"No. It's time you went. I've got to get up for work tomorrow."

"Please," he asked coquettishly. It was so ridiculous to see this grown man begging him to screw him. "Just put it in," the man insisted, "You want to. You know you want to, don't you," he wheedled.

Matt didn't want to; discounting one disastrous encounter in France, Alex was the only person with whom he had ever had intercourse. With everyone else, including Piet, it had only been foreplay and wanking. Intercourse was something special for him, an expression of love; of spiritual oneness.

He looked at the man lying naked in front of him and begging him to screw him. All he wanted to do was to get rid of the intruder. Fuck it, he thought: "Alright. But then you have to go."

The man sprawled prone on the Axminster as Matt served him brutally and mechanically. He was appalled at what he had done. He had used his penis as a weapon to punish that man for his presumption and the bastard had loved it. Apparently satisfied, the man left Matt to contemplate his position. There was little doubt in Matt's mind that he was considered as little more than a whore in that town. Nauseated, he sluiced himself in cold water in a vain attempt to flush his shame away.

CHAPTER 6
1982, REHABILITATION

Feargal was slightly crazy; of this, Matt had little doubt. Obsessed with sex, he talked about it incessantly and his drinking habits made Matt's excesses look like prudent self control and yet Matt never thought of Feargal's behaviour as the least bit inappropriate, as it fitted his Bohemian image. Matt could always find Feargal, alone or in company, any night he chose to go down to Micky's and then they would end up at the flat. Feargal was indirectly responsible for many an unsober morning of teaching. He kept a stock of Cokes in the prep-room fridge, so he could sneak out for a reviving can at critical times when the in-skull throb, combined with the bedlam of a rowdy biology class, became unbearable.

Weekends were a bit more rational. They would head out to a dance somewhere, Ballyshannon was favourite but Enniskillen, Omagh and Donegal Town were all well within their range. More often than not, Feargal would pick up a woman and they would all head back to Matt's flat. Feargal would restrain himself until Matt had gone to bed then screw his conquest on Matt's living room floor. Matt preferred the rare occasions when Feargal didn't score for then he had his full attention for the night.

Feargal had the knack of befriending total strangers and enticing them back to Matt's place. He was brilliant at latching onto anyone's hang-ups and drawing them into a deep conversation about the most personal things. He had a unique insight into the little triggers that would hoist an apparently innocuous being onto his high horse. Because he was so seemingly degenerate, people felt they had the moral high ground. Through Feargal, Matt learnt what it was like to be in the Provos, what one of his colleagues' wives was like in bed and what went on in a local witch's coven, the existence of which had only been rumour until then. Feargal's piece de resistance was to entice a couple of Mormons back one night and proceed to shake their absolute certainty in their mission. Many of these blow-ins didn't have much respect for Matt's home. He didn't worry too much about the cigarette burns in the carpet or the spilt booze, but it niggled him to think that they probably wouldn't dare behave like that in their own homes.

One Thursday evening, late in eighty-two, Matt arrived at Micky's to find Feargal in an unusually ebullient mood. His parents had gone out and they weren't due back until Friday morning. He had the house to himself, for once, and he was determined to return Matt's hospitality. Matt fully expected Feargal to invite half the pub home after closing time. However none of the usual crowd turned up that night so only the two of them headed for Feargal's house.

It was a prosperous looking bungalow on the shore road with a garden that sloped down to the dark lake beyond. As they entered, Feargal shushed at Matt, indicating that his sisters were asleep somewhere.

"I thought you said you had he place to yourself!" Matt whispered fiercely.

"I have, 'cept for the wee-uns, and they're fast asleep so they won't cause any hassle!"

They crept past sleeping doors to the kitchen. A faint whiff of paint hung in the air; they must have decorated recently, Matt decided.

"There's tins in the fridge."

"Where's the bog?"

"Out there, first right."

When Matt emerged, a ladder had appeared in the hall and a light glowed in the attic. Feargal's tousled head popped through the hatch in the ceiling: "Come on up," he beckoned.

Matt knew him well enough not to question his actions. As Matt cleared the trapdoor a whole new aspect of Feargal was revealed. This was his pad. It could have been a Parisian artist's garret; it certainly had nothing in common with the rest of Ballycol. The faint tang in the hall was a turpentine reek up here. Now Matt understood the cause of the hint of organic solvent that lingered under Feargal's acrid, cigarette musk. He wasn't a closet glue-sniffer after all!

A mattress and crumpled duvet were the only indication that this was also his bedroom. A canvas, flushed with white size, sat expectantly on an easel; he was evidently about to start a painting.

Sheets were draped over more canvases propped against every wall. Matt drifted towards the nearest lot: "Can I see?"

"Sure," Feargal responded with feigned nonchalance. Matt suspected he was quite flattered.

He lifted a sheet expecting to see an great master but it was another blank canvas, as was the one behind, and flicking through the rest of the pile was no more rewarding.

"Plenty of spare canvases," he quipped.

Feargal was leaning on his shoulder, watching his face.

"Smart arse!"

Matt looked quizzically at him.

"Suppose you can't see much in this light," the young artist conceded.

On closer inspection the canvases did have a thin wash of colour.

"They're better in natural light," he explained.

Matt tried to look half intelligent: "What're you trying to show?"

"Rain."

"Rain?"

"Aye! What else in this fucking town?" he chortled

He drew Matt to the huge dormer window and they gazed out over the oily black lake in silence.

"You should see it. It never rains the same way twice. I sit for hours watching the light changing out there," he murmured, wistfully. "Fuck, it's incredible. I have to capture it!"

"Paint rain?" said Matt slowly.

"Nah! The light, the movement when it rains. I used to do the view, Mum liked that. There's some horrible chocolate boxes on the living room wall. I want to get rid of 'em but the old doll says they're the only nice things I've done. Fuck! She has no notion."

Matt felt he had to defend his friend's mother: "I'm sure it's not that. I bet she's really proud of you. Any bets she shows your stuff off to everyone who comes in."

"Too right she does. I fucking squirm. I hate it," he grimaced.

"You shouldn't. It's her way of saying she loves you."

"Is it fuck! It's her way of telling me I've become a no good waster. She never misses an opportunity to get a dig in: 'It's such a shame that he didn't stay on at art college, he would have been such a good teacher,' is one of her favourites!"

"I'm sure you would be."

"No way I'm going to get into that game. Jesus! Can you imagine me in a school? A fucking Catholic school at that!"

Amused, Matt looked at him fulminating: "I would like to see your work sometime. In better light. And when I'm sober!"

"Any time," he offered, zipping the tab off a can of Smithwicks. "Any time you like."

He had a stash inside an old turps bottle. He rolled up and they shared a couple of powerful joints. Lounging on his mattress, they gossiped and giggled until the maniac munches came upon them.

"There's sausages," Feargal beamed.

"Let me at 'em."

Matt dithered at the top of the ladder, he didn't feel too stable: "Woah!" he yelled as his legs thrashed in slow motion, looking for a foothold.

"Shshsh!" Feargal sniggered.

Matt slithered to the bottom of the ladder to find himself facing a very angry middle-aged lady. Feargal was standing there, ashen faced.

"I can't trust you a minute, can I!" she lambasted.

"Aw! Come on, Mammy. We weren't doing any harm."

"Oh no!" she sneered. "As soon as my back's turned you bring your drunken, good for nothing friends in to wreck my home!"

His gore rose visibly: "I was just showin' him my work!"

She rounded on Matt: "Suitably impressed, were you?"

"I... I thought they were very good," Matt stammered.

"They're a waste of time, that's what they are. It's time the good for nothing layabout shifted his rump and looked for a job instead of sapping off me. That place is a tip. I'm surprised you have the shame to let anyone see it. I suppose he," she indicated Matt as if he was a turd on the footpath, "doesn't know any better."

"I'm not going to try to argue with you, Mammy," he spat through clenched teeth. "You've the artistic sensitivities of a blind camel with terminal moronity."

"Don't you DARE speak to ME like that you ungrateful young pup." As she said this, she lifted a wooden clothes brush and went for her son, breaking it on his arm. He tried to fend her off, pushing her aside.

She turned to a quaking Matt: "Did you see that?" she screamed. "He struck me!"

By now, two terrified little girls were peering round a bedroom door.

"You wouldn't do that if your father was here!" she yelled.

"But he isn't, is he?" Feargal sneered nastily.

By this stage Matt had his jacket on and was edging for the front door. Feargal spotted him. "Hang on," he yelled. "I'm coming with you."

The poor lad spent a miserable night in a sleeping bag on Matt's settee. Despite his bravado, he was obviously upset by the experience. Feargal told Matt about his home life, head uncharacteristically bowed, voice not projecting with its normal confidence. He stayed with Matt until Sunday. Over the weekend, slowly and painfully, all the anguish and torment, caused by his father's extramarital affair, surfaced.

Matt sat and listened, sharing his friend's distress. For much of the time he had a reassuring arm round his shoulder. A fly on the wall would surely have chirped, "Oh my! Matt's got another man." But it would have been an understandably mistaken fly. The sensations were pleasurable, certainly, but they weren't primarily sexual. The trust Feargal was investing in him was boosting Matt's low ego. He thought people tolerated him because they felt sorry for him; because he was so pathetic. Maybe he amused some of them or supplied them with sexual gratification, but he was sure that no one in Ballycol respected him or, even less, needed him. But, here and now, Feargal needed him. Not just anyone, him. In realising this, the first stage in his restoration into a valid human being had begun.

CHAPTER 7

SPRING 1983, FORCED MOVES

The first day back in eighty-three, Mary cheerily greeted him: "Did you have a nice Christmas?"

"Not particularly!" he replied sullenly. Other than her party at the end of term, it had been pretty dull. His former pupil and friend, Simon, had only been home from college for a couple of days so he hardly saw him. Alex was a bit better with him but he was still hard work and in any case, Sandra seemed to have a monopoly on him. Willy-John and Louise had had an intimate little Christmas for two. In the absence of any of his old mates Matt had been reduced to boozing with Feargal in Ballycol, which wasn't much different from the usual run of things.

Mary was in charge of health education and she had booked a speaker from the Northland Centre to give form five a talk on alcohol abuse. Matt happened to teach them the morning of the talk, so he had to sit in on the lecture. There were actually two people doing the talk; a fairly cute young man and an older, middle-class woman. The woman started with an academic account of what alcohol did biologically. She moved onto the dangers of drinking too much and explained what was deemed excessive. He wasn't surprised to note that his consumption was way over what was considered wise but he was a little alarmed to see how much over the 'safe limit' he had gone. He consoled himself with the thought that his consumption was nothing when compared to Danny's. Danny had been Matt's best friend at primary school but they had drifted apart more than once. Last time he had seen him he had been drinking heavily, and they had been incommunicado since summer eighty-one. Matt had tried to phone him on innumerable occasions but he could never catch him. To Matt's great relief, the cute young man stood up after the break. Russell had been drinking since he was fourteen. He had discovered that he was an alcoholic at the age of twenty-four. Slowly at first, then with increasing confidence, Russ took the audience on a nightmare journey from his early beginnings as a schoolboy boozer. He told of his graduation to drinking every day and of the lengths to which he went to find drink when all the pubs were closed. He described the blackouts. They hit an awful chord; Matt had mornings when he couldn't remember anything about the night before. Clearly and dispassionately he described his nadir. He had woken up one morning in a strange hotel room; he wasn't even in Northern Ireland and he couldn't remember how he got there! Russ had grabbed Matt's attention; he felt he could well be on the way down the same dreadful road and said so to Mary: "I'm in a rut," he complained, "My life's just not going anywhere. I'm not meeting the sort of people I want to be with. My only friend here is Feargal and, with his drinking habits, he's a liability."

"Make a New Year's Resolution," she advised, "Find friends who aren't boozers."

"How?" he whined. "I need to be where people get pissed, to meet people without them being freaked out."

"Why do people have to be drunk to get on with you?" she asked incredulously.

"Because I'm gay and it's only when they're pissed that they lose their fear of me."

"That's nonsense!"

"It's not. I can see the looks when I go into the pub."

"Come on, be sensible," Mary demanded. "I don't believe that's true, but, even if it is, who wouldn't need to be drunk to socialise with you? Think."

"No one in their right mind." he sulked.

"Matthew!" she squealed.

"I was only joking," he assured her. "Other gay people, I suppose. And broad minded straights like you, but they're pretty rare."

Mary managed to keep her patience: "And where will you meet these people?"

"Straights or gays?"

"Either," she almost snapped in exasperation.

"That's the problem, isn't it. There aren't any gay people in Ballycol."

"I'm sure there are," Mary said more gently. "But even if there aren't, what about Enniskillen? Omagh? Dungannon? Even Derry! You go there some weekends, don't you, there must be gay people there, why not socialise with them?"

"I suppose I could phone Cara-Friend again. You know, that gay help-line in Derry. They might have forgotten that time when Piet made such a spectacle of himself in the pub."

"Do it." she commanded, "Make that your New Year's Resolution. I'm sure they won't hold Piet's behaviour against you!"

Matt perked up: "I will. What's your resolution then?"

"Ah-ha," she smiled secretively. "Promise not to tell?"

"Go on."

"I'm getting out of teaching this year."

Matt was appalled: "What will you do? I can't imagine you not being a teacher!" He thought she was crazy to give up teaching. In the short time she had been at the school she had leaped up the promotion ladder and she was head of home economics as well as teacher in charge of health education.

"I'm going to use the money from Dad's will to open a whole-food shop."

"Great, where?"

"Right here in Ballycol," she beamed.

His face dropped.

"What's the matter?"

"Do you think they want whole-food here?"

"I've been laying the foundations with the pupils. There should be enough of a nucleus of health conscious kids here now to make it work."

He was impressed by her enthusiasm, but he wasn't convinced.

Micky's was packed, as it always was on Friday nights. Matt was sitting with Feargal and a crowd of his friends when the babble of the pub was silenced by an almighty, gut-wrenching boom which flung the doors open and rattled the glassware and bottles behind the bar. The momentary silence was followed by a hubbub as everyone streamed out to see where the bomb was. Matt had become blasé about explosions by then and assumed that this one was somewhere in the main street or up near the army base. Someone bustled over to fill them in: "Red Hand Bar and Auchinleck's," she jabbered. "Bodies in the rubble. Terrible mess."

Biologically, a surge of adrenaline caused a constriction of his superficial skin capillaries, diverting heat from his external thermoreceptors; Matt's blood ran cold.

He followed the crowd to the Diamond where a white tape, guarded by policemen, flapped limply across the end of Cavanagh Road. Matt gabbled something about living there and the young constable let him pass.

It was an eerie sight. The street lamps were out but the scene was being swept by the blue beam of an emergency vehicle's lamp. The throb and roar of a helicopter thrashing the air above the street dominated everything, and its searchlight bathed the end of the street in its Star of Bethlehem light. Every window was gone and curtains flapped purposelessly in the breeze. Shattered glass was strewn over the road like a fresh fall of snow, it crunched under his feet as he picked his way along. Windowless cars were islands in the sea of shards. His end of Auchinleck's was standing but at the far end was a gaping hole. Opposite was a great gap where the Red Hand Bar had been. Ambulances had reversed as far down as they could and people were swarming like ants over the rubble that once was the bar. An occasional flurry of activity would accompany a stretcher as another victim was ferried to a waiting ambulance which wailed off towards the hospital.

Matt pushed his front door, which yielded without recourse to the key. He flicked the switch, knowing that no light would appear, and felt his way up the dark stairway. When he squeezed past the dislodged living room door he had expected to see chaos but the reality shook him. Even in the eerie, flashing half-light the devastation could be seen to be complete. Shredded posters dangled from his walls. The contents of his cupboards were strewn over the floor and his plants had all disappeared from the window ledge; they had been sucked out by the blast. Most terrible of all, was the monstrosity in front of the hearth which was strewn with bricks and soot. Almost pulsing with menace, a tangled lump of metal straddled his shattered settee. It was the back axle of the van in which the bomb had been planted.

The kitchen was as bad. Every cupboard had been sucked open and one had collapsed into the sink. He felt helpless in the face of such destruction. Going into his bedroom, he threw the glass-strewn counterpane from his bed, crept defensively under the sheets and sobbed quietly to himself. After a while, he decided that he had had quite enough of feeling sorry for himself and it was about time he started to tidy up the mess. It was then that he heard someone moving about in the flat. As he pulled the covers around him he heard footfalls in the passage. "Who's there?" he called.

A light flashed in his face.

"Are you all right sir?" a Ballymena accent enquired.

"Perfectly, thank you."

"No injuries?"

"No. None."

"Where were you when it went up?"

"In the bar."

"How did you get out?" the policeman asked, incredulously.

Matt realised he thought he meant the Red Hand: "Micky's!" he explained. "Is anyone hurt?"

"Three dead so far. Still digging," the policeman reported grimly.

"Fuuuck!"

"You shouldn't be here, sir," the constable went on. "They shouldn't have let you back in. There could be gas, you know. Have you somewhere you can go?"

"No. I'll be alright here."

The policeman sat down on the bed. He talked to Matt as if he were a child: "They've opened the church hall in the Diamond. You had better go there," he insisted. "Do you know if there's anyone else in the building?"

The church hall was filling with the stunned residents of Cavanagh Road. He wasn't there long before Simon's father arrived to take him up to their house where he was given Simon's room and told to stay as long as it took to find somewhere else.

Somewhere else turned out to be seven, Richmond Villas, one of the four-storey, Georgian, town houses overlooking the lake. It belonged to a family called Pollock. Their son, Richard, had been one of Matt's more successful pupils and his Granny had left him the house in her will. It had lain empty for a couple of weeks but the family were worried that squatters might move in, so they had been taking it in turns to sleep there. Matt's need was their fortune. He could stay there, rent free, as a sort of caretaker until Richard decided what to do with the house.

Despite the bitterly cold wind which whipped across the lake and found its way between every window frame and under every door, he liked living in Richmond Villas. He could certainly see why the Pollocks preferred their centrally heated house in Bel Vue but the view of the lake from the front window was spectacular; worth every shiver and crick in the neck.

He made the first floor front room into his sitting room and slept in the room above it. This meant that he could keep his eye on the pageant of the lake's moods and fauna. Time and again, mysterious misty mornings and pyrotechnic sunsets sent him rushing for his camera; he certainly appreciated Feargal's need to paint the lake. After a few weeks he could have done an entire portfolio entitled, 'Views From My Window'. Binoculars hung in permanent readiness. Usually the flotilla of duck was mallard but it could just as well be scaup, teal, pochard, goldeneye or widgeon. To Matt's surprise, David called to his new home to see how he was and offer him his support. After that he began to pop in every now and then for a cup of tea and a chat. It was odd, because he had always avoided Ballycol, saying it wasn't safe for RUC men. He *had* come to Mary's Christmas party, though and he hadn't seemed to mind chatting to Feargal and some of the other Catholics, there so perhaps he was mellowing in his old age.

Living so cheaply, Matt would soon have saved enough to get a car but then his father intervened, loaned him what he hadn't yet saved and soon he was the proud possessor of a vivid scarlet, flat windscreened Beetle. Mobile at last, Matt rang the Derry help-line and asked for Kevin, the guy who had met him and Piet a few years earlier. He wasn't on that night but the man to whom he spoke was very friendly. Matt quite fell in love with his voice. Barney, for that was his name, told him about gay discos being held at Magee College and promised to meet Matt the following Friday, to take him there.

CHAPTER 8

SPRING 1983, CHRIS MCDAID

Magee College was Derry's centre of higher education. The main college building was Victorian Gothic, in the same style as the Methodist College in Belfast, but in sandstone. It occupied a commanding site. From its proud frontage, a great expanse of parkland swept down to Lough Foyle. At least, it would have done had someone not built a road along the shore and lined it with warehouses and terraces. However, the panoramic view was blurred by teeming rain the night that Matt's little car chugged up to the imposing building. Barney was sheltering in the vaulted portal. As Matt drove up, he threw the hood of his Parka over his head, dashed over to the car and got in.

Barney was much younger than Matt had expected. He was slim, acned and had a slightly slack mouth. Brief introductions were made, then Matt asked him if the disco was in the main college. It wasn't.

"You don't mind driving down, do you?"

Matt drove about fifty yards down the hill to a sinister shell of a house he'd never seen before.

"Park here," Barney commanded.

Matt looked around him. Other than the old house he couldn't see anything. "Where is it?" he asked.

"Round the back."

Barney shot out of the car, called, "Follow me," and disappeared into a shadowy doorway.

Dubiously, Matt began to lock the car. After all, what did he know about this guy? He had talked to him once on the phone. He had no proof that this was even the same guy he had spoken to. Barney looked too weedy to do anything to Matt on his own but he might have friends in that derelict building. It could be a terrorist trap. Perhaps, with his hint of an English accent, they thought he was a soldier. He lost his nerve, unlocked his car and got back in. This is bloody stupid!

he said to himself. If I don't do this I can forget ever meeting other gay people in Derry. Anyway, what the fuck do I care if I do get killed? It's better dead than living like I am at the moment. He relocked the car and headed for the black doorway.

The room was dank and dark. He edged into the blackness, listening to the dripping rain. Suddenly, a dark figure stepped out in front of him, Matt's heart missed a beat as he saw a face covered by a mask.

"What took you so long?" Barney asked, unwrapping his scarf. I'm freezing my bollocks off here! Come on, it's round the back." He trotted out of the door and disappeared along a poorly lit, slippery path, with Matt on his tail.

What looked like a concrete blockhouse had been added on behind the derelict house. Strains of music seeped through the double doors. As Barney pushed the door open, Matt's senses were assaulted by disco lights and sounds. Adjusting to the light he saw that the doorman was Kevin. He greeted Matt like a long-lost friend.

Magee was very different from the Queen's discos. The atmosphere was more of a house party than a commercial venue. To his left a serving hatch, presumably from a kitchen, was doubling as a disco console and a soft drinks bar. Low tables skirted three sides of the parquet dance floor. A few dozen women and men occupied stacking chairs scattered around the tables. Each table tended to have a more or less homogeneous group. One seemed to be well-dressed middle class men, another was occupied by women in jeans and T-shirts and the far corner of the disco was the domain of a fairly aggressive looking crowd of punks swigging from vodka bottles.

Matt had the strangest feeling of deja vu. It was like that first dance on the Waterside, just over ten years ago when he was a naïve sixth former. There he was again, making tentative first steps into a new life. If seventeen-year-old Matt could have seen himself at twenty-seven he would have probably given up then and there!

Kevin left the door, to chaperone Matt for a while then disappeared off to talk to someone. Matt feasted his eyes on the banquet of men set before him. Couples of all three possible combinations bopped and weaved. Clean-cut couples in suits and ties boogied, long haired, leather-clad youths head-banged and punks pogoed.

"I didn't realise that there were so many gay people in Derry," he shouted to a young man next to him.

"Place's full of queens," he replied. "But not everyone here's gay. Students get in free, and the punks come here 'cos it's the only place'll let 'em in."

Looking at the exotic creatures, he wasn't very surprised. He had thought that punk had gone out ages ago but it had, evidently, a residual following in this remote corner of the empire and they were really not a very attractive lot. They seemed to go out of their way to make themselves look ugly, they looked intimidatingly violent and most of them were staggeringly drunk. It was obvious why they weren't welcome in "normal" society.

Matt became aware that one of the punks was staring at him. He averted his eyes, not wanting to draw unwelcome attention to himself. He worried that they might get heavy if they thought that a gay man was eyeing them up! Shit! Matt thought. The punk was coming over to him; he prepared himself for evasive action. To his alarm, the punk stared penetratingly at his face then grabbed his arm to shout in his ear.

"Hello, Matthew,"

Confused, he responded.

"Don't you know me?" the punk roared above the music.

Matt didn't know anyone with lilac hair, not in Derry at any rate. He peered at the punk's face, it was familiar but he couldn't place it. He was too young to have been at school with him. He had evidently suffered from dreadful acne in his adolescence. His mouth was sullen but his eyes sparkled. Even in that light he could see they were porcelain blue. "Sorry. I just can't place you," he yelled.

"Fucking brill, that! You've known me since I was knee high to a grasshopper and you don't even recognise me."

It dawned on Matt that it was Danny's wee brother: "Christopher?"

"Aye. Got it in two!"

"I wouldn't have expected to see YOU here!" Matt blurted. "Of course, I imagine you punks have a hard time of it in Derry," he added lamely. "How's Danny?"

"He's grand," he started. Then he said something that was drowned by the thump of the disco beat. He grabbed Matt's arm and steered him towards a door.

Chris took him into what he had supposed was a kitchen. In fact, it was only a small room, and the main thoroughfare to the toilets at that. Evidently, this was the recognised spot for conversations. The walls were lined with little chatting knots.

"Bit too noisy to talk out there," Chris grinned.

"It's not much better here."

"You don't usually be at these, do you?"

"This is my first."

"Thought I might have seen you here sooner."

So. Danny told him about the misunderstanding, Matt thought.

"Why did you leave it so long?" Chris asked.

"Having too much craic in Ballycol. And I don't come home much. Anyway, I didn't know they were on."

Glancing away, Chris said, "Not a bad disco, eh?"

"Seen worse."

"Specially in Derry."

Matt brought the subject round to Chris: "What're you doing at the moment?"

"Government artist."

Matt looked puzzled.

"Drawing the dole!" he laughed.

"What about Danny?"

"Same. He's looking for work, though. Got an interview at Dupont's next week."

"What as?"

"Same sort as thing as before, I think."

Chris must have seen something in Matt's face. He smiled and said, "He's alright now. He's off the drink; properly off it."

"I'd like to see him again," Matt said cautiously. "Do you think he would see me?"

"Don't see why not."

"I've written loads of times but he's never replied. I thought he mustn't want to know me any more."

Chris looked serious for a moment: "I don't know for sure but I don't think you're right about that. Tell you what. I'll see what I can do. How can I get in touch with you?"

"Give me a ring at Strathbeg; number's in the book. I'll be there till Sunday evening but I'll be out most of the day because I'm going to see a friend."

"Boyfriend?"

Matt smiled broadly: *"Unfortunately*, no. School friend, actually. He was in an accident, he's in a wheelchair."

Danny rang when he was at Alex's. He left a message for him to ring back but, before he got the chance, Danny called again: "How's me old mucker?"

"Great, really great. How about you?"

He hesitated a moment: "I'll tell you when I see you. How's about next weekend? Will you be up?"

Matt wasn't intending to come home the next weekend, but with an offer like that, he could hardly refuse.

The rendezvous was Saturday lunchtime, in a pub called the Townsman. Matt left the car in the big car park next to the Guildhall, went through the gate in the old city walls and up Shipquay Street, one of Derry's main shopping streets. About a third of the way up the street, steps plunged down to the left, parallel to the pavement. Matt ventured down. The dimly lit bar was done out in plush velvet, holed with cigarette burns. Despite his neat, short haircut Matt recognised Danny immediately. Even in the weak light filtering through the basement window, Matt could see the old glow of his burnished coppery locks. He had lost the flab too. He looked fit and well and Matt told him so.

"Not looking so bad yourself," he retorted.

"It's great to see you. I'm really glad you rang."

Danny smiled sadly: "I wasn't sure."

Matt shook his head despairingly and looked at him dolefully.

"Sorry. Should have known better, shouldn't I?" Danny mumbled. Then he brightened up "How is me old mucker, then?"

"Great," he said. Then, without thinking: "Don't you want a pint?"

"Just a coke for me."

Matt decided to cover: "Driving?"

"Nope."

"Anything to eat?"

Matt ordered a shandy, a Coke and plates of sandwiches.

Matt filled Danny in on most aspects of his life over the last couple of years. He hadn't heard about Alex.

"Fucking shame, that," Danny responded. "He was O.K. Despite being a pig."

"He's coming on quite well," Matt explained. "It's beginning to look like he might walk again. Sandra says his legs are responding to physiotherapy. But what about you?"

Danny looked embarrassed, scanned the table and said, "I wondered when you'd ask." They had been close at primary school, then they had lost touch. They had met again at university but Danny's drinking had subsequently come between them. The last time they were together Matt had tried to get him to face up to his situation. He thought he had got through to him but there was an embarrassing incident and, afterwards, Danny had become totally incommunicado. Matt decided that he'd chased him off.

"What happened, Danny?" Matt asked softly.

Danny looked at his old friend: "This is going to be really hard."

"Don't talk about it if you don't want to."

"I wouldn't be here if I didn't know I had to; wanted to. I owe you, of all people, an explanation." He looked at Matt with his big, pale blue eyes. "You know I was drinking? Of course you knew! Jesus! Can I still delude myself?"

Matt didn't flinch.

"You got a tiny taste of what I was like when I was on the bottle. Mammy and Chris had it all the time. They were glad when I got home, at first, but I was soon up to my old tricks. Mammy hid her purse from me but I still managed to steal cash from her. You know I stole from you, don't you?"

Matt nodded.

"Chris and I got into a scrap, it was fierce. He beat the crap out of me. I should have been able to slaughter him but I was slowed up and he made a mess of me. Then he took me to the hospital. I wasn't that badly hurt but they kept me in a few days and he sat with me. Day and night I lay there, and he talked. He tried to make me see what I was doing. I couldn't see it. I thought everyone was ganging up on me, I thought they were imagining it. I had the horrors in hospital." Danny looked at Matt, wide eyed: "Fuck, it was hell."

He shivered to think of what Danny had gone through.

"They let me out after some counselling which I totally ignored. I *knew* I could handle the drink. Chris wouldn't let me out of his sight. He was like a mother to me, no, like a shadow. No matter how full I got he was there with me. He never stopped me boozing, he helped me home when I couldn't find my own way and next day he told me everything I'd done, everything I'd said and told me about all the people I'd pissed off."

"That's dedication for you."

Danny began to look incredibly uncomfortable: "Chris tried to find out what happened between you and me." He stared at his Coke, slowly rocking his head. "I'm sorry Matt." He couldn't look at him. "I.... I told him you... you raped me."

"Well it's true. Sort of," Matt murmured.

Danny shook his head; he looked as if he was going to be sick: "You were getting pissed off with me. I knew you loved me and I thought you'd let me stay longer if you thought you could have me. How sick is that? I offered you my body in exchange for a place where I could drink! Shit, I feel really bad about it, Matt. It's the worst thing I ever did."

"Did you ever tell him the truth?"

Danny shook his head in shame: "I was so ashamed. I couldn't bring myself to tell him."

"I don't get it. He never liked me. I'm surprised he doesn't loathe me now. He was really civil to me last week!"

"You're wrong about him, you know. When I said what I said he didn't believe me. He said he didn't think you would do that. He tried to get me to tell the truth. I didn't, but he did make me face up to the games I'd been playing with you and, once I'd faced that, the rest started to become obvious.

After Christmas, twelve months ago, he had me convinced. He got me to go to the Northland Centre. Know what that is?"

"Aye, we had a speaker," Matt confirmed.

"It was pretty heavy, Matt. If you think Chris was putting me through it, you should see what they did!"

"What?"

"It was all about getting you to face up to your drinking. There were encounter sessions where you had to expose all."

"Where do you join?" Matt said coquettishly.

"Not like that, you pillock!" Danny laughed. "You don't change, do you? I don't know, you might actually find it quite useful doing something like that. You have to explain to the others what was inside you. It's funny but when you start having to explain it to others you start to understand it yourself. I told them about everything, Lisa, lots you don't know about, about you, too, Matt."

"Oh, God," he half sniggered.

"Don't worry. No-one will ever say a thing. The whole point of the exercise was that there was a contract not to talk about the session outside. It means you feel safe to say anything."

"Was it important, about me?"

"Not really."

Matt looked deflated and Danny smiled: "You're important. But I had already faced up to what I'd done to you, and why. I had to think about what I was trying to escape from, trying to avoid."

"What is it?"

He half smiled and tilted his head, "I'll tell you when I know."

"What're doing with yourself now?" Matt enquired after a suitable silence.

"Got back into Gaelic, doin' a lot of training, bit of soccer."

"Don't those boys booze a lot? Isn't that a bit hard for you?"

"Aye, but I can't wrap myself up in cotton wool, can I?"

"So where are you at now?"

"I haven't had a drink since December eighty-two!"

"Not one?"

"No."

"Can you keep it up?"

"I've got to Matt. If I go back on the drink, I'll kill myself!"

CHAPTER 9
SUMMER 1983, PAINFUL REALITIES

He hadn't intended to go back to Derry the following weekend but, as Friday evening wore on, the thought of seeing Danny became more appealing than a lonely night in Ballycol. He drove up contemplating his next move; he would go to see Danny on Saturday morning and to Alex's on Sunday.

He got up abnormally early on Saturday morning and headed up to Rosemount. Danny wasn't in but Chris insisted on his staying for a cup of tea and some idle gossip. In the cold light of day Chris wasn't nearly so exotic. To his surprise, Chris' conversation was interesting and it was only when Mrs. McDaid asked him if he was staying for dinner that he realised how long he'd been there. They had started on Danny's cure and drifted from there. He realised that Chris and Danny were very alike. On a superficial level, he was the easiest person in the world to talk to but, as with his brother, Matt sensed that there were hidden depths in his personality he wasn't willing to expose.

Matt made his duty visit to Alex but, when he arrived, David was there. Unlike the Beetle, David's car would take a wheelchair so he offered to take them all for a spin. They went to Portrush where they took turns to push Alex along the promenade and onto Ramore Head. They gazed over the churning sea. Other than complaining about being too hot, Alex hadn't said much on the drive. Now he said he was too cold.

Matt sprinted back to the car for a blanket and, after covering Alex's knees, he crouched down next to him. "Beautiful, isn't it?" he said. "Look at THAT one!" he directed Alex's gaze towards the waves breaking over the Skerries, "They must be going up fifty feet!"

"I want to go back," Alex retorted.

"Sure. You ready, David?" Matt asked.

David didn't seem to hear: "Remember Rathlin?" he breathed.

Matt wouldn't have thought he would have wanted to remember Rathlin. Whether or not he admitted it, that trip must have been a blow to his ego.

Alex laughed. It wasn't a real laugh; he hadn't laughed naturally since the accident. If he thought the situation warranted it he would force a harsh, "Hah, hah, hah." This time it was worse than hollow.

"I missed my chance there," Alex said in a strange, lecherous voice. "Only had two of you. Could have had all three! Hah, hah, hah."

Matt didn't dare look at David. He'd forgotten Alex's suspicions about David that dreadful evening of Alex's accident. "That's not a very nice thing to say, Alex," he whispered fiercely. "Have some respect for David's feelings, for goodness sake!"

David's granite face was resolutely seaward.

Matt hunkered down in front of the wheelchair gripping its arms. He stared into Alex's watery brown eyes which stared back earnestly as he said, "Ask him if you don't believe me. He's queer....," He turned to David, "aren't you?"

Matt searched Alex's flaccid face for a trace of emotion. Perhaps it was his idea of a joke, ribbing his chum, but no, in his mind he was stating a fact.

"Listen," he started, "You and I had sex. That doesn't make you gay, does it?"

"No."

"Well then, why say David is?"

"You both want my cock. You got it, he didn't."

Matt was cross: "It wasn't just me, you know! You had something to do with it. Don't you remember? I loved you... I still do.... Doesn't that mean anything to you?"

A troubled frown passed over Alex's usually impassive face. Once passed it cleared again, he had come to a conclusion. "I wasn't getting any," he explained. "It's alright now though. I've got Sandra. I don't need it from you."

He glared at the churning water: "I want to go back to the car."

They walked back to the car in silence. Matt was desperately attempting to rationalise Alex's bombshells, Alex was his usual silent self and David didn't look at all happy. By the time they reached the car, Matt had reconciled himself enough to be able to make conversation with Alex on the journey home. They could sort it all out when Alex was better, this was neither the time nor the place to start a row. But if Matt could find it in his heart to let what he had said pass, not so David. He never said a word all the way home and he was driving far too fast. At the house, Matt brought the wheelchair round and David dragged Alex out of the car, plonking him in it like a sack of spuds. Matt started pushing Alex up the path but he turned to see David was ready to drive off, so he left Alex where he was and stopped David.

"Wait for me," he commanded, "I won't be long."

Half an hour later he prised himself away from the grateful Mrs. King and was surprised to find David still waiting as ordered.

"Sorry I was so long."

"No matter."

"Are you O.K.?"

"Aye."

"I'm going to my parents'. It's only round the corner, follow me up will you?" he asked.

David nodded and his smart blue coupe trailed the battered beetle to Strathbeg.

They settled in the parlour with a pot of tea and a plate of Jaffa Cakes.

"He's still not himself, you know," he tried to convince David. "He doesn't mean what he says."

"I think he knows damn right well what he says. He means it alright!" David scowled.

"The person that's sitting there means it. But that's not Alex yet, not the real Alex. He's confused and frightened. He's trying to make sense of what's happened to him and his poor brain's not working properly. It's not true what he said about him and me." David looked dubious.

"No, no. I don't mean that. We did have sex together. What I mean is, it wasn't just him letting me have his cock. He wasn't screwing me as second best 'cos he couldn't find a woman."

Matt's voice was cracking up: "For some reason, he can't remember the affection part of it. It was there, I promise you!"

"Do you think he's shagging Sandra?"

"Do you mind?"

"Is he, though?"

"I suppose he might be. I don't know any details about which bits of him are in working order. They did have something going before the accident. You knew that?"

David nodded.

"On the other hand, it could just be wishful thinking. The poor bastard must be as frustrated as hell. He always was a randy old stud," Matt grinned, a little too wistfully.

"I don't know how she puts up with him," David spat.

"Possibly she loves him."

"But he's..," he hesitated, "He's like an animal!"

"Come on," Matt remonstrated.

"He is! Haven't you seen him eating? He's like a pig! You could put swill in front of him and he would gobble it up all the same. He shovels it down him like a half starved convict. He's the same with drink too. And the way he talks about it, I bet his fucking is the same. Get as much spunk in, as quick as he can! Perhaps that's all she wants." He was sitting erect in his chair, staring past Matt, a flush on his high cheek bones, a slight flare of his nostrils his only outward sign of emotion.

Matt was shocked, he had never seen David like this and tried to reason with him: "I can't pretend to be a neurologist. But Sandra has been keeping me abreast of what's been going on. It's as if all his brain functions were shut down by the accident. Slowly, ever so slowly, they're coming back, one by one. But he's got to learn how to use them all over again. Or, rather, he has a memory of how to use them but it has to be jogged. The most basic, almost animal, functions were the first to come back. He can talk, but he hasn't the subtleties of conversation yet. He can think, but he has yet to regain reason and etiquette. He gets hungry and he wants to eat but he's not remembered how to savour good food. I suppose he feels sexual desire but he can't temper lust with what we call self control and reason. What we have at the moment is a few little bits of the Alex we love. The other bits, the fine edge that makes him special, are still there but they are dormant. Sandra has faith that they will come back."

"What do you think?"

"I hope so. If I believed in God, I would pray for it like I had never prayed before."

"Why does he have to be so bloody rude and insulting though? We're supposed to be his friends!" David said in a hurt tone.

"I don't think he was. In his mind he was stating a fact, he was making a conversational gambit. He can't see that what he said would cause embarrassment." Matt paused, then asked tentatively, "Er. Why do you think he said that about you?"

"I haven't a notion," David snapped. "As you say. He's confused."

Matt knew he was lying, was he feeling guilty, he wondered? Did he think that his pass at Alex sent him off on the binge that led to the accident?

"Try to be patient with him. He needs friends and I know he is fond of you. Will you go and see him again?"

"Aye. I suppose I will." He paused, composing his next contribution: "It's all his own stupid fault, you know!"

"What do you mean?"

"He was high as a kite." .... "The night of the crash."

"How do you know that?"

"Stands to reason, doesn't it. It was common knowledge at the barracks that he drank and drove, and one of the lads at the scene smelt it off him. No-one knows for certain where he was that night. Probably with his bit on the side."

Matt's stomach sank, but what David said next threw him: "He was seeing some woman somewhere. I reckon she was a Taig: he kept it dead quiet."

What the hell was he up to? He knew about Alex and him, didn't he? Why was he saying all this stuff? Was he trying to tell Matt it was his fault? Well, he wasn't going to start taking the blame. If Alex hadn't been so pig-headed he could have stayed over that night, no problem.

He wasn't going to let David know he'd rattled him: "If that's true," Matt said innocently, "Why wasn't he done for driving under the affluence of incohol?"

In reply, David gave him a disdainful stare. "I must be heading," he declared suddenly, standing up.

Matt had a horrible feeling that David was about to disappear for ever and, despite the last uncomfortable hour, he didn't want to lose contact with him. "Still in Skintown?" he asked.

"Aye."

"I'll give you my number. Perhaps we can meet up for a drink...... Somewhere safe. Omagh's O.K. isn't it?"

To Matt's relief, David accepted his phone number gratefully and promised to get in touch.

He watched David's car sweeping down the lane and felt a warm glow of satisfaction at a job well done. If nothing else, he had perhaps saved a faltering friend for Alex. He'd really earned Brownie points that day!

At the next disco, Chris came over as soon as he saw Matt. Danny had been sorry to miss him and he wanted to know if he would go out with him next Friday night; Danny usually played Gaelic on Sunday, so Saturday nights were out for him. He played soccer on Saturdays too, but that was in the afternoon and he didn't take that as seriously.

Business over, Chris said that he'd never seen Matt dancing; didn't he like dancing? Matt told him he didn't know anyone to ask. Chris laughed: "What do you come for, man? If it's not to meet people?"

"I know," Matt admitted. "But this just isn't my milieu."

"What is your mill-whatever you said?"

"I dunno. Quiet chat with friends somewhere. Pub, party, in front of a roaring fire at someone's. But not here. You're O.K. You look great in a disco, you fit in here, I don't."

Chris grabbed Matt's hand and dragged him towards the floor, "Wanna dance?"

A little taken aback, he followed him onto the dance floor and tried to copy his frenetic dance style. There were four fast numbers before a slow one drove him off the floor.

Matt wondered what the punks thought of Chris dancing with him but, as they didn't seem to worry whom they danced with, he decided it probably didn't bother them. Chris divided his time between the punks and Matt. He was the only punk not getting absolutely off his head.

Next Friday night couldn't come quickly enough for Matt. They met up in the Carrick which wasn't far from Rosemount. Matt hadn't expected Chris to be there too. He wondered if he was still shadowing his brother. It was the first time he had been in their joint company since primary school days.

Danny had got the job at Dupont's and he could hardly believe his luck.

"I don't see why?" Matt remonstrated. "After all, you always were smart. You sailed through at Lancaster. They must have seen they were on to a good thing with you and they snapped you up. It's as simple as that."

"But it isn't," he insisted. "I had to tell them about London."

"So?"

"Why I left.... you know."

Matt recalled his out of control boozing and workmates trying, unsuccessfully, to cover up for him.

"The interview was quite heavy. The guy was dead straight with me. He had a report from personnel where I used to work and I had to tell him it all. He wanted to know if he could contact the Northland Centre."

"And?"

"Well, he must have done. You don't understand what getting this job means to me, do you, Matt?"

"Of course I do. It's really shitty being out of work. Dead boring. No cash. Suppose you feel useless too."

"Yeah, yeah. But that's not the important thing. It means that other people - people who don't know me - have enough confidence that I can do it. That's the biggest boost I've had, Matty."

"I know you can do it," Chris chipped in. "You do too."

Chris, the sullen youth of only a few years ago, had stolen some of Danny's sparkle, his wit, his joie de vivre. Matt had wanted to talk to Danny alone and, initially, he resented the fact that Chris had turned up. But, to his annoyance, he found his attention increasingly being taken up by the young punk. He seemed to have more to contribute than Danny. Could it be that, by taking the drink out of him, the life force had somehow been drained too?

Friday nights became a regular fixture with Danny and Chris. He got to know Danny all over again. He hadn't really changed but, like his hair, his sparkling personality had toned down a bit. He was quite happy to chauffeur Chris and Matt. With Danny driving they tended to get further afield, although Matt preferred the evenings they spent together at Strathbeg. The biggest surprise was the interest Danny took in Alex. It began when Danny asked what he was doing one Sunday.

"I've said I'll go and see Alex," Matt apologised.

"Can I come?" he asked carefully.

"I don't see why not," Matt replied, although he wasn't sure how Alex would take Danny.

Alex evidently remembered Danny but whether he was delighted or disgusted, he showed no signs. Once they left his house Danny had no such reservations. "Fuck, it's not right!" he exploded. "If it had to happen to somebody why could it not be one of the thousands of out and out bastards in the police?"

"Fate doesn't work that way, you should know that." Matt paused and continued slowly, feeling his way: "In a way, you know, you and he are victims of the same thing. Me too!"

Danny looked interested.

"I wonder," Matt started.

"What?"

"I dunno. It's stupid, really."

"Go on."

"Well, we're all twenty-seven. Other than that we're really not all that similar but we've all had a pretty rough time and, to a greater or lesser extent, we've taken to booze. I don't really know what your hassle was, I've an idea what Alex's was, still is, for all I know, but I know exactly what mine was," he smiled.

"Being gay, you mean?" Danny asked curiously.

"Aye."

"But you've known that for ages, haven't you?"

"Oh, I've known, alright. But I hadn't accepted it until recently. I was always ashamed of being gay. I was afraid of the consequences. I can't really explain it but I knew in my heart that I wasn't accepted as a valid human being by the society I was trying to be a part of and I simply couldn't cope."

"Can you now?"

"I think so.... I know I'm not perfect. But I'm as right as anyone else and I can, and will, live my life in the certain knowledge that I have every bit as much right to my views and lifestyle as anyone else."

"What about Alex? And me?"

"I don't know any details but I'm pretty sure that Alex had some problems reconciling his own sexuality with the accepted norm."

"Is he gay?" Danny asked in surprise.

"I don't think so, not really. Just a bit unconventional, which didn't really sit very comfortably with his role as a representative of the Ulster establishment."

"What about me, then?"

"I don't really know that. Do you?"

He pulled a face and nodded.

"Just think," Matt speculated, "ten years ago, if you'd known what you know now, do you think it would have happened?"

"There's no way we would have been able to understand it at that age. No, we had to make our own mistakes and learn by them. You're alright now, I'm alright. It's just poor Alex who's been fucked!"

CHAPTER 10
AUTUMN 1983, ROMANCE

Danny must have taken Matt's theory about their common bond to heart because he joined him, whenever he could, on his visits to Alex and began to call in on Alex during the week. Danny wasn't the only one to make new friends that summer. David and Matt began to meet regularly in the Royal Arms in Omagh and he saw Chris every other Friday at the Magee discos. Chris got less punky as the year wore on. If anything he was tending toward hippiness with loose, baggy clothing from Oxfam. He was heavily into natural fibres and stopped dying his hair. Then, to his mum's dismay, Chris went vegetarian. The discos were stopping for summer and it was the last one. Matt and Chris were dancing when the set of slow numbers that signified the end of the night came on. As usual, Matt moved to sit but Chris restrained him and they smooched until the lights went on. Matt melted into the big man's arms and luxuriated in his affectionate kisses.

"You're the first man I've ever kissed," Chris whispered.
"Was it O.K.?"
"Oh Aye!"
"Want to try again to make sure?"
"Oh Aye!"

It was a very innocent courtship. Matt had been slow on the uptake; even after that smoochy dance he hadn't twigged what was going on and it wasn't until Chris rang him to arrange to go up to Belfast that they started seeing each other. Chris didn't want anyone to know about their relationship, so their courting was initially limited to furtive snogging sessions in the Beetle. Matt would have loved to have gone all the way with him but Chris didn't seem to want to get too heavy in the car. It wasn't very romantic and, if they were caught in flagrante, so to speak, they would be in serious trouble. Despite the law having been brought into line with English law the previous year and even though they were both over twenty-one, they were in a car and, in law, that was not considered to be in private. The same would apply to them as to those men who were caught having sex in public toilets. They would have been prosecuted for gross indecency and Matt would lose his job, for sure.

Chris was reluctant to come to Ballycol; how would he explain going to see Matt to his brother? Matt finally persuaded him to make up a story about going to a party in Belfast. Matt felt like a teenager again. He even went back early on Sunday to get the house ready for Chris' visit. He was at it all Monday night too. Although he was sure that Chris would sleep with him, he made up a spare bed in one of the other rooms, just in case. As he scrubbed and dusted he anticipated being able to show Chris off round Ballycol. Not that he would say, 'Hi kids, this is my new boyfriend!' No. But it would be so obvious that they were in love.

Matt worried a bit about what people would think of Chris, he wasn't nearly as beautiful as Danny. He supposed that people would think he had a peculiar taste in men; maybe he did! They might be nice to his face but then they might talk about him behind his back. That would annoy him. And if Mary realised he was seeing Danny's brother, she would probably think Matt was asking for trouble. It would be easier if she didn't know who he was just yet, anyway. And how should he behave with Chris in public? If Chris was a girlfriend he could hold hands; they might even kiss occasionally, but they couldn't do that. If the pupils saw them there could be hassle. If the parents didn't kick up, some of the bolder boys could give him a rough time. Not that he couldn't handle that, but, life would be easier without it. Matt went over every conceivable eventuality and finally decided that he would have to be circumspect when he was out with him. If he was in company he would be sure to give his time evenly to everyone. He hated being with a couple who were so wound up in each other that they had no time for anyone else and he had no intention of behaving like that!

He flew down to Micky's after school on Tuesday. Chris hadn't arrived but he was sure he would turn up soon, so he nipped over to the house to get changed and was back within fifteen minutes, but there was still no sign of Chris. He was well into his second Guinness and deep in conversation with Micky when Chris made his tentative way in.

"Pint?" Matt demanded, slapping him on the back.

"Dead on."

Matt thought they must have sounded frightfully heterosexual. "Good hitch?" he queried.

"O.K. as far as Omagh. Then I couldn't get a lift out. I was stuck for about an hour, then it was all wee jumps. You know, farmers and the like."

"Oh well. You're here now. Hungry?"

"Nah. Not yet."

"I've done you a veggie lasagna."

"Oh!" he paused. "That sounds nice."

Chris was nervous and the conversation didn't flow nearly as well as it should have, so Matt was relieved when Chris drank up and they could leave.

The big Georgian front door of 7, Richmond Terrace clunked, shutting out the hetero world. Chris was gazing up the stairwell in awe; you could see all three floors from there.

"How many live here?" he whispered.

"Just me," Matt replied, slipping his arms round Chris' waist and kissing the prickly nape of his neck. "Hello," he squeaked in a jokey voice. Chris soon relaxed and Matt was able to welcome him properly. "Come on," he said. "I'll show you round."

He gave him the guided tour of the museum-like rooms which he didn't use.

"When will you have to move out?"

"Soon, I'm afraid. Richard finishes at University next June and I suppose he will want to sell it then."

"Why don't you buy it?"

"I don't know. I don't suppose I could afford it. It must be worth a bomb and I dread to think how much it would cost to run."

"I don't know." Chris pondered, "This house isn't exactly in tip-top condition and this doesn't look to be the best part of the town. The house at the end is derelict! If the property was *that* valuable it would have been snapped up by now."

They had reached the second floor and were entering the front room. "And this," he swept his arm dramatically, "is my room." He looked at Chris, "Er. Do you want to sleep here too?" he asked warily.

"If you want me to," he said shyly.

"I do. Come on. Let's eat."

The atmosphere relaxed as they ate. At a suitable lull in the conversation Matt suggested that they went to the pub; he was surprised to see it was nearly nine-thirty.

"We'll probably meet Feargal there. He'll be interested to meet you. I met him through Danny. You'll like him."

Chris looked uncomfortable: "Don't say I'm Danny's brother."

"O.K." He looked carefully at Chris and enquired cautiously, "Why not?"

"I don't want him to know, that's all."

Matt had forgotten what the paranoia of being in the closet was like.

Feargal was in top form. He had been invited to submit some work to an exhibition in Enniskillen. To hear him talk you would think he'd been selected for the Royal Academy. This was it, his big chance. He was going to break into the art world at last. Chris was impressed. "When you're famous I'll be able to say that I knew you when you were nobody."

"FUCK! Nobody is what I am now, is it? When you're somebody you'll be more of a nobody than I ever was!" Feargal chortled.

"No, no," Chris laughed. "I didn't mean that, man! To me and Matt you're important." He glanced fondly at his boyfriend. "To them's out there, them that don't know no better. They don't know you yet, that's what I meant."

The glance wasn't wasted on Feargal. Matt watched realisation dawning on his freckled face and, for the rest of the evening he watched the couple like an anthropologist. He pointedly addressed his conversation to both of them and was uniquely reluctant to go back to the house when the pub closed.

Matt cracked a bottle of Jenever he had brought back from Holland and made them drink it like the Dutch do. When Chris went out to the toilet, Feargal chuckled conspiratorially, "You're a fly man. More power to you."

"What are you on about?" Matt asked quizzically.

He winked: "Getting him well oiled."

"I don't need to," Matt grinned.

"I'm pleased for you, he's dead on."

"He is nice, isn't he?"

"Aye but why aren't you sitting with him? You know! You should be having a wee court. I don't mind what you do, as long as you don't start screwing on the carpet! I might have to join in!" he chortled.

"There's no danger of that. He's a bit shy. I'm his first."

Feargal roared, "You bad bugger. Pardon the term. You took his virginity, did you?"

"Not yet," Matt winked, "not yet."

They fell into a guilty silence as Chris returned and sat next to Matt. "What do you think of this?" Matt asked as he scrubbed his fingers in Chris's recently shorn head.

"Great. As long as no ones going to mistake you for a Brit.!"

"No fuckin' chance," Chris spat.

"Chris's brother was shot by the army," Matt explained, sliding his hand down his neck. Chris tensed but didn't pull away.

Feargal sounded interested, he wanted to know more.

"Killed in action," Chris stated.

Feargal realised it wasn't a subject for discussion and asked, "How did you two meet?"

Matt remembered he had to avoid mentioning Danny: "At the gay disco in Derry."

"Pick you up, did he?"

"No. I picked him up," Chris grinned.

"Well done!" Feargal smiled. "It's about time. This young feller's been going to waste for far too long. I'm telling you. If I was gay I'd have been in bed with him like a shot years ago. Might still," he glinted.

"You might not be my type!" Matt lied, kissing Chris's temple.

"Fuck! Now he tells me. And there's me thinking he had the hots for me all these years."

"Hard luck, Feargal. Not everyone's queuing up to jump into bed with you. Most, but not all!"

"That a challenge?"

"Not when Chris's around, it ain't."

Feargal exploded, "Thank fuck! I thought I had just talked myself into bed with you!"

The ice had been broken, Chris snuggled into Matt and the evening went far more smoothly. Feargal, had an ostentatious yawning fit at an unusually early hour for him. "Time I hit the road to Denver."

Matt saw him down to the front door. Feargal hugged him and planted a big kiss on his lips. "Have a really good fuck," he ordered and disappeared into the night.

Matt was naked when Chris came from the bathroom. He threw his downy arms around Chris' prickly neck, rubbing his naked body against his coarse clothes. Chris didn't quite know what to do. Matt kissed every inch of shaven head, working down his face to his Adam's apple. Chris surrendered as Matt slid his hands under his vest and slid it up, feeling his warm trunk as he did. Torso stripped, Matt was free to kiss from his smooth shoulders down his silky sides to his tight little belly button. Matt surveyed Chris' physique. Where Danny was Caravaggio, Chris was Botticelli. Even at his flabbiest, Danny had a better body. Despite the unfavourable comparison, Matt buried his face into Chris' amply hairy chest and drew in a draught of air, warm, heavy with his fragrance; a faint tang of sweat and soap. Chris clutched Matt's head to his chest like a mother with a new-born babe. A brief fumble undid the belt and released Chris from his jeans. Pushing them down, he slid down his trunk until his cheek nestled against his briefs. Matt drew Chris into his the big bed pulling the duvet over them.

"Will you put the light off?" Chris murmured.

"If you want," he said, darting across the room to complete the task.

Still, Matt had to do all the work. Chris was turned on, there was no doubting that, but he simply didn't seem to know what to do. Matt didn't expect to have intercourse with Chris straight away. Alex was the only one he had ever let do him, he blamed the experience of being raped by a soldier when hitching in France for that. Since the arrival of A.I.D.S. he didn't want to do it with a one night stand anyway. One day he would meet a man whom he could love as much as he had loved Alex and then he was sure it would happen again.

Matt wanted Chris to know the pleasure he'd had with Alex and Piet but, no matter how hard Matt tried, Chris didn't seem to be enjoying the experience. For a few excited, guilt ridden moments his body thrashed before he shuddered and came. Then he fell into an exhausted stillness, leaving Matt to satisfy himself. Once the actual sex bit was over Chris seemed happier. He snuggled up to Matt, the two of them curled up together, and they fell into a cosy sleep. Next time, Matt thought as he drifted off, would be better.

It wasn't. The next night was just as dismal. Matt tried to coax him into reciprocating but he remained inert until his little climax and then lapsed into total inactivity. If Chris worried about his performance in bed, he never showed it. Matt excused him on the grounds of inexperience.

Chris left Matt on Thursday with promises to return for the same again soon. Was it worth it? Matt wondered.

The following Friday night's conversation was a minefield for Matt. In Danny's company he couldn't mention anything they had said or done on Chris' visit. The pecks and cuddles which had enriched Chris' stay with him were out of the question. When Danny went to the bar, he rounded on Chris. "This is awful," he complained. "I just don't feel comfortable. I don't like deceiving Danny."

"Stop trying so hard, man" he whispered fiercely. "You're making it worse. He's going to notice you're behaving oddly. Just talk about the sorts of things you normally talk about. And stop acting like a fucking interviewer giving us each equal time. It's fucking ridiculous, man!"

"It would be a damn sight easier if you would tell him!"

"No! I've told you."

"I know. But I don't get it. I can't see why you're so freaked out by the idea of Danny knowing. He's been great with me, why should he be any different with you?"

"God! You're thick, sometimes, you are."

"Maybe I am, explain please."

"I don't want Danny to know, that's all."

"Why not?" Matt insisted slowly.

"You're his best mate, man! He wouldn't like it."

"He might be a bit surprised, but he prefers honesty. You *know* that. He would respect you for being honest with him, wouldn't he now?"

"Nah!" he barked, "He would go fuckin' bananas. One of the things that was really crackin' him up was what happened at your place that time, you know, *that* night."

"I know. I was pretty ashamed of myself. I wasn't even sure if he knew what I'd done."

"What you'd done!" Chris exclaimed. "That's not it at all, man! It was what he did to you that was worrying him. He said that if anyone else used you the way he had, he would do for them. He meant it, Matt.

If he thinks I've mucked you about he would do me serious damage, I know he would!"

"But you're not. If anything it's me taking advantage of you."

"Fuck off, man! You know him as well as I do. If he gets an idea fixed in his head it don't shift."

Matt was sure Chris was wrong about Danny but he couldn't force him to come out to his brother. The whole hassle of being gay is that first tentative step out of the closet and you can always find reasons for not doing it. Perhaps there were other reasons for Chris not coming clean with Danny. He had an unpleasant thought. "Are you gay or aren't you?" Matt enquired.

"Now you're trying to put me in a neat little box, gay or straight," he chided. "Well you might be happy enough with a little label. I'm not gay, I'm not straight; I'm me. I'm going to do what I like with who I like, is that alright?" He softened, "And at the moment that means you."

"Suits me fine," Matt smiled. "But why be so secretive about it! It's not Danny now, be honest."

"It is. And it's other things too. I have to live in this city. How long do you think I would last if they knew?"

"Who?"

"Anyone."

"There's stacks of gays in Derry."

"Aye, and look at them. I know them, remember, man. I seen them at Magee. Scarcely a week goes by but one of them's given a kicking somewhere."

"That's just a fact of life. If you're gay you get beaten up. It happens, you're sore for a bit and its over. But what's worse? Being bruised for a few weeks or being oppressed for a lifetime? There's only been one gay actually killed for being gay in Northern Ireland, and a few in England. It was you that said you wanted to be yourself, well, do it for Christ's sake. Don't let them stomp all over you." Matt spotted Danny weaving back from the bar and paused. "He's coming, but listen to me. It's tough at first. You get hassles, but in the long run it's worth it. You'd be amazed how different life is, facing it head on instead of waiting for the next insult or jibe."

"A lecture on gay liberation?" Danny quipped as he plonked the tray down. "You'll have to watch him," he grinned, "he'll be converting you next!"

"No chance!" Chris laughed.

"I was just making a statement of principle," Matt replied haughtily.

Danny put a friendly arm round his shoulder, "Something we have in common, isn't it Matt?"

"Principle?"

"Well, coming to terms with something inside us. You and me both had to admit an unpalatable truth before we could start to really live."

"Yours was tougher."

"I had help." He smiled at Chris. Matt smiled at him too. He hoped he got the message.

CHAPTER 11
SPRING 1984, TROUBLE BREWING

Exactly when the persecution began, Matt didn't rightly remember. Once established, it happened too often for him to recall any one specific incident. The typical train of events would begin when he least expected it. Having wound down for the evening he would be relaxing in his lounge. He might be dozing but, usually, he was engrossed in a book or watching television. Whichever was the case, he would be light years from Ballycol. In the warm room, curtains pulled and washed with mellifluous sounds, he could forget the nasty reality of Ulster. Out there might be Ambridge. Or he could imagine Lucia and Georgie tripping below his window in their promenade along Tilling High Street. At a push, the lough could be the Dal Lake at Srinagar where Sarah Layton encountered the baby of that Manners girl. Then the doorbell would drag him back to reality. Matt would assume it was a visitor and hoist himself out of the comfy Chesterfield for the trek down to the front door. The first flight of stairs had a landing and the porch door was always stiff. He had to keep it closed to minimise the gale which whistled under the great, ill-fitting front door. Obstacle course negotiated, he would heave at the great oak door to reveal the deserted vista of the lake. He soon learned to lean out of the window before going to the door. It was irritating but nothing more than that. Being on the way to the park, youngsters were passing the house at all hours and Matt supposed that every house in the row got the same treatment.

The pranksters graduated to snowballs the January after he moved in. Chris had bought him a kit for Christmas. He had always fancied making one of those spindly early flying machines and this was an AVRO Aveling. He was in the middle of a delicate bit of glueing when a fusillade of thuds rattled the window. The percussion was so sudden and unexpected that he practically threw the filigree kit into the air. He never saw its shattering nose-dive onto the hearthrug for he was storming to the window, in time to catch sight of a gang of hooting kids scooting round the corner. He soon calmed down. After all, he thought, boys will be boys. He could put up with doorbells and even the odd snowball. Providing there was nothing worse.

But there were other things; niggly, little things. They were nothing on their own but, all together, they gnawed at his self confidence. There was this guy called Enda, who thought himself a bit of a stud. All of his crowd were of a type; beefy hunks with hairy chests and woolly minds. Every Tuesday, they assembled in Micky's after working out at the gym. Their uniform was tight fitting track suits in shiny pastel shades and glossy sports bags that appeared to be empty. Enda wasn't that good-looking, in fact he was downright ugly, but one of the clan *was* very attractive. A good six-footer, he had tight blond curls and was perfectly proportioned. He always wore a vaguely bored expression which Matt took to stem from the tedium of the company. Matt couldn't help but notice him; his attention would drift from current conversation, to his sinewy neck, pert little bum and chunky legs. But the macho brigade noticed Matt's interest and a time or two he caught one of them glancing over in his direction in the midst of conspiratorial sniggers. To avoid hassle he tried to ignore their Tuesday floor show.

Enda always made an entrance. It was as if he was physically incapable of walking normally. He would strut in and arrange himself between his friends, and he always seemed to find a spot where he could watch Matt. Matt wondered if Enda fancied him and was trying to give him the eye; he even started weighing up whether or not he could bring himself to go with him. He was a bit too short but he had a nice body, even if all that weight training had made him a little top heavy. Matt began to feel sorry for Enda; he imagined him as a closeted gay trapped into a macho stereotype by his hetero friends. Perhaps he, Matt, was his one chance to escape. If he was gay, Enda evidently hadn't the courage to make an approach, possibly that was why Matt was getting longing stares. Matt reckoned that, given the chance to talk to him alone, Enda might be less reticent.

One night Matt had had enough to make him reckless so he followed Enda into the toilets. Abandoning his usual caution, he sidled up to him at the urinal. "Hi," he grunted, nodding to Enda as he fumbled with his zip. Enda ignored him and scurried out. He had no reason to think Matt was trying to pick him up, everybody says, 'hi', when they go in for a piss. It always amused Matt. When standing next to someone you wouldn't dream of talking to outside, no matter who they were, they seem compelled to hold a conversation with you as they drained off their night's investment. Matt had given Enda a chance and he had shunned it. Maybe he was wrong about him.

He was soon to find out just how wrong he was. The staring continued, but now it was tainted with a glint of malice. Matt was uncomfortable and deliberately chose seats where Enda couldn't watch him. Then Matt began to hear stories about him. Not only was he excessively proud of his physique but he revelled in demonstrating his prowess. He bounced at local discos which gave him ample opportunity to use his brawn and he was notorious for starting fights. Sometimes, Matt could sense that they were talking about him. They would glance over, sneeringly. Enda wasn't present when the first actual insult came. The physical jerks were at the bar when Matt arrived. As he walked past them, he heard, "Mind your arses!" Not a major insult but it made Matt seethe and it took a couple of gins to calm him down.

Emboldened by their success they escalated their campaign. Initially, they scored with discrete little comments. One or another would utter 'pouf' or 'bum-boy' if he thought Matt was in earshot. They didn't confine this to the pub either. Like much of Ballycol's youth, they spent much of their free time lounging in shop doorways along the main street. Enda's gang occupied the prime position, the entrance to the sports emporium. In winter they sheltered under the wrought iron awning but summer would see them displaying tanned, muscular bodies on the wide steps. Matt didn't know where to look when he passed; he didn't want them to think he was ogling them! Summer or winter, he could almost guarantee that one of them would insult him as he passed and he began to organise his shopping trips around minimising the number of times he had to pass that cursed door.

Matt baiting was soon taken up by all the town's corner boys. One man in particular undertook to make his life a misery. His great talent was his ability to dodge unseen along the street yelling insults whilst keeping well out of his sight. Matt only ever saw him once and he was shocked that he was at least twenty-five! He had another notable quality. Never in his life had he heard such a powerful voice. Every time Matt went into town he would hope that iron lungs wasn't there. He was rarely so fortunate. Going about his shopping, the stentorian voice would carve its way into Matt's heart. "QUEER BOY... MATTHEW," he would bawl, "QUE..EE..ER BOY!" Matt assumed that he had a problem; that he was gay himself and was trying to deflect suspicion. It didn't help, though. Shopping became a nightmare.

When Matt was on a downer he would find excuses not to go into town. He would eat nothing but toast for days on end because he simply couldn't face going to the shops. It didn't stop him going to Micky's, of course. He didn't tell anyone there about it. He wasn't about to let the town's morons know they were succeeding in their battle to intimidate him. He was sure they would get bored if they thought it was having no effect, so he didn't do anything. Eventually Enda and his friends grew out of it but other louts grew into their shoes; he wasn't able to walk through the town absolutely free of anxiety for years. Enda's mob jogged in the park so he suspected they were the doorbell ringers but he couldn't prove it. Once or twice, he hid for hours in the downstairs front room, lights out, curtains open, but the only person he caught was a surprised wee tinker selling sticks.

Matt bought the house and Mary came to lodge until she had the flat above her shop done up. Mary's arrival coincided with an escalation in the hassle he was getting at the house. Their evenings would be punctuated by the ping and thwack of missiles hitting the window. It was a war of attrition. No one incident merited police attention. It would happen once or, rarely, twice in a night and not every night, by any means. Pebbles and apple cores were the principle ammunition, although he dreaded a higher calibre as he had just spent a fortune on double glazing for the sitting room. That, plus the abuse he was getting around the town started to get to him. He planned little revenges, fantasising about mining the footpath outside or pouring boiling chip oil over the little fuckers.

One night he got back from a parents' evening to find Mary in a terrible state. After a bath, she had been lounging in front of the fire downstairs when, with a crash, the front door was smashed open. She was terrified. Sitting there half-naked, she was sure than some gun-toting terrorist was about to burst in on her. When nothing happened, she ventured into the hall to see the door lying wide open. The wood round the lock had splintered and a big boot-mark was embedded in the door panel, about eighteen inches up. Some one must have taken a run at it to do so much damage. By the size of the boot, he must have been a big feller too. After that, she avoided staying in on her own at night and moved into the Sunflower sooner than she had planned. This time, the police were called in but they couldn't do much. They suggested it was being done by his pupils, but Matt was sure they were wrong.

The door was a one off. The window assaults went on for months without getting any more serious. But Matt felt vulnerable and worried that there was more to it. Could it be orchestrated by the I.R.A.? He hadn't a clue how they behaved towards people they didn't approve of. He knew that Sinn Fein had an official pro-gay policy but did that carry through to the Provos? What level of control was there over terrorists? He couldn't believe that the provisional IRA's volunteers were any more tolerant of gays than the rest of the town's youth. What if some young turks had taken it upon themselves to victimise him? He guessed that, if the I.R.A. really wanted him out, he would know about it by now, but he would still lie awake at night and worry. Any sound from the street below would bring him scuttling to the window to check. He worried that someone might pour petrol through his letter box and light it, and became so paranoid that he fixed a smoke alarm in the porch.

He kept his fears to himself in Ballycol but he had no such reticence when he got home. He was telling Alex and David about a particularly trying night the previous week, when his windows had been assaulted with a veritable goulash of rotten fruit and vegetables.

"Fix up a surveillance camera," David suggested.

"Come off it. I couldn't afford that! Anyway it's not all that important. It's only silly little boys."

"Sure of that, are you? You don't think it's anything more sinister?"

"No," he laughed. "It is kids, really!"

"I could get you a camera, you know. There are always old ones lying about. You don't have to have it on all the time. Just having it will discourage them."

Matt didn't want to install a camera. It would be admitting they were getting to him and he wasn't going to let them win. It might even make attacking his house more of a challenge.

Despite everything, Chris and Matt's relationship survived. Chris would sneak down to Ballycol for the odd night or two and Matt went up to Derry every weekend. Chris even began to join Danny and Matt on their visits to Alex but Chris steadfastly refused to tell Danny about their relationship. Sex remained a one-sided activity but Matt needed affection and he did love snuggling up to Chris at night.

Chris had a very different solution to Matt's problem; one that was equally unacceptable to Matt. "Tell Sinn Fein," he insisted. "If they don't already know who's doing it they'll find out and stop the fuckers. The police'll do fuck all." Chris would never forgive the British for shooting his older brother, Patrick, who had been killed in action with the Provisional I.R.A.

Annoyingly, Matt could appreciate Chris' point of view. Any Sinn Feiners he had ever met cared deeply about their community and they would move heaven and earth to help anyone who went to them. They got things done and, if it was a matter of simple policing, as this would be, Matt supposed that they had the Provos to use as a lever. However, the use of terrorists was anathema to all Matt was brought up to believe.

"You know I won't and you know why," Matt glared.

Chris shook his head in despair, "I'm telling you. If you want it stopping, tell them. If it's as bad as you say, they'll do it."

Matt's breathing shortened as his anger increased: "By going to Sinn Fein I would be saying I tacitly approve of what they stand for, and that includes terrorism. You know damn..."

Chris cut through his protest in hurt tones, "I'm only trying to help!"

"I know, I know," Matt said wearily. "I've heard it all before. I *will not* be seduced by easy solutions and be indebted to the provisional I.R.A.!"

Matt expected an angry retort but Chris hugged his unyielding waist, lowered his voice and crooned soothingly, "I know, I was only trying to help, honestly, man. I don't need all this agro from you. Let's drop it, hey?"

Chris pulled Matt's face into his shoulder and massaged his neck as his angry heaving subsided. Calm at last, Matt looked him in the eye. "Fuckin' Nor'n Ireland," he snarled, and kissed him.

Matt adopted neither strategy and lived with the constant, low level harassment. It would stop for a while, only to resume with a spate of nightly attacks. The cycle of lull and storm continued for almost a year before it escalated.

Chris and Matt had been together for nine months and yet things were still not working in bed. Matt was very fond of him and he loved being with him all night, but he needed something back from him. Matt tried to talk it through with his lover but when it came to the crunch and he asked him why he was so reluctant he simply replied, "Just." He even tried the "Don't you love me?" angle but that just insulted Chris. He did love him and Matt knew it.

Matt convinced himself that it was because of his friendship with Danny and he was becoming increasingly aloof. Perhaps Chris was right and Danny suspected what was going on. Perhaps he wouldn't tolerate their being lovers. If Danny was putting pressure on Chris, that could explain his hang-up about sex.

"Perhaps it would be better if I stopped coming to Derry at the weekends," Matt suggested.

"What for?"

"I don't think Danny's that fussed at the moment. It might be easier if I stayed down. You could come down for weekends, then. I'd much prefer that. Not having to leave you in the morning to go to school."

Chris was dubious but Matt was sure that, without Danny's disapproving aura, their sex life would improve.

Chris came up to Ballycol on Friday and they got quite drunk in Micky's. It certainly loosened Chris up, but they were so pissed that they fell asleep as soon as they collapsed into bed. On Saturday they didn't get so drunk, and Matt thought he was making a little progress, but Sunday morning was a near disaster. They should have been able to luxuriate in each other all day, instead of which Chris was restless and at half-nine he got up to make breakfast. Matt was getting really pissed off! He would give it one more try next weekend.

Chris couldn't make it up until Saturday. This time they stayed in and supped wine cuddled together on a sofa in front of a roaring fire.

Chris was so relaxed and compliant by the time they got to bed that his inhibitions evaporated and, for the first time, Matt felt that he actually enjoyed the sex. Matt was tempted to attempt intercourse but his integrity prevailed. Afterwards Chris slept peacefully in Matt's arms; he had broken the ice and he relished Chris' awakening.

When it came, it was abrupt. The doorbell rang at some ungodly hour of the morning. Matt staggered down to find a policeman at the door. "Have you seen this, sir?"

He couldn't very well miss it. Scrawled across the door in red spray paint were the words QUEERS LIVE HERE.

"Bastards!" he growled.

"You don't have any idea who is doing this, do you?"

"Nothing definite. I've my suspicions, that's all."

"Do you know why they're doing it?"

"Because I'm gay. Do they need any other reason?" he replied to the nonplussed officer.

"Have you anything to get it off?" he asked.

"I've some turps, I could try that."

"No good. It won't take it off. We've some stuff in the mobile. I could let you have some."

He disappeared into the grey, armoured Landrover and returned with a bottle of solvent.

"Thanks. What else have you got in there?"

The policeman was puzzled.

"Is this a mobile hardware store or a police car?"

The policeman explained that rioters threw plastic bags of paint at the Landrovers to try to obscure their view, so they kept the solvent in the windscreen washers to clean it off.

Matt's instinct was to slip back into the warm bed and leave the cleaning until later. But, if Chris saw the mess they would have the whole Sinn Fein thing over again so he set to and cleaned the obscenities off as best he could. Unfortunately he removed a layer of the door paint and patches of dull blue showed through the cream. The door would need repainting.

It was still only just after nine and Matt was wide awake and ready for sex. Pushing the door open, his nostrils were assaulted by the room's atmosphere. Beery breath and stale sweat mingled with the pungency of spilled semen. Due to the heavy curtains, dark still reigned. He picked his way over their scattered garments to the heap of crumpled duvet under which his pleasure slumbered.

"Where have you been, man?" Chris demanded, wincing as Matt's extremities sucked heat from his body.

"Someone at the door."

"Who?"

"Nobody as important as you. Warm me up."

"Time is it?"

"It's early."

Chris reached for his watch. "Fuck!" he said slipping over Matt and grabbing for his pants.

"Where're you going?" Matt asked indignantly.

"See you later," he called, heading for the door.

Matt jumped out of bed and caught him up in the hall, grabbing his arm. Chris stopped and looked at him through guilty eyes.

"Where ARE you going?" Matt asked in bewilderment.

"Mass."

Matt's eyebrows shot up, "What for? What about breakfast?"

"It's Sunday. I won't be long. I'll have breakfast when I get back."

And at that, he was gone.

Matt was stunned; he'd known Chris for a year or more and the subject of religion had never come up. Mrs. McDaid was always very devout but Matt had assumed that her offspring had shunned mother church. She had, doubtlessly, drummed religion in to him but why was it surfacing now? Had something happened?

He was back within three-quarters of an hour. "It's a gorgeous morning!" he beamed as Matt let him in. "What happened to the door?"

"It's the wind," he lied. "More effective than paint stripper. I'll have to repaint it before winter."

In the kitchen, he broached the subject. "What made you go to Mass?"

"It's Sunday. Mass is on Sunday."

"You've never gone before."

"I've never been with you before, on a Sunday."

"Last week!" he reminded him.

"I wanted to," he said sharply.

"It's none of my business. I'm just a bit surprised, that's all. Do you believe all that stuff?"

"I believe in God. I don't like a lot of what the priests say but they know the fundamental truth, don't they?"

How could Matt have known him for so long without twigging that he was a closet Christian? "Do you go to confession?" he queried.

"Sometimes."

"Do you tell him about us?"

He nodded.

"What does he say?" Matt asked gently.

"What do you think?" he said in evident distress.

"I haven't a clue, tell me."

"It's between me and my conscience, isn't it?"

Matt tried to cuddle him but he wasn't having it. He was as gentle and wheedling as he could manage under the circumstances. "Please Chris, tell me what your priest says."

His eyes filled with tears. "What do you think he says? It's a mortal sin!" His cheeks reddened as he got into his stride. "Do you expect him to say, man? Go ahead, Chris." He threw out his hand in offertory. "Screw away. God'll let you off because you're special. You're doing it with a prod, one of us to purgatory and one of them. Fair exchange? Like pairing in parliament?"

"Hey, hey. Don't take it out on me, love," Matt whispered.

Chris planted a tender kiss on his lips, "Sorry, man."

At last, Matt knew what was wrong. God was coming between him and his love.

The door of the Sunflower was painted an appropriate yellow. Matt hammered on the big knocker and Mary threw the window up and grinned down at him. They were soon clattering through the wonderful sandalwood-and-cinnamon-scented shop. Her living room was like an extension of the shop. Aromas from below mingled with potpourri and boiled beans. Brown dominated; rush mats, hessian bean bags and anything that could be made of cane was so made. Slumped on a bean bag he sipped the lapsang souchong and poured out his heart to her.

What could he do? She had no easy answers, she never had, and he wouldn't expect her to. She listened patiently, steering him in the right direction with an apposite question here and there. There was nothing Matt could do about Chris' hang-ups. He had to work them out himself; all Matt could do was be patient with him. If he really loved him it would come right in the end.

"Why *is* the church so anti-gay?" he asked Mary.

"It depends on what you believe, there's the rub," she smiled. "If you are a committed Christian you have to believe that all the bible is true. Have you ever read the Bible, Matt?"

He stifled a forced laugh.

"You should; you might understand. The language is obscure to say the least. The King James's version was translated from the Greek in 1611, and the Old Testament had already been translated once from the Hebrew. It was a different world. Language is more than words, the ideas behind them are so important. Look at yourself, Matt. When you use the word gay you mean a happy and well adjusted homosexual. Go into the street to one of the corner boys and to them it means an unimaginable pervert. My old dad still thought of gay people as being the bright young things of the twenties!

If one word can have so many difference nuances here, today, what did language three hundred and fifty years ago mean? And they were translating from things written fifteen hundred years before in a culture of which they could have no concept! The Catholics have a Latin Bible, translated into the Latin in the fourth century!"

Fascinating as it was, this history lesson didn't seem to be getting him very far.

"What's the point of reading the bible then? If it's so archaic?"

"That *is* the point!" she continued. He shifted, sipping the tea as she developed her theme. "No ordinary person could hope to understand the bible so there have to be experts, teachers, that's why there has to be a church, a hierarchy of cognoscenti. If you believe that, by the guidance of God, they are infallible, you have to accept all the nonsense they put out. If you suss that they are only men with male power trips and male sexual hang-ups you start to see where it all comes from. They make the bible say what they want it to say. Why do you think there are so many different Christian sects and schisms? Every time someone thinks *he* has a different interpretation that suits *his* purposes better, *he* starts a new church. You should study the history of Christianity. It would be funny if it wasn't so tragic!"

"What has this to do with gay persecution?"

"There's some anti-gay stuff in the bible. All you have to do is look and there it is."

"As far as I can remember there's anti-everything in the Bible, why pick on us?" he complained.

"Ah!" she exclaimed, finger heavenward in a declamatory gesture.

"Again, it depends on what you believe. If you think that priests and ministers have a direct hot line to God the answer is swift and obvious. God doesn't like you, either, and what God says goes!"

"Fuck 'em!"

"Sweet thought. But you can't do that. There's too many of them, even for you to take on."

"What's the other view?"

"God is made in *man's* image," she smirked.

Matt was surprised: "Bit iconoclastic, even for you!"

"True though. My God has nothing to do with all this condemnation and hatred. *Men* are adept in using religion in their power games. There's a censure in the bible for every occasion and you can bet that if a religious person wants to make a point, he can back it up with the good old book!

Many men are terrified of their true sexuality. You know, better than most, that the hundred per cent, lifelong heterosexual is a pretty rare species. The church law makers must have had the same feelings. Can you really believe that no pious acolyte ever found himself lusting after a young choir boy or novice? You know, impure thoughts. It must scare the willies out of them. If I, one so pure, have these feelings, what baser lusts lurk within the breast of the common man? They fear and loathe the homosexuality in themselves, so they try to make damn sure that no one else is going to express it.

All it needs is a few centuries of condemnation from the pulpit, backed up with scraps from the scriptures, and they can throw in that homosexuality is to blame for the fall of the Romans and Greeks. Then, Bob's your uncle, homophobia is fixed in western European culture. It permeates the law and practically every other aspect of western society."

"So you blame everything on the church, then?"

"Most certainly."

"But I don't see *why* they do it. What harm are we doing? Why pick on us?"

"You have the right word there, Matthew, *us*. You and me; gays and women. The power of any church is based on them having numbers. To keep their numbers up, all the women have to be baby factories. Anything that threatens that, is quashed. Abortion, contraception, divorce and, of course, homosexuality; every one a threat to their numbers. It's alright to go to war, note. It's fine to massacre hundreds of thousands because that strengthens the church, if they win."

"Hold on, though," he objected. "If it's all selfish oppression, how come the population put up with it? Tyrants get overthrown in history with monotonous regularity. The Church has lasted two thousand years."

"They're sneaky. Firstly, they have Christendom conned into this idea that, if you suffer on earth, you will get your reward in heaven. People will put up with astonishing levels of privation, believing that the next life will be better. However, they would find it tough to suppress the most natural biological functions of human kind. Your field here again, Matt, what do you teach? Every single action of an animal or plant is geared to optimise the survival of the species. Sophisticated as we are, it's still the main drive in life, the need to reproduce which, in human terms, is the need for love. Luckily for the church, love usually produces more babies; not always, though. We humans are more complex than that. Some of us love in a way that doesn't make babies and they can't allow that, can they? They intimidate their followers, to deflect any unconventional sexual urges into productive sex." She smiled knowingly at him.

"I still don't get why we gays seem to get such a raw deal out of it. I'm sure stacks of Catholics use contraception and get divorced, even have abortions, but they don't get as much hassle as we do."

"That's the clever bit," she nodded. "The church is telling most people to do, more or less, what they want to do anyway. So they'll put up with the odd minor conflict between beliefs and desires to keep in with God. It's a bit different for you. The minor conflicts are things people do, homosexuality is what you are. It's only when the church's dictates absolutely contradict you that you feel totally stomped on. There's not all that much intimidation needed to stop you popping a condom on, or make you feel like a murderer for having an abortion, but they have to work damn hard at it if they're going to completely negate someone's sexuality. All society has to join in; and they do, with a vengeance!"

"You've really gone into this in a big way, haven't you?"

"Assertiveness and consciousness-raising sessions!" she explained. "You should get involved, Matt."

"So all I have to do is explain all this to Chris and all will be fine and dandy."

She shook her head, "No, Matthew."

"You then, you do it for me. You're so much better at it than I am."

Again, her head oscillated: "You can't talk like that to someone who has been brought up to believe that all the church says is true. If you did convince him, which is very unlikely, he could be shattered. Anyway, you would be more likely to find that he wouldn't take a blind bit of notice. You can't just tear down the whole edifice; a lifetime of beliefs." She paused, "Perhaps if you offer him a way out.... I don't like making suggestions but if you made it possible for him to reconcile his beliefs with his sexuality, maybe things would get better. Talk to your help-line friends in Derry, they might be able to help."

The help-line people knew a priest who would listen sympathetically to gay Catholics but they didn't hold out much hope of his toning down Chris's Catholicism. He was a priest after all, and he was bound to toe the Catholic line to a certain degree. It was worth a try, though. Anything would be better than the present state of affairs.

Broaching the subject with Chris was less difficult than he had feared. One Sunday, he asked him if he found it difficult to confess to his priest when he knew he was going to get an ear-bashing and Chris opened up. The guilt tortured him. Sometimes he concealed the extent of his transgressions and then felt worse because he could deceive the priest, but not God. When he did tell the priest what he and Matt had done, he could imagine him on the other side of the screen, tight lipped, shaking his head in disgust at Chris's revelations. Every time he confessed, he promised to try to resist in future. But as soon as he met Matt his resolution faltered.

"Not completely," Matt observed.

Father O'Connell was young. He must have had gay friends, he might even have been gay himself because he seemed to understand what it was to be gay. Visit by visit, he peeled away the layers of Chris's guilt. As the shell dissolved, he became more accessible and

Matt didn't need to get him drunk to relax him. Then, one joyous May night, Chris took the initiative and Matt knew that his hang-ups were fading.

By June their relationship was blossoming. Matt couldn't imagine being happier. Mornings were his favourite. For drifting hours they lay together, meandering conversations filling the tactile time. Sometimes they didn't bother stirring until hunger drove them out into the afternoon lull of the town.

The bells of Saint Theresa's twanged lazily off the rooftops. "No mass?" Matt grunted dopily.

Chris engulfed him, "Coming with me?"

"Mmmm. You start."

"Stop it!" Matt giggled, as Chris tickled him with a lascivious chuckle.

"Matt?" he asked.

"Mmm."

"Still going to Holland?"

"I promised."

"Oh,"

"Don't you want me to?"

"Nah, nah, man. Just wondered."

Matt relished Chris' hand working gradually down his front, his slow breathing was deep.

"Will you sleep with him?" Chris whispered.

"Who?"

"Your man. You know who I mean."

"Don't you want me to?" Matt said, in mock surprise.

"Course not, you're mine."

Matt turned to face him. "I'm not anybody's. I love you and I love Piet but it's different with you and with him."

"You can't love two people."

"I can, and I do. I love Piet as a really good friend but I love you as a lover!"

There was a long silence.

"He's right," he mumbled.

"Who?"

There was another pause.

"He said this could happen."

"What would?"

"Promiscuity," he hissed.

"I'm not promiscuous!" he objected. "Piet's an old friend, we go back a long way. What did who say anyway?"

"Father O'Connell. He told me that homosexual relationships can never really work like heterosexual ones."

"Of course they can't, they're different. That doesn't mean they're any worse, though."

"It's no good for me Matt. I need one person."

"Listen, love. You don't want me to sleep with Piet and I won't," he promised.

His reward was a gentle kiss.

CHAPTER 12

SUMMER 1984, FRIENDS IN TURMOIL

Matt genuinely believed that he would keep to his word, a conviction that strengthened when Henk told him that Piet had a steady relationship. Henk had broken it to him gently, thinking he would be devastated, and was most impressed at his stoic acceptance. Piet was in Spain with his new man so Matt and Henk went on a little jaunt down to the Ardenne until Piet got back to Holland. When they met he gulped. Piet sported a shirt, tie and jacket, and his hair was immaculately cut and topped off with a seductive quiff! He looked stunning.

"Oh, very nineteen-forties!" Matt smiled.

Piet appraised Matt's customary jeans and sweatshirt, "You English are so casual!"

Piet flung his arms wide to receive Matt. As soon as they kissed Matt knew that all his resolves and promises were in jeopardy.

As usual, he stopped off at his uncle's in Kendal on his way home. His cousin's children monopolised him as soon as he arrived.

"You would make a wonderful dad, Matt," Mandy teased.

"I prefer being an uncle, thank you very much. I don't mind the kids but, what you have to do to get them! YECH!"

"You should come over more often, you know. Not only for them; we love having you."

"Isn't it about time you came over to Ireland? It's years since you've been. Now I've a house, I could put you all up, no problem."

"Yes. We've heard so much about Ballycol and all those weird and wonderful people you know. I've not seen Willy-John and the rest for nearly ten years. Remember the time Danny was supposed to come here?"

Matt cringed: "How could I forget!"

"I'd love to meet his brother. He sounds lovely. I'm really pleased you've found someone at long last. Looking forward to seeing him again?"

"Yes," he said slowly.

"You don't sound too sure."

"No, no. I am….."

"Go on, tell me," she suggested.

Matt thought for a moment about telling her about Piet but she'd think him a slut. She couldn't be expected to understand the special relationship between him and Piet; neither could Chris, unfortunately.

He sucked air through his clenched teeth, "He's been seeing this priest...... At my suggestion."

"Sounds a bit odd for you."

"I know. I don't regret it. He had an awful hang-up about being gay and Catholic. This priest is helping him come to terms with it."

"But..........." she added slowly.

"Yeah, *but*!" he sighed. "I don't know. It feels wrong, somehow. The church is intrinsically anti-gay. I don't trust them. I wonder what this guy is trying to do to Chris."

"What do you mean, do to him?"

"Right!" he said, trying to lay out his arguments as clearly as he could. "Chris is gay, they accept that. Now, when they make public pronouncements on homosexuality they are really anti. They do their level best to stop anyone who is gay, realising their sexuality. You with me so far?"

She nodded.

"But now they're faced with Chris being gay as a fait accompli. If they followed the logic of their public pronouncements he should be shunned as hopeless sinner, but he's not. I can't put my finger on it, but it looks as if they're steering him into a particular life style; a more morally acceptable way of conducting himself. I think they're trying to sell him a parody of the church's ideal of heterosexual behaviour. I can't believe that they'll let him think of himself as morally equal to hets and, let's face it, the church oppresses hets as well!"

"How is he taking it?"

"It was great at first. Once he was conned into believing that the church was accepting his sexuality he was so much happier. Sex was great!" he grinned. Then his face fell, "Recently, he's started coming out with odd little statements."

"Like?"

"He's started going to special prayer meetings with other gay Catholics. He told me about some American Priest who was blessing gay couples. I got the feeling that he would like us to go through something like that!"

"How sweet!" she chuckled.

"Oh aye! Who'll wear the wedding dress?"

"It's ridiculous. How can anyone be duped into that?"

"I don't know," Matt said, "I don't know!"

As soon as Matt got home, Chris called round to Strathbeg. After a hug and a kiss he looked him in the eye: "You slept with him," he said resignedly.

Matt couldn't lie and he couldn't admit it. He'd blown it!

The relationship didn't collapse there and then. Chris showed Matt Christian forgiveness but, as September went by, Matt realised that the relationship wasn't working anymore; Chris was increasingly distant. His friendship with Danny wasn't doing much better. Matt concluded that Chris must have told Danny about it all.

By autumn eighty-four Alex was walking; albeit shakily. However, his mind was recovering, so visits were less trying. Matt arrived at Alex's one Saturday to find Danny's car parked outside. They were out, he was told. They had gone to Limavady with David.

There are only two shopping streets in Limavady so, once he'd checked North-West Books, it was a matter of tracking them down in a coffee shop or a pub. He was making his way up the wide main street when footfalls thudded up behind him and his name was called. Danny was trotting up to him.

"Danny! Where were you?"

"Sports shop. He's buying a track suit."

"Taking up jogging, is he?" Matt quipped.

Danny wasn't amused, "Might be."

"Seriously?"

He pursed his lips momentarily then smiled, "No, I persuaded him he'd be comfier in a track suit. Truth is, Sandra says he finds it a hassle getting jeans on. Track suit'll be easier."

"You're great, you," Matt smiled.

"Am I?" was his cold reply.

Track suit purchased, David led them round the corner where they settled in a pub. It was a very sober round. David and Matt were driving, Alex couldn't drink and Danny didn't. Matt carried the tray of orange juices and cokes to the table. Matt surveyed the sullen faces. "Cheer up!" he chided.

Danny scowled. The only one who didn't look totally depressed was Alex.

"How's Sandra?" Matt asked.

Alex's face fell: "Alright."

He decided he'd better not ask any more; he turned to David: "Good summer?"

David was equally uncommunicative: "Not bad."

"What is wrong with you lot? Dare I ask you how your job's going, Danny, or will I get my head bitten off?"

"Don't be so fuckin' sensitive," he snarled. "Perhaps we're knackered. Some of us do a full day's work every day you know."

"Pardon me for breathing!" Matt complained.

"Sorry," Danny said. "What have you been up to?"

"Usual. Nothing special. I started going to night classes, would you believe?"

"Needlepoint or Ancient Russian?" Danny laughed.

"Ancient Russian Needlepoint," he smirked. "Painting, actually. I've always wanted to paint and Feargal's taking the class so I thought I'd give it a go."

"I can just imagine you in a smock and beret, *what a queen*!" Danny mocked. The others smirked.

"I have to try to integrate with Ballycol society. I'm thinking of joining PHAB. That's thanks to you, Alex."

David spoke, "What's PHAB?"

"Physically Handicapped and Able Bodied," Alex chanted. "They tried to get me to go to the one in Londonderry but I didn't fancy it."

"Too many Fenians, eh?" Danny said with a hollow laugh.

"It's not funny," David snapped. "He could never be sure if he was safe. Some of those murdering bastards would jump at the chance of murdering a cripple."

Danny looked annoyed but Alex was really angry: "I'm not a cripple."

"No, I'm sorry, you know what I mean, though," David apologised.

"That's why I didn't go. I won't have people treating me as a cripple. And that includes you two!" he said glaring at David and Matt.

"Be fair, Alex," Matt objected. "I only meant that after seeing the hassles you've had, I wanted to help others in the same boat. And you can't claim that you are exactly able bodied at the moment, can you now?"

He pointed at David: "*He* called me a cripple!"

"He didn't mean it like that. He was only making a point, weren't you David?"

"Aye," Danny chipped in, "that you can't trust Fenians!"

The way David looked at him needed no reply.

Alex broke in, "Danny, give us a hand to the bogs, will you?"

David and Matt watched Alex's progress. He needed two sticks to walk and even with those, he wasn't too steady so Danny hovered to catch him if he fell. It was painful to watch. It would be so much easier for him to use the wheelchair, but that was Alex.

David tried to break the ice: "He's got some guts, hasn't he?"

Matt nodded begrudgingly. "What sort of summer *did* you have?"

David squinted at him: "You asked me that once. I said O.K."

"Are you alright, David?"

"Why shouldn't I be?"

"I don't know. You seem to be rubbing everyone up the wrong way today."

The muscles of his square, imperious jaw tightened as he clenched and unclenched his teeth. He was staring at his empty glass.

"That Danny. He doesn't understand. In their books Alex's still a cop. It's not safe. Danny's probably O.K. but you never know. Did you know his brother was in the I.R.A.?"

Matt nodded, wondering how David knew. He hoped he wasn't going to imply that because Paddy was, Danny was. "My brother's a boring prat, so that makes me one, does it?" Matt demanded.

"You said it!" David murmured.

"Charming!"

The young policeman smiled for the first time: "Joke."

It didn't sound like it, but Matt let it go.

"He lives in a Republican area. If he says anything about Alex they could use him to get at him; or me for that matter."

"He's not daft, you know. He..." Matt was cut short by his friend's shambling return.

"Danny's got to get back," Alex announced. "Do you mind taking him Matt?"

"No prob."

"Will you take me to North-West Books, David?"

"You should try Bookworm in Derry," Matt chipped in. "They've a good selection there, they even sell Gay News!"

"And Republican News!" David said. "I've heard all about that...."

"Fenian hole?" Danny finished for him. "Come on Matt, let's go."

Danny was silent as they chugged out of Limavady. At Ballykelly forest he pulled into the same lay-by where he had told Alex he was gay, many years before.

"Come on. Out with it," he said

Danny sounded surprised: "What?"

"I've hardly seen you since summer and, when I have, you've made a Trappist monk seem like a chatterbox!"

"I've been busy."

"You seem to have plenty of time for Alex. He was telling me you're never away. That's why David's so suspicious."

"He's an ignorant gulpin. He would be suspicious of the angel Gabriel himself."

"That's not what's bugging you though, is it now?"

"Nah."

"Have I done something on you?" Matt begged. "It hurts, you know! You're my best friend and suddenly you cut me off, apparently in favour of Alex and you two hated each other's guts at school! It doesn't do much for my self-esteem. I've lost you twice, I don't want it to happen again."

Danny frowned at the view ahead: "You're head's away, young feller!" he blustered unconvincingly.

"Is it Chris?" Matt ventured.

Danny started: "EH?"

"Is it me and Chris?"

Danny seemed almost relieved: "Fuck no! You two do what you want to do."

"You know, then. Did he tell you?"

"No. I'm not an idiot, though. He's had the hots for you for years," he laughed. "I began to think you'd never get off with each other!"

"Nearly didn't. And I think I've ruined it now."

Danny was astute; he skillfully sidetracked Matt into pouring his heart out about Chris. He was not at all worried, if anything, he was sorry it wasn't working. "You're not Catholic," he said. "You don't know the power they have over us."

"You don't seem to be too worried."

He winked and grinned: "Ginger sheep of the family!"

"Chris isn't exactly a conformist!"

"Isn't he?" Danny questioned with puckered lips and raised eyebrows. "When we were wee'uns mum used to send us to see a priest, because we weren't at a church school, you know!"

Matt nodded.

"He tried to explain about the soul and sin." He thrust his clenched fist into his chest. "He said the soul was here, like a white ball at our heart. Every time we sin, a black patch appears on the soul and the bigger the sin, the bigger the blotch. I can remember how scared I was. Every time I told a lie or used a bad word I could feel another black spot growing like a cancer. That's why we had to go to confession, to clean the spots off. You see, if they grew together it would kill us!"

"Come on, you were *not* told that!" Matt said in disbelief.

"We were! God's honour."

"That priest must have been a bloody loony!"

"No way! It was a pretty smart way to explain the soul to wee boys. The Church always did go in for overkill."

"O.K. but you *do* know it's crap now, don't you?" Matt asked tentatively.

"I do. But I'm not too sure about Chris. If you asked him he would pooh-pooh the idea, no doubt. But it's still there in him, you know. Deep down, in his subconscious, he has his pristine white soul to think about and, every time he slid into bed with you the black spots gnawed at him from inside."

Matt would have liked to dismiss this as fantastic but he couldn't; it explained Chris's behaviour far too well.

He was waving Danny good-bye outside King's before he remembered that Danny still hadn't explained what was troubling him.

A couple of days later, Mary called with him. When he told her about Danny and David, she looked sheepish, not a look he normally associated with Mary!

"I could probably explain David's behaviour."

"*What?*" he exclaimed.

"I've been seeing him; he made me promise not to tell you."

Matt blinked and shook his head as if he wasn't hearing right: "Why did he say that? What the fuck's he at?"

"Don't blame him."

"Come on, he's an adult! He doesn't have to keep secrets from his friends!"

"He's very innocent in some ways."

"Immature, you mean."

"No," she insisted, vigorously shaking her head. "He thought you would be offended."

"I'm sorry, Mary," he laughed. "I just can't take all this in."

"I'll explain. Remember my Christmas party?"

"The first part."

"That's right, we put you to bed about three, didn't we?" she smirked.

"O.K., don't rub it in."

"I was chatting to him in the kitchen, remember? You kept singing, 'Always in the kitchen at parties' every time you came in to get a drink."

"I usually do."

"After the party he started visiting you, didn't he?"

"Not a lot."

"No, but more than he did before."

Matt nodded; he thought it was odd at the time.

"Well, I didn't realise at the time but he was coming because he wanted to see me. And when I moved into the shop he used to call there."

"Randy old sod!"

"It wasn't like that," she insisted. "More's the pity!"

"Yeah, he's quite a hunk, isn't he?"

She looked reprovingly at Matt: "He's very sensitive."

"He hides it well."

"He's frightened of you, you know. I think he would love to talk to you, but he's scared to."

"Scared I'll jump on him!" Matt smiled.

She wiped the smile off his face: "I'll come to that later. Do you want to hear this story or not?"

He nodded contritely.

"Shut up and listen, then. All he needed was someone to talk to. Alex was his only confidant and then something happened when you two went to stay at Portrush. He never told me what it was, but it really freaked him out."

Matt detailed the events of that weekend and she took it all in without comment.

"Joking apart. Maybe he does think I would jump him. Once, just once, on Rathlin, he started to talk openly with me and then I went and made a joke about raping him. Do you think I freaked him out?"

"No," she said curtly. "Shall I go on?"

"Please."

"He dropped in here a few times. He would always turn up with a really good bottle of wine and we would sit chatting to the early hours." She paused, distinctly uncomfortable. "Then one night one thing led to another," she confessed. "I don't know how it happened, Matt." She looked at him balefully, "but happen it did."

"It's quite natural, you know," he smiled.

"For me, perhaps," she sighed. "I shouldn't have let it get that far. I fancied him and his poor ego didn't let him resist."

"Come off it. What's this? You are the last person I ever expected to be worried about having sex?"

"It wasn't right for him. He only did it because he thought he ought to. He's not been near since, I think he feels guilty now. I reckon that's why he was so ratty with you. Now he's put this barrier up to you; the one person he should have been able to talk to."

"Why don't you make the first move. Tell him it was a one off; there's no harm done!"

"There is."

"Och, not really. He's a big boy, he'll get over it," he assured her.

"He didn't have a condom and I let him think I was on the pill."

Matt's initial reaction was to berate her for being such an idiot but that wasn't what she needed. He'd no doubt that she had been suffering acute self-recriminations ever since she realised her predicament. Her predicament! He shook his head slowly: "Oh, no!"

She nodded ruefully.

"Are you sure?"

"First period was iffy. Second should have come last week. I got a Clear Blue. It couldn't be bluer if the bloody thing tried."

"Now I see why he's in such bad form. What did he say?"

"I've not told him."

"Ah!"

"It's best he doesn't know. I'll have to get rid."

Matt was shocked. "Oh, Mary! *Could* you?" he asked gently.

She buried her cheek in her hand. She couldn't look at him: "I can't have it!"

"You don't like him... ?" Matt started. "I mean you wouldn't....? No. I should know better."

"Yes, you should. If you're suggesting marrying him."

"Well, that's what people would say."

"If they knew, and they won't." She spun the subject through one hundred and eighty degrees: "Matthew, do you think David's gay?"

He prevaricated.

"You do, don't you?" she said.

"There're a few things, right enough. Nothing concrete."

"*I* think he is, but he doesn't know it. Help him, Matt," she pleaded. "You're the only one he can turn to now and, I promise you, if you can get through that hard front he puts on, he's the gentlest, kindest man you'll meet."

CHAPTER 13

AUTUMN 1984, MARY AND DAVID

The end of eighty-four was dramatic, to say the least. Mary was going through a gruelling and humiliating experience. Unlike in England, a woman in Northern Ireland could not get an abortion for anything but the strictest medical reasons. Mary had to go through a tortuous process of finding a pregnancy advice service, going to Belfast for counseling, and then getting the money together for a trip to Manchester, where she would have the operation. Her decision to go ahead seemed contrary to all she had always stood for. She worried that her friends would think ill of her for acting against her principles. To Matt it seemed obvious that she didn't want to go through with it, and he wondered why she didn't have the baby and then give it up for adoption. He didn't dare say anything though; after all he was a man, and a gay man at that. He would keep his mouth shut and respect her decision.

The dreadful night in October came and Matt called round to the Sunflower. She was to fly to Manchester the next day.

Little Paul opened the door with a most grown-up decorum.

"Is your mummy upstairs?"

"No, she's working in the back," he replied, running into the store room.

Carmel emerged, holding a scoop of mung beans and a cellophane bag. Carmel was about fifty and had brought more than her fair share of kids into a household dominated by a violent husband. Family more or less safely raised, she had taken control of her life, gathered up Paul, the youngest, walked out on the brutal man and moved into the women's refuge where she met Mary. Everything she involved herself in fell under her spell and, as soon as she discovered Mary's plight, there was nothing she wouldn't do for her. She moved in to the Sunflower and undertook to accompany Mary to Manchester.

She peered over her specs: "Hello Matthew," she smiled. "Then she nodded towards the stairs: "She's upstairs, go on up, there's a love. She'll be glad to see you."

He started up the stairs and Paul trailed into the store after his mother. Approaching the top, he called, "coo-ee Mary," and tracked her down to her bedroom. She looked ghastly.

"Hi," he smiled weakly.

She swept him into her arms and hugged him tightly. They stood silently for an awkward few seconds.

"I was just doing some last minute packing," she sniffed.

"Oh."

"Tea?"

He nodded and followed her into the kitchen.

"Have you heard from him?" she asked, falsely airily.

"I wrote last week but no reply since."

She turned sharply: "You didn't say anything?"

"Of course not. I tried ringing a time or two but he's always either off duty or out on patrol and he never returns my calls. Alex hasn't seen him, either. He's seen plenty of Danny though, which is more than I have! They're still bosom buddies," he finished, dryly.

She looked gloomily at the hand on her stomach: "I hope he never finds out!"

Matt put his arm round her: "How could he? I won't say anything, will I?"

She tried to put on a brave smile: "It'll all be over soon."

He couldn't stand it.

"Can I ask you something?" he asked, warily. He had her full attention. "I'm sorry to be so blunt but exactly why *are* you going through with this?"

She shook his arm off and rushed to her room. Horrified at what he'd said, he followed, to find her sobbing on her bed.

"I'm sorry," he crooned. "I just hate seeing you putting yourself through this. I don't understand why you're doing it."

She glared at him, "I don't want to.... I'll probably hate myself for ever, but I can't have it. Please, believe me, *I can't have this child*."

He said nothing but his eyes said, 'Why?'

"Oh Matt. Can't you see what would happen if I have it?"

"You would have a child to care for."

"Two children! This, and David!"

He couldn't think of a suitable riposte so he wagged his head in despair.

"You know what he's like. Him and his overgrown schoolboy honour, he would do the right thing by me. I would be a ball and chain on his life. He doesn't need that."

"He might want to but you wouldn't *have* to let him."

"You don't understand, do you? I couldn't hurt him like that. He would want to marry me; he's like that."

"And you don't like him."

"Of course I like him. I don't sleep with people I don't like."

He flushed as he thought, and I do!

"I didn't mean it like that, Matthew!"

A wave of his hand dismissed her comment and accepted her apology.

"What I'm afraid of is that, if I have his child, I couldn't keep it a secret from him. I would feel terrible not telling him and, even if I didn't, he'll know it's his anyway and he'll feel duty bound to care for it and me. I don't need that, and neither does he. It'll be a disaster for both of us."

Matt heard her anguish but he couldn't give her the support she had given him. He felt so pathetic.

She was back from Manchester sooner than he expected.

"How do you feel?" he asked, cautiously.

"Fine," she beamed.

He was somewhat taken aback. This resilience was the last thing he expected. She's putting on a brave face for me, he decided. She's trying to make out that I didn't upset her the other night.

"Poor Matt," she grinned. "You do look a picture! I'm sorry, Matt, here you are with all your guilty sympathy and I'm letting you suffer. I didn't do it!"

Matt beamed, "You mean?"

"Yes Matt. I'm having the baby. I can handle David but I couldn't handle the guilt of killing my own child."

Mary was a changed woman. All her enthusiasm for life had returned and much of her energy was being directed into the task of preparing for the arrival of a new life. And David remained blissfully ignorant of his paternity.

David was not in the habit of arriving unannounced on Matt's doorstep. When he did, and in a state of evident agitation, Matt prepared himself for, 'I've just discovered I'm going to be a father.

The two of them faced each other over the coffee table making the smallest of small talk.

Matt decided to break the ice: "What brought you here? Not that I'm objecting, it's nice to see you.... after so long."

"I wanted to talk to you," David stammered.

"Go ahead," Matt said, coolly confident that he already knew what he was about to say.

"I'm in bother."

Matt calmly waited for the story.

"I've done something really stupid." He gathered his thoughts and began to chew his knuckle. "I got drunk a while back."

"That's not like you."

David pulled a wry face: "That's not all that isn't like me."

Matt raised his eyebrows: "Oh yes?"

"I tackled someone."

"Hormones out of control, eh?"

David ignored him: "I made a real ass of myself. I can't go back. I have to but I'll never be able to look at them straight."

"Come on, you aren't the first and you won't be the last. Half the guys in your station have probably done the same at some time or another. You got caught, so what?"

David was looking at him with incredulity: "Do you think so?"

"Aye, of course. Once the old hormones get going, anyone can get carried away."

"I don't think you're right. I got a wild lot of stick from the other guys when they found out. He dobbed, you see."

"Who?"

"Raymond, the guy I, er, made a mistake with."

Matt blanched and swiftly rearranged his thoughts; had David told this guy about Mary? Did he know about the baby? "Exactly what did you tell him?"

David was acutely embarrassed. "Well, it started a couple of months ago, I suppose. I've been getting very close to Raymond. He's a nice guy, you know, good craic. Knows more jokes, you know. Most of the other guys don't talk to me, but he does. I like him; you know what it's like, Matt, like you like Alex."

Matt drew in a deep breath and nodded a grim smile to him.

"I got pissed, I was feeling horny. We were in my room and..."

The realisation broke on Matt: "And you made a pass at him."

"More of a lunge actually," he said nervously. "Pinned him to the bed and tried to kiss him."

Matt was impressed: "What did he do?"

"Told me to fuck off. Said I was a queer bastard."

"Poor old David. Is that what Alex was on about that time?"

"Aye. Fuck! What is wrong with me, Matt?"

"There's absolutely nothing wrong with you. Most men find themselves attracted to other men at some time or another."

"It's not sometimes."

"No?"

"No."

"Ah."

"Yes," the young policeman said with relief.

"Join the club."

"It's not one I want to be a member of."

"It can be tough but it's worth it in the long run."

"I don't know if I can do it, Matt. If they find out they'll have me out of the force. I will be disgraced."

"They don't have to know. You can pass that incident off as a joke. Great laugh, you know. Ha, ha, poor old Ray; had him thinking I was gay, Ha, ha, ha."

Matt's humour wasn't going down well.

"Here! Cheer up. It's not the end of the world, you know. It's quite nice being gay."

"You could have fooled me. All I ever seem to hear is you moaning about how unfairly people treat you."

"That's just me going on."

"What about all the agro you've been getting at the house? That's been bugging you for ages, is it still going on?"

"O.K. There are hassles, a lot of battles to win, but they're outweighed by the pluses. I'd've given up years ago otherwise. Being gay, I can't take anything for granted. All my life I've been told how to behave by straight society on the assumption that I was straight. But their rules are largely based on the assumption that my sole aim in life is to get married and produce a family. I'm not going to and their standards aren't mine. The vast majority of straights take the line of least resistance. Their goals coincide with society's plans for them, it makes life easier if they conform, or at least seem to conform. I've been forced to think about every aspect of my role in society. I know that every action, every attitude is *mine*, not the church's or the government's or some snotty buggers who think that they have a divine right to tell me how I should think; how I should feel!

When I first realised I was gay I felt wretched about it. I was scared shitless, too. My opinion of myself was a reflection of society's. I thought I was a worthless lump of shit. You don't have a clue what I was like in those days; I was a total wimp. You can't function if you don't feel good about yourself; it's called self-oppression, ask women about it, they've been fighting it for years. That's why I get on so well with people like Mary and Feargal; they are those rare creatures, thinking straights. Take the chance David, find the real David Robinson. It'll be well worth it in the long run."

Over the next few weeks, David visited Matt every time he was free and they talked the nights away. Bit by bit David's hard, protective shield vanished. Mary was right about his warmth and gentleness and Matt realised he was becoming really fond of him. He fancied him too but he knew he hadn't to seduce him. Matt was David's only tenuous link to the gay world. If they did have a fling which didn't work, David might find it difficult to talk to Matt in future. Matt saw it as a race against time. How much gay consciousness could David develop before he found out he was a father?

CHAPTER 14

SPRING 1985, DAMIAN KELLY

"I see Martina's one of your friends!"

Matt looked up from his marking and stared confusedly at his colleague, Robin, "Eh?"

"Martina Navratilova. She's gay."

"So?"

"Just thought you'd be interested, I read it this morning."

"In the News of the Screws, I suppose," Matt sneered.

"The Sun, actually. Us P.E. teachers aren't intellectual enough for the Guardian."

"Ha, ha. I don't know why you read that rag. What the hell does it matter who she sleeps with? What difference does it make to her tennis?"

"Jesus, you're so bloody sensitive. It's just a bit of craic, that's all."

That was about the level of it, Matt thought, exposing somebody's sexuality to ridicule for the titillation of mindless Sun readers. He was sure he wasn't over-reacting. The mindless yobs of Ballycol saw no difference between press harassment of famous people and their persecution of him.

It's all too easy to underestimate the effect of chronic harassment. Each individual incident is, on its own, insignificant. Matt's friends witnessing the odd event would brush it off as unimportant and interpret his anger as unreasonable paranoia.

"They're stupid wee hellions, you don't want to let them worry you," Robin instructed.

"Ignore it, they're not doing you any harm," was Danny's solution.

Finbar, a sporty lad who frequented Micky's, was more pragmatic: "Everyone gets abuse from time to time. It's irritating but that's all. You're too sensitive."

Of course he was sensitive. Each stone that hit his window, each jibe and catcall in the street, was a statement and the statement was, you're queer and worthless! Matt knew this wasn't so, but that didn't stop the anger and the fear. To all intents and purposes they were treating him as something subhuman. If that was how they saw him, what consequences might ensue? Only fifty years ago, the Nazis had been able to persecute the Jews (and homosexuals) by convincing the German nation that they were inferior. Once dehumanized, the Nazis could do what they liked with them. Matt worried that he could easily become the target for more serious attacks. He might be assaulted, he worried, even murdered!

Was it because he had come out? Would it have happened if he lived in England? Reading Gay Times, he had to conclude that it might have; there was a definite rise in anti-gay sentiment throughout the land. Some people blamed it on A.I.D.S., others pointed to the increasingly high profile that gay people had achieved, nationally. Whichever was the case, there had been an increasing vilification of homosexuals in the popular press.

By the late seventies, a sort of acceptance had developed. However this had been a generally young middle class thing that hadn't impacted on the vast majority who had never knowingly met a gay person. They were exotic denizens of another world and their only knowledge of them was from the telly; comic creations; mincing parodies of men who could not control their lust for any other male of this, or any other, species. Then a new sort of gay appeared on the scene; the loony left, the black lesbian and gay activist. In their attempts to discredit socialist councils, the right wing press dwelt upon the fact that many gay activists were socialists. The idea that filthy queer commies were diverting healthy heterosexuals' rates into their subversive schemes was fertile ground. The tabloids had hit upon a feared minority, the punters loved to be told how disgusting the queers were, and they would buy the rag to get more and more. The advantage of queer bashing was that there were no laws against it. Sun readers hated blacks, too, and Jews and Indians and anything that wasn't the same as they were, but there were laws against racial hatred so the editors had to be a bit circumspect in their exploitation of those fears. It was open season on the nancy boys and the militant lesbian feminists.

God must have been a journalist at heart. Just when it was most profitable, he sent the 'gay plague'. Maxwell, Murdoch and company must have fallen to their knees in thanks. Not only were homosexuals using up their taxes but also they were spreading contagion and certain death!

Incredibly, the situation deteriorated. The campaign was so effective that, by nineteen eighty-eight, the Conservative government was able to openly use homophobia as a vote catcher. In a party political broadcast they pushed the idea that socialist councils wasted money on gay and lesbian groups and clause twenty-eight was conceived. Britain soon had a law that made it *illegal* for local government employees to treat gay relationships as equal to straight relationships. The effect was that teachers were terrified to talk about homosexuality in class or support gay pupils, in case they were prosecuted. The law didn't apply to Northern Ireland; it didn't need to.

Matt knew he had to break the cycle of victimisation, but how? There was no one to appeal to. The police were powerless, Sinn Fein were out of the question and the only other authority in the town, the church, implicitly supported the persecution of homosexuals by their explicit condemnation of the gay lifestyle. Matt decided to modify David's idea, to find out who was persecuting him. He borrowed the video camera from school and set it up in the front window, the lens just peeking through the curtains. He bought three, three hour blank tapes and simply kept the thing running all night, changing tapes as they ran out. That way he could cover the critical hours of six p.m. to three a.m.

Needless to say, he chose one of the lulls and it was nights later before he got the first shots of them. Eagerly, he banged the tape in the video recorder and peered at the shadowy image. Too bloody dark, wasn't it! Next day, he went to the electrical store where Finbar worked and purchased an elegant light to go above the front door. Fin helped him put it up. It was practically a floodlight; it worked like a dream and within a couple of weeks he had a video dossier of the doorbell ringers and stone throwers.

Then he had a culprit-spotting party. Finbar brought some of his mates round and they sat, identifying the little shits that were doing it. Surprisingly, Paddy and his thugs were not in the cast. The culprits were mostly wee boys, mostly in their late teens, who lived quite close.

Matt then indulged in a few weeks of extremely pleasurable counter-harassment.

He kept an eye out for faces he recognised and would stop them: "Martin Donnelley and Vincent Rossi!" he called, and two startled boys swung round to face him.

"What." Vince said cheekily.

"Stop making nuisances of yourselves."

"Don't know what you're talking about."

"Yes you do, you've been ringing my bell and throwing stones at my windows."

"Fuck off. It wasn't us."

"Yes it was, I've got you on video and if it doesn't stop, your parents will have a private showing."

Of course, it was going far too well, he should have known there would be a hitch.

He was up in Derry for the weekend when Mary phoned to tell him that someone had smashed his front window on Friday night. He was seeing Alex on Sunday, and he didn't worry about rushing back because Finbar had boarded it up for him. The insurance covered the cost of repair, but that didn't stop him being really rattled by the experience. He found it distinctly unnerving to think that there was someone around who hated him enough to lift a potted plant from someone's garden, for that's what it was, and carry it the length of the town to hurl it through his window.

The police couldn't do much about it, and Matt thought it unlikely to be any of the kids he'd already tackled because they would think he still had the camera on. He decided to bluff. He collared Vincent and his mates. They were only about fourteen but they were as hard as nails. He tried to sound as macho as he could, "Look boys, I know it wasn't you. I don't know the names of the boys who did it but I'll be able to find out, just like I got you boys."

They looked at him suspiciously.

"I'm not asking you to grass on anyone, but if you know them you can tell them that they come to me or I hand the tape over to the peelers."

It didn't look like it was going to work then, one day, as he was about to wheel his bike down the passage, a gangling youth in Dr

Martens and denims sidled up. Matt didn't know his name but he'd seen him around quite a bit. He was a bit of a loner.

"Hello, Matt," he said.

Matt pretended to recognise him: "Ah yes! Hello. I don't know your name but I DO know your face."

"I didn't do nothin'. You didn't see me doing anythin' did you?"

"No, I don't have pictures of the plant pot being thrown. Just faces."

"God's honour it weren't me. I was just follerin' them, honest."

"Well you'll have to tell that to the police because I'm going to hand the video over to them if the culprit doesn't come to see me. Which one actually threw the thing, anyway?"

"You won't tell him I grassed?"

"Of course not. He'll think it came from the video, won't he now?"

He nodded pathetically: "It were Frankie McSorley."

"That was the boy carrying the pot, was it?"

"Aye."

"Where did he get it."

"House on the Shore Road."

"Don't worry, I'll keep your name out of this," Matt smiled condescendingly.

As soon as the youngster was out of the way, Matt whooped and did a little dance of glee. "Got the fucker by the short and curlies!" he crowed to himself.

In Micky's Matt told Finbar the story. He knew Frankie McSorley alright: "It's Paddy's wee brother. Not so wee, actually."

Ah!" Matt exclaimed. "Remember there was one guy on the video we couldn't pinpoint, tall lanky geezer."

"Ah-ha."

"Bet you that's him. He's about eighteen, drinks in Hannah's. Should we go and have a look?"

They finished their pints and made their way up the main street to a trendy pub half way up. He felt very out of place there; they were nearly all Fin's age and he seemed to know most of them.

"There he is," he whispered, pointing to a six foot version of Paddy. Frankie didn't share his brother's complexion. His almond shaped face was as smooth as a peach. He had a tight little mouth surmounted by the merest suggestion of a moustache. His nose was as flat as any seasoned pugilist's and his eyes were deep in dark sockets.

The innocent texture of his skin threw his pugnacious features and his harshly cropped black hair into sharp relief.

"Ach! I know him. He's always making smart-arse comments in the street, I didn't realise he was Paddy's brother. Had I known that, I would have understood! Should I tackle him now?"

"I wouldn't if I was you. He's on home territory and he's probably half cut. He usually is."

He took Fin's advice and hung on until he saw him in the Diamond a couple of days later.

"Frankie?" he said.

The boxer looked him up and down.

"Have you something to tell me?"

"Fuck off you queer bastard."

"Would you prefer to talk to the police?"

"I don't know what you're fuckin' well on about. Now, fuck off."

"O.K. then, don't say you haven't been warned!"

The police were very interested. They wanted to know how he got a name. Matt explained that he had promised to protect his source. They said that they couldn't do very much without proof so Matt told them that Frankie was seen taking the plant from a garden.

Next evening, the doorbell rang and Frankie stood on his doorstep with a very angry father. Matt invited them both in. Mr. McSorley launched straight in: "We've had the police at our house tonight. They say you have accused my son of damaging your property." He turned to his son: "Did you do it, Frankie?"

"No Da."

"So it's your word against his. I could sue you for slander," threatened the angry father.

"Look," Matt started, "I don't know what he's told you but he's not nearly as innocent as he lets on. I don't know if you know this but I'm gay."

Mr. McSorley was obviously embarrassed by this revelation but he made conciliatory noises.

"Your sons know this and they don't miss an opportunity to remind me of the fact." Paddy verbally abuses me in the pub and Frankie does it in the street. What was it you said to me the other day Frankie?"

Frankie was suffering: "Can't remember," he mumbled.

"I'll remind you, should I? It went something like this, Hey big boy; do you want to suck my stiffie?"

Mr. McSorley looked appalled: "Is that true?"

Frankie was white as a sheet as he nodded.

"That isn't the only thing. Do you want to hear more?"

Frankie shook his glum head.

"Do you want me to show your dad the video?"

Matt explained to Mr. McSorley, "I have been tortured for the last two years by youngsters yelling abuse at me, ringing my doorbell, throwing things at my windows and, once, someone sprayed 'queers live here' on my door."

"That's terrible. I might not agree with what you are but what my boy's done's not right," he said.

"Yes, I got fed up, so I set a camera just inside the front window. I have some interesting videos, would you care to watch your son at work?"

Mr. McSorley didn't want to hear any more. He turned to his son: "What have you to say to this man?" he demanded menacingly.

"Sorry."

"Is this all true?"

The guilt-ridden boy nodded.

"Let's hear you say it."

"Aye Da."

The embarrassed man turned to Matt: "I'm very sorry. I never thought he would do something like this. We've always brought him up to behave himself. It's a bad crowd he's been running with. Well he won't be running any more, you can be sure of that. Well, boy. You're in trouble now. Mr. Woodhead was quite right to go to the police. You're lucky he didn't go elsewhere!"

Matt tried not to smirk as the defeated couple left, and wondered idly what Paddy and Frankie would get from their dad when they got home. If he had known what would happen to Frankie, he wouldn't have been so gleeful. Two days later, Frankie turned up at Matt's door. He looked as if he hadn't slept for days and he had a black eye.

"What will the police do?" he asked.

"I don't know. It's not up to me now."

"Me dad says I've got to pay you for the window. How much did it cost?"

"It was a lot. I claimed on my insurance."
"How much?" he insisted.
"A hundred, it was double glazed, you see."
He let out a long low whistle, "Shit!"
"I'll give it you. Dad'll kill me if I don't."
"If you insist. I'm sure the insurance will be delighted not to have to pay."

It was ridiculous. Matt had the young thug exactly where he wanted him and yet Frankie was so pathetic that he felt sorry for him. As he saw him out he said, "Are you alright?"
"Yeah."
He pressed him: "You don't look very well."
"I'm O.K."
"Listen, I'll talk to the police," he promised. "They might drop it if I tell them you've owned up and paid."

The police were no bother. They said that they couldn't do anything without witnesses and were happy enough to forget about the whole thing. Frankie turned up every pay day, regular as clockwork, with the next instalment.

By nineteen eighty-five Matt was quietly confident of his position in Ballycol society. He assumed that everyone who mattered knew he was gay and, despite the continued low-level verbal abuse, he felt that there was little significant opposition to his stance. Nevertheless he sometimes wondered where all the gay people in Ballycol were. In the old days he could pick a man up, no bother, but recently he had noticed that he wasn't meeting them any more. The few men who he did know for certain were gay, had started to avoid him. He had to expect it. He was openly gay and as such he was a threat to their anonymity. Also, he was twenty-nine; no longer one of the bright young things and the crowd in Micky's was looking distinctly young. At one time he could slot in with almost anyone in the pub. He could drift round from one company to another joining in with the craic. Now he could go in and not see one person he could honestly say that he knew well enough to talk to. It was possible that this was simply due to his being older than the clientele. However various little birds had told him that he had a rather fearsome reputation amongst the youth of Ballycol.

Despite feeling rather like an ancient retainer, he still liked drinking in Micky's. The popularity of Micky's with the youth of Ballycol meant that there were always attractive young men to look at. There was no chance of anything more than looking, but it's human nature, even if it is appallingly sexist!

There were a few who were particularly exquisite. Two extraordinary characters had added themselves to the ranks of the beautiful the previous September. The pair stood out because of their hair. By the mid-eighties most trendy males had little more than bristles on their heads. These two still had flowing tresses, reminiscent of the hippy days twenty years before. The brown-haired one was nice looking but fairly ordinary. When he first saw him, Matt assumed the black hair belonged to his girl-friend. Then, as he was chatting away to Finbar, the shock of black hair rose to its feet to reveal a slim, masculine form squeezed into a pair of black denims. He glided to the bar where he leaned earnestly on the counter. As he waited, he nervously rubbed his upper lip with his knuckles tickling an embryonic black moustache. The boy's enormous, liquid-brown eyes were fringed by long black lashes. He had astonishingly prominent, high cheek-bones. Despite his pale, Irish complexion, this gave him a vaguely oriental aspect, North African, maybe. The exotic in him appealed to Matt.

This Adonis and his mate became regulars in Micky's; he was called Damian Kelly and his friend was Stevie Brolly. Matt worked out that he lived in the old town. He knew that, because he used to see him walking home from work. He worked somewhere on the Omagh Road; it must have been manual labour because he wore overalls and carried a tatty metal lunch box. Stevie and Damian had plenty of girls in tow but never any one in particular. Then, when Matt came back after Christmas, Stevie had a girlfriend. At first Stevie, Damian and the woman would be in a threesome, and then Matt noticed that Stevie and his girl would sit apart from Damian and he would have to find others to talk to. Damian was friendly with Elis, and she was very often with Finbar, which meant that he was in the same sort of company but Matt still didn't get to meet him.

Then came the fateful evening. Matt was sitting with Finbar and Feargal and he could see Damian sitting in his favourite stall talking to someone Matt didn't know. Damian's companion left, but he sat on in the emptying bar, drinking alone. Matt watched Damian's eyes straying round the bar until they rested on him. For a moment Matt held his gaze, then Damian went back to his pint. Often, when he glanced up, he would catch Damian whipping his head round. Was he imagining it, or was Damian watching him? Finally, Damian glanced at Matt, drank up, pulled on his black, leather jacket with the fringes, and left.

Some madness came over Matt. He jumped up, said, "I'm off now, see you tomorrow," and left.

He didn't see Damian at first. The shore road was deserted, silent but for the lapping of the choppy lough. He turned to walk homeward and spotted a figure on one of the benches by the water. Crossing the road, he walked casually along the shore-line until he was opposite the bench.

"Are you alright?"

Damian didn't reply. He was stock-still. Matt approached him: "You O.K.?"

Still no reply, so he shook his shoulder.

"Wha?" he said as he came to.

"Are you alright, Damian?"

"Yeah. I'm fine."

"You don't look it." His heart was thumping: "Come in for a coffee." He held his breath, waiting for a reply. Damian rose to his feet somewhat unsteadily and followed Matt to the house, without a word.

Now he had achieved his ambition, Matt wasn't sure what to do. He had the exquisite drunk in his living room but he wouldn't dream of touching him. "Feeling better?" he asked, as Damian slurped his coffee.

Damian peered at Matt from under his luxuriant eyebrows and nodded slowly.

"You were looking pretty pissed off in the pub," Matt ventured. "Is there something wrong?" Matt thought it was a bit of a cheek asking a total stranger so personal a question, but it was that sort of evening.

"Just split with me girlfriend."

"I see," Matt said, nodding, as his heart sank. "Were you going with her long?"

"Two years next month."

Matt showed he had been watching Damian by telling him that he hadn't seen him with any particular girl. Whereupon Damian explained that her parents wouldn't let her go to pubs. Matt thought it odd that he should stick with a girl when she couldn't go out with him and said as much.

"I've been going with her since we was at school. Didn't matter as much then."

Matt was grateful that he hadn't tried anything on with Damian. All this time he'd had a girlfriend and Matt had been imagining he wasn't interested in girls. He'd had a lucky escape; he would let Damian drink up, then ease him out gently.

It didn't happen like that, though. The coffee brought him round and, once he'd started, he didn't want to stop. Slowly, Matt learnt a lot about Damian's life. At first he seemed angry that Maire had ditched him. But, as he recounted how many times she had not done something he'd wanted to, or vice versa, he began to change his attitude.

"Did you love her?" Matt wondered.

"At first, aye, I did. Then, later, I don't think so." He turned to look at Matt warmly, "Funny, isn't it. I would've gone on the same way and got married. No one said it but you could see them thinking, what a nice pair we made. I've nothin' in common with her now, you know that?"

"Perhaps it's as well, then."

"Fuckin' right it is."

At four o'clock Matt decided to suggest that Damian should leave. The conversation had ranged through relationships, sexual and emotional, to politics, religion and sundry other fascinating topics. Matt saw him to the front door where he stood as if unwilling to leave.

"Thank you," he said, "for a really interesting time."

"I enjoyed it too."

He opened the door to let him out. Damian hesitated, darted in, kissed Matt full on the lips and left him standing there, somewhat dazed.

The nature of his departure put all sorts of disturbing questions into Matt's mind. He couldn't help but think that Damian had a gay streak in him. He told himself that young people today were far less inhibited than his generation had been and that Damian might do that to any of his friends, but he didn't convince himself.

If Damian was gay; what then? He was nineteen; ten years his junior. Matt couldn't believe that such a beautiful young creature could ever find him attractive, and there was another thing that worried Matt. At nineteen, Damian was a treacherous two years below the age of consent and any sexual liaison with him would be risky in the extreme.

Next time he went down to Micky's, he was a trifle apprehensive about seeing Damian. He went in on his own and sat by the bar. Damian wasn't there but nor was there anyone else he knew. He soon found someone to talk to but it was a conversation on which he only half concentrated; he had one eye on the door. When he came, it was with Stevie and two girls, neither of whom was Stevie's woman. Damian said hello to him, smiled pleasantly and went off with his friends into the back room.

He noticed the girls leaving alone and, later, the boys drifted out. Ah well, he thought, you can't expect any more. He drank up and left, himself.

Matt was putting the key in his lock when Damian appeared out of nowhere.

"Any chance of a coffee?" he asked.

With less alcohol consumed, the conversation was a little slow to get going but it was, eventually, as friendly as before and this time there was no talk of girls and Matt's homosexuality was what Damian wanted to know about. Matt had the full attention of Damian's gentle face as he recounted the joys and pains of being gay. That was what was so special about Damian; his face. All the other lads in Ballycol went around with a hard, set expression, as if to smile would be a sign of weakness. If they did smile, it was a sneer or cruel mockery. Damian's face was so soft; when he smiled you saw all his pearly teeth and, even when serious, his upper lip had a little upward kink revealing his two upper incisors; it gave him the air of a startled rabbit.

Matt found himself being drawn to Damian. There was a palpable sexual tension between them. Matt wondered if Damian could sense it. He would have loved to stroke his gorgeous hair, to touch his lips, to caress his slim body. Matt thought that, if he knew what he was thinking, he would run a mile. He had had years of practice at school and he wasn't going to let one pretty boy expose him.

This time, when Damian left, the kiss was longer and lingering, leaving him in no doubt at all.

The following Friday, Damian was overtly friendly in Micky's. Matt was introduced to Stevie and a few other friends of theirs. When the pub closed they all went up to Matt's for coffee and craic but, on Saturday, the youngsters were going to a disco and they disappeared at about ten. Matt drifted home well after midnight and sat up watching a Frankenstein movie. The doorbell went at ten past one and Damian was standing there with a bottle of wine.

They sat on the floor facing each other, basking in the fire's warmth. Damian looked nervous; Matt asked him why.

"Just tense, that's all. Can you do massage?"

"I don't really know how."

"Have a go," Damian said coyly, "Maybe you can relax me."

"Come here, then."

Matt sat on the couch and Damian settled himself between his legs. Matt gripped his bony shoulders and started to massage the tense muscles. Damian rested his head in Matt's lap, snuggling into its hardening contents. Unperturbed, the young man smiled blissfully up at Matt: "My shirt's in the way," he said, "take it off for me."

Matt unbuttoned the denim shirt revealing Damian's white torso. He slipped the garment off Damian's shoulders and gently caressed his pale body. I'm being seduced by a nineteen year old, he thought, and it's wonderful.

The beautiful boy twisted and glided up Matt's body until he felt his warm breath on his face. He kissed Matt with his sumptuous mouth. Matt was amazed; no one had ever kissed him like that. Matt felt that Damian had given him his very life force through that mouth. Matt wanted his whole body to be in Damian's mouth but all he could get in there was his tongue.

Without being fully conscious of what they were doing, they stripped each other and writhed, naked, in front of the fire, kissing as if their lives depended upon it. Then there was ecstasy and warm slipperiness flooded into their groins. They prised themselves apart and lay on the floor, breathing deeply.

"Will you stay?" Matt asked.

"Nah, I gotta go now." Damian said kissing Matt's cheek. "Don't want to. Me Ma would kill me if I stayed out all night. Can I come again?"

"I don't know, try!"

"Argh!" he shouted leaping on top of Matt, nearly breaking his ribs. He scriggled the hairs on his chest, kissed him, finally, and leapt off him.

"Don't get up," he commanded as he pulled his things on, cried "See yah!" cheerily and was gone.

Damian became a permanent fixture at number seven. At first they would meet up in Micky's but soon number seven became his first port of call. Like Matt, he was infuriated and frustrated by attitudes to gay people. They spent hours over steaming mugs, putting the world to rights. He may have only been nineteen, but he was a damn sight more politically aware than Matt had been at that age. His politics were green tinged with red, pale at first but deepening with time. Chris had been a silent Sinn Fein supporter, rarely expressing his views on the subject, but not so Damian. He was the first person Matt knew who openly expounded the Sinn Fein line. His father had been exploited, as he put it. Then, when crippled with bronchitis, he had been thrown on the scrap heap. That was long before he was born; he could only ever remember his mother being the bread winner. Despite being bright, he had left school instead of going on for 'A' levels and was now stuck in a tedious job in a brickworks. He blamed the Protestant capitalist mill owning bourgeoisie for all his family's misfortunes and the Kelly ills were symbolic of Ireland's struggle. A revolutionary heart beat in Damian's handsome chest and, when roused, its zeal burned in his dewy eyes. Britain was responsible for maintaining the status quo, they had to be removed and, much as he regretted people having to die, you had to break eggs to make an omelette. The army was one of occupation and the police were collaborators; he hated them with a vengeance.

Sometimes he would turn up at Matt's house incoherent with rage at some incident or other, although even Matt could find the soldiers irritating at times. For a start, their radios caused him endless annoyance. As they passed the house their transmissions reduced Radio 4 to the gibbering of manic dolphins. But he didn't have to have the radio on for them to intrude into his home. The joy of patrolling Richmond Terrace in the wee small hours of a shining summer's morning was obviously too much for the squaddies. Raucous English regional accents would slice into his sleep. When it was bawdy rugby songs he could sneer, turn over and try to get to sleep again but, more often, it was tantalising snippets of conversation;

"Did 'e?" a Yorkshire lad shouted under his window.

"Did 'e 'eckerslike!" laughed another.

"What a Wally."

"'e couldn't could 'e," the first roared, "'asn't got the equipment!"

Then, less distinct as they progressed along the terrace, "Is that so then, Dusty?"

Dusty's reply was lost in the alarmed quacking of a family of mallards flushed from their dawn dabblings.

Poor Dusty. Matt wondered if he was the unfortunate soldier Mardy had met a few weeks previously. Coming out of school late one evening, he noticed a soldier, barely out of teens, cowering in a doorway. In itself, that was unusual. Unlike Matt's school, the Christian Brothers' was hostile territory for the army. Mardy, being Mardy, smiled and passed the time of day, only to see a tear trickle down the youth's cheek.

"Are you alright, young feller?" he asked, looking round for the rest of his patrol.

Eyes full of fear, the lad stammered, "They've gone without me and I don't know my way back."

Mardy loaded the frightened teenager into his car and drove him round to the barracks. An act of kindness but also an act of extreme courage. Most of Ballycol wouldn't dare be seen "collaborating"!

When he heard stories like that, Matt could feel great sympathy with the Brits; at other times he shared Damian's fury and disdain for his fellow countrymen. One such incident was on a Monday morning. He had been home for the weekend. He had been held up in Castlederg and he was late for school, Piet was staying at the time, so he was with him in the car. He was nearly at school when he ran into a checkpoint. There was a queue of about seven cars, most bringing pupils to school. The car crept up to the soldiers and had stopped before he realised that he hadn't got his licence with him.

"This is ridiculous." he exclaimed as the sergeant asked him for it. "I don't have it with me and I'm late for work."

"We'll see how ridiculous it is," the soldier said grimly. "Would you get out of the car, sir?"

Matt growled under his breath.

"Would you open the bonnet, please, sir?"

Matt stood fuming as the soldier searched through the engine compartment.

"That's the engine," Matt said trying to make a joke. Unfortunately, it came out as a sour rebuke.

"Now your boot, sir," the militia insisted.

As he opened it, he grimaced at the car-loads of grinning pupils building up behind him.

"What's in here, sir?" he asked, indicating the compartment for the spare wheel. Matt was tempted to say Semtex but he kept his mouth shut and opened it.

His patience waned as the soldier thoroughly inspected his few tools. "You're just being awkward," he said.

"Just doing my job, sir," he replied in grim satisfaction.

By now, Matt was seething. Typical thicko, he thought. Give 'em a bit of power and they just love to use it. I bet he knows damn well I teach at the school, and he's just doing this to get back at all those poor teachers who were evidently totally unable to penetrate the layers of bone and blubber to his minuscule brain.

At long last, the search was over but the soldier hadn't finished the humiliation process. "What's your passenger's name, sir?"

"Piet van Vondel."

"Would you get out of the car, please, sir?"

Piet thought this was great. He'd read all about the forces of occupation and now he could go back to Holland and tell them all how true it was. Piet was perfectly polite but, for some reason, the soldiers took a dislike to him. They made him take every single document out of his wallet and lay them on the car roof. It was drizzling so his papers were soaked. The ink on his driving licence ran and a photo of his current affair was a soggy mess, after. Eventually, they let the car go. Matt was furious. He even considered complaining to the barracks but he decided against it on the grounds that the soldiers might, subsequently, single him out for extra special attention.

Matt was perceived as a member of the loyalist community and that sort of thing didn't happen to him too often, but the same didn't apply to Damian. And it wasn't only the army; the police would single him out for the same sort of treatment. Every day, Matt saw the way they worked in the street. They would approach a group of youths who were doing nothing more threatening than standing in a group on a street corner. The patrol would question them and write it all down. Matt thought it had to be so infuriating to be treated like that on the streets of your own town. He once asked David why the police did it. He said that it was to keep the terrorists on their toes. If the Provos knew that the police and the army were there and that they were doing their job, they weren't as likely to try anything on. David just couldn't see that, every time a youngster was stopped in the street, it simply reinforced his support for the forces that would eventually bring about their downfall.

Damian reckoned that there was an unofficial policy of physical abuse against Nationalist youths in the town. David said it was all Republican propaganda, but Damian would shake his conviction by quoting cases where his friends had been beaten up by soldiers. The only first hand account he ever heard was Stevie's. Matt thought Stevie quite handsome in a traditional sort of way, although he hadn't noticed this until Stevie got his hair cut. There was even talk of his doing some modelling professionally. One night he came into Micky's looking a terrible mess. He had broken teeth and his badly bruised face had a great gash, criss-crossed with stitches, across the cheek. He told Matt that he had got into an argument with some soldiers and it had culminated in him being knocked to the floor and having a rifle butt smashed into his face. Stevie claimed that the attack, which the army denied even happened, was unprovoked but Matt was confident that he must have been pretty abusive to the soldiers to get treated like that. Despite that, Matt couldn't help worrying that the soldiers shouldn't have done that. It just wasn't cricket, was it?

CHAPTER 15

SPRING 1985, DANGEROUS LIAISONS

David began to call at Matt's house more and more. Delighted as he was to see David, his visits made Matt uneasy. Every time he came, the probability of his bumping into Damian increased and Matt dreaded that. Matt respected Damian's innocent outrage at injustice; revelled in his energetic enthusiasm for sex and adored his fiercely individualistic good looks. At the same time, he was growing increasingly fond of the enigmatic young policeman with his anachronistic reserve and noble profile. David wouldn't be able to cope with Damian's Republican politics and Damian, being Damian, would feel obliged to expound upon them. The fact that David was a policeman was a problem, too. He trusted Damian to the hilt but could he entrust him with David's safety? If Damian knew that a representative of the hated forces of his oppression visited Matt, gay or not, could he trust him not to betray him? What sort of friend was he, that he could think such a thing about him? Of course, he wouldn't deliberately tout on David, but might he let something slip when in Republican company. It wouldn't only be David that would suffer; all of them would be at risk. Fond of Damian as he was, he couldn't take the chance, so he tried to meet David in The Royal Arms in Omagh as much as he could.

Damian wasn't the only person he didn't want David to bump into in Ballycol. Mary was due in April. Matt had vowed not to spill the beans to David but, if he saw her, he was bound to guess. Matt dreaded David's asking him about her, but he never did; Mary was evidently another of his little secrets. It was far better to meet up with David at Alex's but even that had its drawbacks. As soon as he arrived Alex would tell him about Danny's latest witticism or escapade. He had to listen patiently to amusing stories about his friend whilst wondering why he was shunning him. What had he done to deserve this? It couldn't be because of Chris, could it? Danny had seemed to take it O.K. Could he have been putting up a front? Deep down, was he angry with Matt for seducing his kid brother? Perhaps Chris had said something to him. Maybe he had insinuated that Matt was to blame for the split. Yes, he thought, Chris had told Danny about him and Piet and Danny despised him for doing the dirty on his little sib. But it didn't ring true; Danny didn't think like that. The only explanation was that Danny was bored with him. Whenever they met, all Matt ever talked about was how rotten it was being gay in Ballycol. He supposed that Danny had got really pissed off with hearing the same old story, week after week. He could hardly blame him for wanting to avoid him. Next time he saw Danny he would have to make an effort not to harp on about it but, at the rate things were going, he was hardly likely to see him again.

It was taking David a long time to come to terms with being gay. He was sexually and emotionally frustrated. Matt coaxed him into admitting that he had been in love with Alex and could never quite forgive Matt for having won Alex's affections. It was useless his trying to explain the unique nature of their relationship, he couldn't see how they could have been lovers if Alex wasn't actually gay. He didn't tell David how badly Alex had reacted when he'd made a pass at him. All David could see was that now Alex was crippled, and he'd missed his chance. David never spoke about any other men. Matt tried to find out what sort of man he fancied, half hoping that he might describe him. David was very handsome and, when he opened up to Matt, he found him irresistible. If David had made a single move in Matt's direction he would have been putty in his hands, but David was consistently aloof.

Kevin from Derry Cara-Friend had told Matt something which was never far from his thoughts when he was with David. The help-line had a strict rule about not sleeping with the people that came to them for help. It seemed self-evident that to do so would be highly unprofessional, but Kevin pointed out that they were all volunteers, anyway. It was nothing to do with morality; there was a far more practical reason for the rule. When they met someone, they could be pretty sure that that person had never been able to open up about their sexuality to anyone and, as a result, an intense bond of trust was built up between the client and the volunteer. The client sometimes became infatuated with the volunteer and would try hard to seduce him but the volunteer was at risk too. The caller's sheer vulnerability would make him attractive and it would be all too easy for the volunteer to crumble and fall into bed with him; much as Piet had with Matt. Their relationship had survived that pitfall; more commonly, they didn't. There was always the risk of the newcomer taking fright or being ashamed of what he'd done. Then he would be reluctant to contact the volunteer again and his one tenuous contact with the gay world would have been lost for ever. Matt could see a close parallel between what Cara-Friend was doing and his situation with David. If he did make a pass at him, he might scamper off like a frightened piglet, never to be seen on the gay scene again. Matt wasn't quite sure what he could do for David, other than listen to him. There was no way David could go to the gay discos in Derry; it was simply too dangerous. Matt wasn't sure about Belfast, but he suspected that it would be no better there. He even suggested that David should go to Holland with him the next summer, but he said no.

Matt thought of his weekly visits to Alex as giving Sandra time off. For the last three and a half years she had devoted every spare minute to him. What she got out of it, Matt wasn't sure. Initially, Matt was jealous of Sandra because her devotion had won Alex away from him but, now, he could see it wasn't quite like that. He watched her helping Alex get dressed for him to take him out.

"Aghh!" he winced, "Careful!" He turned to Matt: "She's rough, you know!"

"I'd be rough if I had you to deal with every day."

"She's used to it, aren't you? Goes with the job!"

Sandra took this with equanimity: "There, is that alright?"

"Sock's not right," he complained. His tone was sharp; she'd not done her job right.

The tension made Matt uncomfortable. He tried to side with Sandra: "Can't you dress yourself yet?"

He replied in a stage whisper, "Aye, but it's easier if she does it for me."

Matt caught an angry glance from beneath her big, round specs: "There you are. I'm going into Londonderry, do you want anything?"

He shook his head dismissively

Matt followed her to the front door: "You O.K.?"

"Course! Why shouldn't I be?" she responded airily.

"He's difficult, isn't he?"

She grimaced: "He has his moments."

"Have a nice time," he smiled.

"Don't worry about me," she smiled, "You've got him for the afternoon. I'm off."

With that she was down the path, into her Metro and away.

City of Derry were playing at home that Saturday. Matt had had enough of rugby at school but Alex yearned to play again. Matt thought that watching all those able bodied men would frustrate Alex, but he seemed happy enough to hobble along the touchline cheering his former team-mates along. A good number were at school with them, although there was a new generation coming up. The team always made the effort to come over to chat to Alex after the game, which seemed to give him a boost.

The action was at the far end of the field and Derry was getting hammered. Matt turned to him: "You're a bit rough on her, you know."

"Who?"

"Sandra, who do you think?"

"Ach, Jesus," Alex exclaimed in obvious pain.

"What's up?"

"Ma leg. It's the cold. I need to rest it."

"I'll bring the car over, should I?"

He nodded vigorously, "Aye."

By the time he got the car over, the play had moved closer and Alex was roaring his support for Derry with a healthy gusto. He wasn't the helpless creature of a couple of years ago.

"You want to watch Sandra," Matt continued at half-time.

"She's alright."

"She's too good for you," he admonished, turning to look at Alex. For the first time he was all there, every bit of his old soul was in his dark eyes. A shudder passed through Matt's guts.

Alex's eyes bored into him. "Are you still jealous?" he demanded.

"Of course not. I've still got Piet, and there's..... well there's someone else too," he finished lamely.

"Oh yes?" he grinned. "And who have you been poking on the quiet?"

Matt was embarrassed: "It's not like that!"

"Of course it isn't. It never is with you Matthew. Us mere mortals have sex but Matt has deep, meaningful relationships."

"So what about you and Sandra then?"

He leered horribly. "She gets what she wants."

"I don't know how she puts up with him," he complained to Mary. They were sitting in her flat, an embryonic baby cardigan, spiked on two knitting needles, rested on her burgeoning bump.

"I'd like to meet her. Perhaps I could talk sense into her. I know you're very fond of him but he does need to be taught a lesson, he's being a real brute."

"He has had a rough time."

"And nobody else has, I suppose?"

Matt brushed this off: "She's not the sort of person to lie down and take all that crap. That's what I can't understand. She must really love him more than we can imagine."

Mary shrugged: "Women in this country! I can't believe how many let themselves be trampled over. Carmel's gone back to her man, you know."

"You're kidding. Why?"

"Says she'll give him one more chance; reckoned Paul missed his dad. She's willing to give it a go for his sake."

He blew a dubious puff of air through his lips. "I hope it goes O.K."

"We need a women's centre here," she declared.

"Where?"

"That's the problem. There's only a handful of us. I'm the only one with any capital at all and it's all tied up in here."

"What about getting a grant from the health and social services people?"

"We would need to find premises first. There's nothing in this town. You know how hard it is to find a flat, even."

"That's another thing," Matt commented. "How will you manage here when Junior's born? The place is like a fridge and you haven't even got hot water on tap."

"I'll manage, Matthew. Thousands of women bring kids up in conditions that would make this look like a palace. What would you suggest, anyway? Move into a centrally heated house? I couldn't afford that."

"You could if it was mine."

"What's the matter Matt? Need someone to iron your shirts do you? You poor dear!"

He could never cope with her teasing: "Och, no. I just thought it'd be better for the wee'un."

"You're not getting broody, are you?" she smirked.

"No, of course not!" he blustered. "I was just thinking of you, that's all."

"It's very sweet of you, Matthew, but I couldn't imagine you putting up with a baby somehow. And what about your romantic life? I can just imagine it. Creeping in from the pub with some new conquest warning him, shush or you'll wake the baby."

"The only problem I could foresee would be David."

"Precisely," she smiled, blissfully, "I've kept this from him so far, I don't want to spoil it now."

It was easier getting Mary and Sandra together than he had dared hope. Mary moved in the following Monday and Sandra and Alex were to arrive early the next Friday evening. He decided they would sit in the dining room on the first floor instead of the usual ground floor lounge. Alex could sleep in his bedroom which was just above and only half a flight up from the bathroom. Sandra would have to sleep in the attic room and he would either kip in the lounge or make a bed up in the box room.

When they arrived, Matt was in the kitchen and Mary was upstairs putting her feet up in front of the fire. She had been working in the shop all day and was absolutely whacked. Matt's heart missed a beat as he opened the door; David was helping Alex out of the front seat of his car.

Matt pounded up the stairs. "Quick!" he gasped, "David's here!"

Mary eased herself to the vertical: "What's happening?"

"It's David. He's brought Alex and Sandra."

She collapsed back into her seat: "Kismet Matty, kismet."

"Come on, they'll be up in a minute, you don't want him to see you, do you?"

"Matthew. I'm in no state to go hiding in a cupboard, am I?"

He exhaled exaggeratedly, said, "Right!" and scampered down stairs.

The guests had settled themselves in the downstairs lounge. If he could keep them there...

Alex greeted him, "Where did you disappear to?"

"Um.. Had to.. Um.. put the fire guard up upstairs."

"Why? What's wrong?"

"Nowt. Nowt at all. Just worried about the fire. You know me. Paranoid about fire, I am."

"Should I see to it?" David offered.

"No, no. It's fine now, let's get your stuff in from the car."

"It's all in," Sandra assured him.

"You've not much."

"I'm not staying," David said, "I'm on duty, I just brought these two down. Sandra's car won't take the wheelchair." Matt breathed an audible sigh of relief. "Right! Em.. coffee? tea?" He scuttled to the kitchen, thanking his lucky stars. It looked like they were going to get away with it!

Sandra followed him to the kitchen: "Can I help you?"

"Could you carry the tray?"

"Sure. Where's your friend?"

"Who?"

"The one you said you wanted to meet us, the woman."

"She's upstairs, asleep."

She looked at him questioningly.

"You'll understand, when you meet her."

Entering the front room what he saw or, rather, what he didn't see, nearly made him drop the teapot.

"Where is he?" he demanded of Alex.

"Gone to the bog. Alright?" he asked condescendingly.

"Sure!"

"He won't wake your friend," Sandra reassured.

"Yeah, Mary, she's asleep upstairs," he explained. As he listened he strained to hear any noise from above, none came. At last he heard footfalls on the stairs.

"Coffee or tea?" he asked David as he came in.

"Neither, thank you, I've got to be on my way. I'll see you tomorrow lunchtime, then. Good-bye." And with that, David was gone.

Tea finished, Matt said that he would check to see if Mary was awake and, if she was, they could go up to the sitting room. "Phew!" he said, walking in. "That was a close one."

"Closer than you think!" she laughed.

"What do you mean?"

"He only came in to look at the fire, didn't he?"

"Shit! What did he say?"

"Not a lot. I don't think he recognised me at first. He was a bit flummoxed when he did."

"What did he say?"

"Oh! I didn't know, was his first comment. He hedged a bit, then asked me how advanced the pregnancy was."

"What did you say?"

She laughed, "Some men are dopes. I told him I was six months gone; he swallowed it, hook, line and sinker."

"Didn't he ask whose it was?"

"Nope. None of his business, was it?"

"You're a cool customer. How could you?" he hugged her clumsily, "Mary, you're amazing. Should I bring them up?"

Alex was on his best behaviour, so much so that Matt began to wonder if his attempts to influence him had worked. Mary took the bull by the horns: "Are you going to the pub?" she demanded.

"I hadn't thought of going. I didn't think you'd want to and Alex might not either."

"Do you want to go, Alex?" Mary asked.

He looked happy at the prospect.

"How about if you two go to the pub and Sandra and I can stay and have a nice chat here. Is that O.K. with you, Sandra?"

Sandra nodded.

"Can you make it on foot?" he asked Alex.

He thought he could, so they made their slow way to the nearest bar, which was Micky's.

All the usual gang were there and, to his amazement, all his friends reacted marvellously to Alex. Feargal kept Alex entertained with tales of his outrageous sexual exploits and Finbar talked sport. Feargal knew Alex's saga but it was a horrifying story for the rest of them. Elis' eyes, fixed on his friend's still handsome face, widened in awe as he described his gradual climb out of the confused dream of his coma. He described how it slowly dawned upon him that something was wrong with him, how he sobbed with frustration at not being able to communicate, not even being able to think. He explained how he knew that his mind was as disabled as his body and how he could do nothing about it.

By closing time, Alex was plastered and Damian and Fin had to practically carry him back to Matt's. A cosy little tableau greeted them in the upstairs sitting room. Mary and Sandra had pulled two easy chairs up to the fire and they were deep in intimate conversation. The others fussed round Mary whilst the two lads got Alex safely into an armchair to protests of, "I'm alright, I can manage."

As a social evening it was a success. It was probably the first time that Alex had been in a normal social situation since the accident, and Damian made a significant leap forward that night. Up to that point, Matt was the only person in Ballycol who knew he was gay. As Matt settled on the couch next to Fin, Damian insinuated himself between them like a great, silky tom cat. He wasn't overtly intimate but the others couldn't have been left in much doubt as to their relationship. Matt should have been concerned, but he wasn't.

Damian was deep in conversation with Alex, so he didn't leave with the others and stayed the night. Next day, when they had gone, Mary collared him. "Revelations, revelations!" she exclaimed.

"You mean me and Damian, I suppose."

"That's not what I meant but yes, you naughty boy. That was a turn up for the books. How long has that been going on?"

"Since January," Matt grinned then, turning serious, he said, "Listen, he's only nineteen, you know. If we're caught I could be in real trouble. You know what I mean, don't you?"

"Come on, Matt. What do you take me for? I'm not going to say anything, am I? Can you be sure of him, though?"

"Of course! Well, I hope so anyway. I do hope so."

He turned the conversation back to her first comment: "I suppose you're relieved now that David knows, or rather doesn't know. You don't have to worry about him finding out, anyway."

"That's not what I was referring to, Matthew," she sang.

"What are you on about then?"

"I had a long heart to heart with Sandra."

"And?"

"She didn't want me to tell you."

"Why say anything, then?"

"I persuaded her you deserved to know," she smiled.

"Go on," he said, intrigued.

"Do you want to know why Danny's been avoiding you?"

"Of course I do!"

She smiled, infuriatingly: "It's not your fault." She bit her lip and paused, dramatically. "Hold on to your hat, Matt. Sandra and Danny are having an affair."

"Jesus Christ!" he yelled, "I don't believe it. The randy old bugger. That explains it!"

At least I'm not responsible, he thought, there's a chance to retrieve our relationship. Suddenly his face dropped; a dreadful thought had struck him. What about Alex?

Mary appraised him: "I wondered how long it would take you. You don't imagine Sandra hasn't thought of that, do you? She has been going through agonies. She loves Alex, but not in the way she used to. Now it's like the love of a mother for a child. She couldn't hurt him but she could never marry him. Then Danny came like a knight on a white charger. She's in love. For the first time in her life she's found someone who can return her love, but she won't abandon Alex until she's sure he can cope."

He whistled: "Poor Sandra. What will she do?"

"Wait. And hope."

Sandra wasn't the only one who had to wait and hope. He had thought that Sandra might have said something to Danny and that he would call but after a couple of apprehensive weeks, it was evident that he had hoped in vain. Next time he saw Alex, he was full of the last weekend he'd spent at Matt's. He had liked his friends and was there any chance of his coming for another weekend? Matt was happy to oblige; it would give Sandra a weekend off so she could spend time with Danny. He hoped he would be grateful.

There was no way that Matt could get Alex's wheelchair in the Beetle, so he had to drive to Derry, bring Alex back in his dad's Landover and then reverse the process on Sunday, but it was worth it. Matt had enjoyed Alex's last visit, too.

It wasn't the best weekend for him to come. Mary was now overdue and he expected to have to whisk her into hospital at any moment. He was glad he had persuaded her to move into number seven at least until she had the baby. He had a phone so she could call for help if she started.

"Matthew!" she growled, "I can look after myself. You go and get Alex. If I do start when you're away, I'll call an ambulance. Now stop fussing and go!"

"I'm sorry," he apologised, as he explained the situation to Alex. "I don't think we can go out this weekend. I hope you don't mind."

"No prob," he reassured.

He spent the night waiting on his two immobile friends. Mary retired early leaving the two old friends in their familiar pose huddled around a glowing coal fire with a collection of beer tins. The only difference from the old times was the restrained rate at which they emptied them.

The hour hand crept around another circuit of the old clock's freckled face and Matt was explaining about the changes in the exam system. It was the last year that biology would be examined by two separate exams. The following year the G.C.E. and the C.S.E. would be replaced by what was to be called sixteen plus. The details were so riveting that Alex nodded off.

"Come on," Matt said, shaking him. "Beddy-byes." He shook him gently until he came round. "Come on. I'll get you upstairs." Matt grabbed both hands and pulled him upright with an, "Ups-a-daisy."

"It's early yet," he said drowsily.

"Maybe for you. But I have to be on my toes. Dutiful prospective Daddy!"

That shook him out of his doziness: "Matt, I never realised! You've recovered! You've gone normal!"

"Bastard!" he grinned, threatening to push him back into the chair.

Alex was serious, though; "*Is* it yours?"

"Don't be daft! You should know me better than that."

"Who is he?"

He hesitated: "That's her business. However. I still want to be fully compos mentis for when she goes into labour."

Slowly, painfully, Alex hoisted himself up the stairs. Matt followed closely, tightly gripping the banister to brace himself in case he fell. At last, Alex collapsed onto Matt's bed.

"Need a hand?" he asked.

"Sneakers, socks and jeans." he paused, "If you don't mind."

Without a word, Matt started working at his laces. After his shoes he removed his damp, malodorous socks. He hesitated at his waist. Stupid. Sandra did this for him day in, day out. Alex hoisted his bum up as Matt pulled his denims off and Alex pulled his own shirt off. He's still got it, he thought, as Alex disappeared under the covers.

"Matt?"

"Uh-ha?"

"Where are you sleeping?"

"In the attic room."

Alex grimaced.

"It's not as bleak as it sounds. It's a nice room, actually. If you don't mind walking at a slant."

"You'd be comfier in your own bed," he said quietly.

Matt flinched inwardly, "What are you saying, Alex?"

"Please. Stay with me tonight."

How many times would he have leaped with joy if Alex had said that before? Now, it was with a sense of duty that he stripped off and crept in beside him. Alex's huge arms drew Matt to him; years of hoisting himself round in a wheelchair had given them incredible strength. Alex buried his face in Matt's chest and sobbed.

"What's the matter? Don't cry like that. What's wrong?" he whispered.

He got no sensible reply. Alex choked, "I'm so... so scared," then blubbered like a baby until Matt's chest was wet with tears.

Once the subterranean shudders had subsided, Matt stroked his head and tried again, "What are you scared of?"

"Mam, Dad, Sandra, the future, everything," he sniffed. "What am I going to do? I've nothing left, no job, no life, no friends, nothing at all!"

"That's rubbish and you know it. You've me. And there's David," he hesitated, was this wise? "and Sandra and Danny."

"Not for long," he murmured.

"Don't be silly. We've stuck with you when you were being impossible. Why on earth should we desert you now you're getting back to your old self?"

"Sandra doesn't love me. She's dying to get away from me. I want to tell her to go but I'm scared," he started to sob again. "What will I do if she goes? I'll have no-one."

Matt kissed his forehead; it was wet, hot and salty. "You've got to stop relying on people so much. There's stacks of people with handicaps far worse than yours and they're practically independent. I know, I work with PHAB, remember?"

He didn't speak. He almost crushed Matt's ribs with his ape-like arms, closed his eyes and sought his chest for comfort.

"Matt! MAAATT!" Someone was shaking him awake. Alex was snoring peacefully, clutching him like his childhood teddy. The voice was Mary. Matt peered at her disbelievingly; she was clutching her tummy.

"It's started, Matt."

He shot out of bed before realising that he was stark naked. At that moment another contraction struck. She giggled and winced simultaneously as he tried to grab something to cover himself.

"What are you up to?" Alex moaned.

"Mary's having the baby. I'm taking her to the hospital. Will you be alright?"

"Yes," he said resolutely. "I'm not a cripple, you know!"

With a quick kiss, Matt was gone.

At five o'clock, on a Saturday morning in April Ballycol looked peaceful, even beautiful. The Landrover chugged up the main street, past the pools of yellow light casting brown shadows beneath the discarded beer cans and chip wrappers from the last night's revelries. Beyond the town, the warm yellow gave way to sad little isolated pools of weak blue-white. The journey was almost completed in silence, Mary tried to apologise for dragging him away from Alex, but he assured her that it wasn't what it seemed and that it really didn't matter.

The cottage hospital was on the Enniskillen Road. It looked deserted as they drew up to its bleak, brick frontage. There was a porter on duty and a quick word with him swung the duty staff into action. Mary was on a trolley and whisked down a brightly lit passage before he could even say good luck. He was left alone, wondering what to do.

It seemed to be ages before anyone came to see him, "Mr. Moore?" a nurse demanded.

"No, Woodhead, Matthew Woodhead. How is she?"

"You'll have quite a wait, I'm afraid," she said. "Did you want to be present at the birth?"

"Em. No. No thank you," he said.

She looked surprised. "Is this your first?" she smiled patronisingly.

"Excuse me. It's not my... I mean, I'm not the father. I'm just a friend."

She blushed, "Oh, I *am* sorry sir."

He wasn't sure whether she was sorry that he wasn't the father or that she'd assumed he was.

"How long will it be?"

"It could be one hour or six," she simpered.

"I don't know what to do. I have a handicapped guest. He's on his own at the house. Will you ring me when it happens?"

"Of course, sir," she beamed. And so, leaving his number with the porter, he tootled back to Alex.

It was nearly seven when he crept in to his room to find his bed empty. Shouting for Alex, he got no reply and he was on the way down stairs, when he heard a crash from the kitchen, followed by a loud "SHIT!" Matt pushed the door open to find Alex on the floor. He rushed over to help him up: "Are you all right?"

Alex shook his helping hand away. "Aye." He pointed to a shattered mug in a pool of milk and coffee granules, "Sorry about this, though."

"What happened?"

"I was making breakfast for you; the cup came off the tray."

"Did you fall?"

"Nah! I was cleaning it up wasn't I?"

"Here, I'll do it," Matt ordered.

He pushed him out of the way, "Fuck off. This is my first day of independence!"

As Alex grovelled in his own private regenesis, Bryony Moore was born.

CHAPTER 16
AUTUMN 1985, DAMIAN'S STORY

Every day that Matt and Damian were together brought the dreadful juncture nearer when Damian's family discovered that their son was gay, and they were guaranteed not to handle it very well. Damian felt certain that he would be thrown out of the house, probably with a beating, against which his father's past violations would pale into insignificance. He wasn't the only one at risk. The age of consent was twenty-one and Damian was nineteen, so Matt was in a decidedly dodgy position. If one of his enemies found out, they could go to the police. If he was prosecuted it would be the end of his career, and he could end up in prison. He knew he should put a hold on their relationship, for both their sakes, but a few minutes in Damian's company evaporated his resolve.

Besotted as he was with Damian, he was also wary of him; even afraid sometimes. He wasn't from his world and his thoughts emanated from an alien culture. When Damian talked of his violent home life, Matt tried to envisage what it was like for him but he knew he wasn't understanding. It wasn't the Catholic thing so much as his pure, undiluted, working class background. Class divisions in Northern Ireland have always been secondary to the sectarian divisions. Had they all been English, Alex and Damian would have had more in common with each other and Feargal, by virtue of his family background, would have been Matt's natural peer.

Damian had had a girlfriend but Matt wasn't his first male lover. Matt found it difficult to believe the stories that Damian told him about his school days. He seemed to have had sex with half the boys in his class!

"I'm sorry," he said, "I simply don't believe there are that many gays in this town!"

"They aren't gay, not most of them, anyway," he grinned. "Though I've my suspicions about one or two of 'em!" He paused to observe Matt's reactions. "You know what young fellers are like, they're as randy as fuck and the girls are all pretending to be virgins. It's better than wanking alone! It's traditional round here, you know, look at Jim Cassidy!"

Matt hadn't a notion who he was talking about.

"You know Jim..... Aye you do!"

"I can't place the name."

"Sometimes drinks in Micky's. Tallish guy; a bit overweight. Short black, curly hair and very, very camp."

"I think I know the guy. Face like an uncooked pork pie, drinks rum and black all the time. But he hangs about with Paddy McSorley's crowd, doesn't he?"

"Aye, that's him."

"What about him anyway?"

"He's gay."

"He can't be; he's so camp. How could he get away with it? Those bastards hate me for being gay."

"They all love him," Damian grinned, wide-eyed. "Watch him flirting with them some night. He's safe, you see. He makes passes at all of them. Nobody would suspect them for being seen with him, not like you."

"So he never gets it, then?"

Damian sniggered. "He gets more than me and you do! He's practically a prostitute. Never seen him doing the park or the toilets?"

Matt grimaced: "No. Surely no one would risk going with him. I mean, everyone would know, wouldn't they?"

"He's not going to say, is he? And they're not, anyway!" he laughed.

A thought struck Matt, "You don't suppose that Paddy and Jim...., you know?"

"Probably....... He's had his brother."

"Frankie?" Matt said, in utter disbelief.

He nodded: "He's a great body, you know. All that training he does."

"So Frankie's gay is he? He's the one who broke my window, you know."

"I don't know if he is but Jim said he loved it."

Matt looked at his boyfriend suspiciously: "And how did you find this out?"

"Jim wanted me to go with him. Thought I was Frankie's friend, so he tried to use his tactics with Frankie to persuade me. It was easy from there."

"Did you?"

"Nah!" he shuddered, "give me some credit. You're the only one I've got eyes for," he smiled, snuggling up to him.

But Damian's integration with Ballycol society was not without its problems. Matt lost count of the number of times Damian arrived at his door, shaking with rage at some gratuitous homophobic insult hurled at him in the street. He had always had Nationalist leanings but, now, he seemed to be increasingly identifying with Sinn Fein. Matt supposed that this was a reaction to his experiences; that if he could establish himself as a solid Republican, the town's hard men might stop persecuting him. That wasn't how Damian saw it. He maintained that the laws and attitudes against homosexuality were a product of British colonial rule. Sinn Fein held the moral high ground in Ireland and they had the only real answer to the situation which had blighted the lives of the Irish. When Sinn Fein adopted a pro-gay policy things would improve, he was sure of that.

Damian's sympathy with Sinn Fein only served to magnify Matt's worries about him as a lover. He didn't have any personal objections to Damian's political opinions, but he was well aware that others wouldn't share his liberality. Firstly there was school. The intake had changed over the years and the lower end of the school was verging on being twenty per cent Catholic, and yet the school was still dominated by conservative Unionist types. They would never tolerate his having an affair with a nineteen year old, never mind a nineteen year old Republican! There was the law, too. Had Damian been an ordinary lad, he doubted that the police would ever know about their relationship unless there was a complaint. The security forces were sure to be keeping an eye on the budding Republican. Intelligence in Ulster was second to none! They would know that they were friends and they would probably have a good idea that they were lovers. If they wanted to get at Damian or, worse still, use him in some way, they would have the perfect lever. He didn't want to be a casualty in the dirty war between the Provos and the Brits!

Superficially robust though Damian was, his ego was fragile. Despite his previous sexual exploits, Damian invested a lot of importance in what they had. Matt was the first self-confidently gay person he'd met. He had become more than a lover. He was Damian's guru, on gay issues at least. If Matt said he wanted to cool their relationship he would be devastated and he would demand to know why. Matt couldn't tell him the real reason nor could he let Damian think that he wasn't still in love with him.

They might have struggled along were it not for Matt's uncle Ned. His father's younger brother had emigrated to East Africa about the same time as they had arrived in Northern Ireland, a slightly more extreme move but the motives were the same. On Ned's last visit a plot was hatched between the brothers; they would swap sons for a year and Mark had arrived at Strathbeg in November. Mark was about Matt's age but he was a bit too yacht club, sports car, dolly bird on the arm for Matt. Whilst Mark was having a whale of a time in Northern Ireland, his brother, Roger was miserably homesick. He was on the phone for well over half an hour at Christmas, by the end of which time Matt had been convinced that he should go out to Kenya for the summer. It wouldn't have taken much to persuade him, but money was a major problem and this was where Rodge came up trumps. He rang Matt in May to tell him that he would pay the air fare. He came off the phone stunned by his sib's generosity. "He can afford it!" he explained to a coldly silent Damian.

Matt winced as he saw Damian purse his lips to psych himself up for a tirade: "You British colonialists make me sick!" he exploded. "You're still doing it. Going out there to exploit the natives. And you! You're.... You're collaborating with them!"

Matt thought he was probably jealous but his jibe irked him: "Don't be so bloody silly. They're farming out there, not fucking slave traders. If they weren't there, their workers wouldn't HAVE a job. It's people like Uncle Ned who make Kenya prosperous!"

Damian vigorously shook his head. The swirling of his dense black locks temporarily obscured his angry face. "Typical Prod!" he spat. "Do you really think that the Kenyans couldn't do just as well if they were given the chance? If people like your uncle weren't hogging all the best land for themselves!"

"Come off it Damian," he snapped. "It's a nice idea, but you know damn well it doesn't work like that. Ned told me that the only businesses that are surviving are those run by whites. No harm to them but the blacks don't have the background."

"Just listen to yourself! He would say that, wouldn't he! The British Imperialist system made sure of that! It's the same old story. Keep the natives ignorant, then you can always use that argument, can't you?" he sneered. "They haven't the know-how."

"Jesus Christ, Damian!" he said exasperatedly. "You should hear yourself! You sound like a fucking Marxist manifesto. You're talking in clichés. Don't you have *any* thoughts of your own? Think for yourself, for Christ's sake!"

His eyes blazed, "*ME*?" he yelled. "It's you that's coming out with all the conditioned crap from that reactionary school you went to!"

Another niggling swipe at his Protestant background: "Just fuck off, will you? I don't have to stand here and listen to this crap from you."

"O.K.," he shouted. "I will fuck off." and he stomped down the stairs, slamming the front door behind him.

"Stupid fuckin' idiot!" Matt spat, to no one in particular as the house reverberated to Damian's departure.

Lying in bed, Matt mulled the whole stupid affair over. He couldn't quite work out why they had argued. Why had Damian been so snotty about his going to Kenya? Would he come back to see him? What if he didn't? Well, he thought miserably, at least I won't have to worry any more about people finding out about us. Rationalisation didn't help. He found himself longing for the warmth of Damian's body curled up within his arms. He was so gentle in bed. Damian needed somewhere to hide from the brutal world outside but, in doing so, he'd brought those realities into Matt's haven and now, he'd rejected him.

Damian held no grudge. He was back the next day with some flowers Matt had seen growing in a garden down the road. "Sorry," he squeaked.

Matt couldn't resist the look in those beautiful, big, brown eyes. "So am I," he confessed, "but we have to talk."

Damian nodded.

"What was it all about, then?" Matt asked gently.

He pursed his lips and shook his head slowly.

"We're no good for each other are we?" Matt ventured.

"No," he mumbled.

"I think you need to meet gay people nearer your own age."

"Some chance here," he bemoaned.

"How about Derry?"

His eyes lit up and his frown transformed into a smile. He really was very beautiful and Matt was thinking how mad he was to be pushing him away like this.

At first he stuck to Matt like glue. Then he spread his wings and began to hitch up and down if Matt wasn't going. By July, when Matt headed off to Africa, Damian was well integrated onto the Derry gay scene. He found friends who would accommodate him overnight, as he went through the promiscuous phase that many gay men go through when they first find the scene. Strangely, Damian's freedom brought Matt and him closer than ever. He spent more time than ever at Matt's and treated him to a blow by blow account of all his adventures. Thanks to Matt, he was very conscious of safer sex and was appalled by the number of gays in Derry who conducted their sex lives oblivious of the need to be careful. Damian vowed that he never let anyone screw him without a condom, and Matt hoped it was true. When the whirlwind had left Matt felt empty, but he told himself this was best for both of them.

East Africa was fantastic. Matt drank in the sights and sounds but remained celibate for the whole trip. Rodge had implied that sexual adventures might unfold, with his warning as he arrived. "Don't you go, you know.... abusing the houseboys, you could get yourself in serious trouble!"

Matt was indignant. He had no intention of using his position in the house to entice local employees into sex. If he met someone who *was* gay, that would be different!

However, Rodge had no need to worry. In the whole time Matt was there he never once met anyone he even suspected of being gay. Matt had one significant adventure that summer. Vijay, a Ugandan Asian he knew at school, had convinced him that he had to visit the Queen Elizabeth National Park in Western Uganda and his uncle Ned encouraged him to go. Also, Matt had an overriding ambition to ride the entire length of the old Uganda railway from Mombassa to Kasese. He was badly advised. His Uncle Ned had lived through the Mau Mau and the coup in Kenya a couple of years previously. To him, Uganda was

O.K. and Matt set off with the naive preconception that, if he could live in Ulster, crossing Uganda would be child's play. In fact he had no problems; he sailed through roadblocks in blissful ignorance of the fates of others in similar circumstances. Road blocks on the train journey were, in retrospect, terrifying. Everyone was turned out of the carriage by ragged soldiers, some looking as young as his first formers. Their guns were tied together with string. After seeing these tiny soldiers, never again would the Brits frighten him with their cavalier hefting and pointing of rifles. After the nerve-racking journey the park was a tragic disappointment. Nearly all the animals had been eaten!

A small headline bearing the word A.I.D.S. caught his eye in a newspaper he picked up in Kampala. What, he wondered, could they know about this new disease here? The paper explained to the people of Kampala how this dreadful disease was being brought into Uganda by perverts (by that they meant homosexuals) who had been corrupted by working on ships out of Mombassa. It described how they were being deported back to Kenya, but how they kept sneaking back to Uganda. It wasn't long after he got back to Ireland that the extent of A.I.D.S. in East Africa emerged. To Matt's surprise he discovered that the spread amongst heterosexuals was catastrophic and gay people were hardly mentioned! The media had scapegoated gays but, Matt thought, that couldn't happen here!

Back in Ballycol, Matt bored his friends with endless African tales and tried to impress them with exotic gifts. He had colourful Kangas for Mary and the most beautiful soapstone warrior for Damian. Danny had been lucky to get a postcard; he still hadn't broken his silence. The first surprise of the new academic year came with a visit from Alex and David. Fortunately, he had presents for both of them.

"How did you know I was home?" Matt asked.

"Rang your Mam."

"You needn't have bothered. I'm heading up to Derry on Thursday, but," he smiled, "it's nice to see you anyway. What sort of summer did you two have?"

"Good," Alex said seriously. "Got a lot of things that needed sorting, sorted."

"Sounds fascinating!"

"Later, we want to hear about Africa. David's got to go soon."

They adjourned to the dining room where the first of his holiday snaps were spread over the dining table. David was green with envy at his descriptions of bird watching around Naivasha. He didn't have any photos of the birds yet, so they pored over his Collins guide. He had made notes on everything he'd seen and David was duly impressed.

"The illustrations aren't very good, though. You'll have to come back in a fortnight. I'll have my photographs of the birds I saw by then and I can bore you to death."

"Make sure I'm not here, then," laughed Alex. "I want to hear about the craic not bloody birds!"

Matt winked at David, "Just the two of us, then?"

He saw David to the door.

"What sort of summer *did* you have?" he asked when they were out of earshot.

He looked depressed, "O.K. I suppose."

Matt patted him affectionately on his hard jaw-line; the stubble sent a twinge of lust down his spine.

A familiar voice cut through the little scenario: "Hello!"

Damian was flouncing up to the door with Stevie: "What's all this?" he asked.

Matt was flustered: "This is David, he's just leaving." he turned back to him, "A couple of weeks, then? I'll give you a bell."

The two youngsters followed Matt up the stairs.

"And *who* was *that* hunk of beefcake?" Damian demanded.

"God!" Stevie complained. "What have you *done* to him, Matt? He's man mad these days!"

"Don't blame me. He was a raving queen before ever I met him."

"Aye, but at least he hid it!" Stevie rejoined.

"Fuck off, you two." Damian objected, "Who *was he*? I demand to know!"

"He's a friend of Alex's; he was just dropping him off."

"You two seem very friendly," Damian smirked.

"He's right, you are worse!" Matt commented. "What have you been up to this summer?"

"I'll tell you, when I've an hour or seven to spare!"

Damian bowled into the living room, "Watch it! Matt's getting fresh with your friend," he announced.

"It wouldn't surprise me a bit," Alex smiled.

More coffee and tales ensued until Damian and Stevie declared that they had to go.

As soon as Stevie was out of the door, Alex quizzed Matt: "What happened to Stevie's face?"

Matt lifted his eyebrows and bit his lip.

"What are you making a face like that for?"

"He was beaten up."

"Queer bashed?"

"*He's* not gay; Damian is. No, he got into a scrap with some soldiers and they knocked him about pretty badly."

"Probably deserved it."

"I don't know about that, Alex. I thought that at the time but now I've got to know him better. Well..., I don't think he's like that, I don't really know, so I can't say for sure."

"Nah boy. I know. If he'd been civil he wouldn't have got that!"

"Well. We'll reserve judgement on that, shall we?" Matt changed the subject. "Hey look, I'd better go and get something in for tea. Any preferences?

Matt had never seen Alex trying to help in the kitchen. He didn't know one end of a tin opener from the other, but he did the best he could.

"You said you had got some things sorted out over summer," Matt queried.

He stopped shredding a lettuce, "Aye," he nodded.

Matt sat next to him: "Going to tell me?"

He fiddled with a rapidly deteriorating leaf. "I'm getting a car."

"Great, who'll drive it?"

"I will," he said indignantly.

"Can you? With your leg an' all."

"I've got enough flexibility in this one," he said slapping his left thigh. "I could manage the brake and accelerator with it."

"What about the clutch?"

"It'll have to be an automatic."

"What about the other leg? Can you move it at all yet?"

He shook his head, pummelling the hated limb as if by doing so he could intimidate it back to life: "It will have to sit there and mind its own business. There's a place in England where they adapt cars for you."

"Is it expensive?"

"Aye. I've got it, though."

Much against Matt's nature, they discussed the merits and demerits of numerous makes of car as they prepared the meal.

They were eating in the dining room. Alex sighed, looking across the placid lake: "There can't be many people with a view like that from their dinner table."

"I know. That's what sold this place to me."

They ate in silence for a while.

"There's something else," Alex said.

Matt was trying to dislodge a strand of celery fibre from between his teeth: "Sorry, I didn't catch what you said."

"This view's something else," he said.

"Aye. I'll get the telescope set up after, see what we can see. Might see red throated divers. There was a pair nesting on the lough last year."

"Wow!" he said, sarcastically.

"Sorry. I keep forgetting it's David's into birds."

"Only the feathered variety."

Matt stopped eating and shot him a glance; he knew. "Aye," he said slowly.

"Are you and he...?"

He shook his head: "No, I do fancy him. But I'm just not his type."

"Does that matter?"

"*YES IT DOES*!"

"What about Damian, then?"

"I adore him but he's too young; he's only just twenty."

"You're getting picky in your old age, aren't you?"

"Not really, I slept with you!"

"See what I mean," he smirked, "only the best for you!"

Matt made a jokey sneer at him.

"Anyone at the moment, then?" Alex asked.

"Nope, what about you? How's things with Sandra? You haven't even mentioned her, yet."

Alex inspected his plate for a moment, then resolved to speak: "Gone off with Danny."

Matt looked intently at Alex: "Ah."

"You knew, didn't you?

"She told Mary that night."

Neither of them said anything for a good minute, then Matt broke the silence: "How do you feel about it?"

"I'm not over the moon," he brooded. "I'm not sick as a parrot, either! I sort of knew, you know. I said to you didn't I? I've been watching how Danny was reacting to me. I expected it, really."

"Do you still see Danny, then?"

"Aye. That's the funny thing," he laughed. "They both come round and we all pretend nothing's happened. Danny and I go to the rugby club every Monday night for a game of pool. He's good, you know. The car was his idea."

"You're lucky. At least he wants to see you. I don't know what's got into him. I haven't seen him since spring. What's wrong with me, Alex?"

"Nothing. He's busy, that's all."

"Too busy for his oldest friend."

"To hear you talking, you'd think you didn't have any friends."

"Danny was special."

"Wasn't I?"

"Aye, you still are, but it was different with him. I grew up with Danny and I can't understand why he seems to have shunned me."

Media prurience reached new lows in the summer of eighty-five. Rock Hudson was dying. It became evident that he had A.I.D.S. and the scandal rags let everyone know! "ROCK; THE TRUTH AT LAST," screamed the Star. "I SAW ROCK WED MAN!" proclaimed the News of the World. The Sunday Mirror contributed with "SECRET TORMENT OF THE BARON OF BEEFCAKE. The Sunday Express informed the great British public that Rock hadn't gone out of his way not to place 'innocent' people in danger. What was meant by innocent, Matt was never sure. Presumably homosexuals were guilty and deserved all they got. Not only was Rock Hudson's demise a God-sent chance to gloat over gay people's misfortune but it opened up endless avenues for speculating about other stars' sexuality. Every week seemed to bring another famous name into question. The papers were almost willing them to die horribly; it made such good copy! The level of anti-gay hysteria was being turned up by the media notch by notch and the consequences for the gay denizens of Ballycol soon came.

There was nothing Matt hated more than being dragged out of bed in the middle of the night by the telephone's ring, unless it was being dragged out of bed in the middle of the night by the ringing of the doorbell. The bloody thing wouldn't stop and it was half past one on a Wednesday morning. He dragged himself out of bed and grabbed his dressing gown, the bell was still ringing. He threw the window up, expecting to see one or other of his drunken friends but it was Damian.

He bawled down to him in an irritated tone, "What the hell do you want at this time of the morning?"

"Matt. Let me in," he cried. "Please," he added pathetically.

"Just a minute, then," Matt replied tersely.

Grumpily, he tugged the door open. "This is bloody ridicul....," he tailed off as he saw Damian's blood streaked face.

As he staggered in, he stated the obvious, "I've been beaten up."

Matt led him to the kitchen: "Sit down, let me clean you up."

He looked worse than he was. There were no deep cuts; most of the blood came from a graze on left of his forehead. He was going to have quite a shiner in that eye. His jeans were badly torn and bloody too. "Don't get excited," he quipped, sorely as Matt removed his pants. He had a ragged gash in his leg.

Matt did an inward whistle: "What did that?"

"A boot," he replied sullenly.

Cleaned and patched up, Matt gave him a mug of sweet, steaming tea. "Who did it?" he asked. "And why?"

"Frankie McSorley and his mates, why do you think?"

"I don't know. Why?"

"Because he's a fucking, ignorant, fascist, anti-gay, insecure, fucking, fucking bastard, that's why."

"We already know that, but what gave him the excuse tonight?"

"Was in Micky's with Elis and Stevie and Catherine. The stupid old cunt tried to tackle Trish McHugh at the Manor House disco last week. Elis was telling us about it, he was really shown up! The fucker must have seen us looking at him and laughing."

"What did he do?"

"Nothing there and then." Damian bobbed his head left to right in embarrassment. "I went to cruise the park later. He was there."

"Cruising?!"

"I thought so, aye. He came over to me, I thought he was trying to cruise me."

"He wasn't?"

"His fuckin' mates were behind some bushes. This'll teach you to talk about me, he shouted and they all started kicking the fuck out of me."

"Was it planned, do you think?"

"Nah, I've seen them there before. They take a rake of carry-outs when the pubs shut."

"You were lucky they stopped, you could have been badly hurt."

"Someone came and they ran off."

"You've a witness, then. Did he know who they were?"

"Oh aye."

"You haven't been to the barracks yet?"

"Fuck off!"

"Aren't you going to report it?"

"Am I fuck?"

"You should do, you know."

"I'm not going to the pigs. They'd be bloody delighted, they would. Get three nationalist youths for assault and then do me for cruising."

"You don't need to tell them you were. You could have been out for a stroll!"

He looked at Matt as if he were a half-wit.

Matt was torn between his need to sleep and Damian's need to talk. He was slightly pissed and a bit stoned too; they'd been smoking at Stevie's house after the pub. It was a rambling, repetitive monologue. He wasn't seriously hurt. He would be a bit sore for a few days but Damian felt he had been violated; almost as if he'd been raped. The thugs had assaulted his sexuality and his self esteem hurt more than his wounded body.

At three in the morning Matt decided to ease Damian out. He hugged him. "It's time I was asleep," he whispered.

He looked lost and lonely. "I'd better go, then."

"Aye," Matt nodded. "Come round tomorrow."

"I'd better go, then," he said wistfully.

Matt considered the frightened child before him. He was so in love with that dangerous boy. He wanted to envelope him, shield him, and protect him from that horrible homophobic world out there. It would be so easy to let his resolve crumple and take him to his bed.

He couldn't look him in the eyes as he mumbled, "Yes, you'd better."

At the front door he held Damian to him. Clutching him, he fought with his emotions. Logic won. He kissed him gently on the forehead and pushed him off on his way home.

Damian had the last laugh on Frankie and his friends. One by one they were pulled out of discos or pubs by masked men and threatened for their antisocial behaviour.

"You went to the IRA, didn't you?" Matt said, one evening.

Damian put on his inscrutable look.

"I thought so!"

CHAPTER 17

WINTER 1985, OIL AND WATER

The photos arrived on the Monday, so Matt rang David and arranged a night for him to come over. This was the first time David had agreed to stay overnight. Matt had a vague notion that something might develop between them. David was definitely mellowing but having an affair with a policeman would be as risky as the one with Damian, albeit in a different way.

David was looking well. Crisply pressed, light Chinos complemented a white Lacost polo shirt. His short, spiky hair was razor neat. As he strode in a waft of musty, sweet aftershave excited Matt's nostrils.

They spent a pleasant evening reliving Matt's safari. David was attentive but unresponsive. Matt realised that they weren't clicking.

Fin had declared Matt's fund of Africa stories inexhaustible. He didn't actually say boring but that's what he meant; David seemed about to prove him wrong. He listened in silent appreciation as Matt's monologue meandered across the Serengeti, up Mount Kenya, along the sun-drenched coast and through the swamps of Naivasha. On the rim of Longonot the end of his rambling narrative loomed. An unreasonable sense of panic began to well up within Matt, as he realised he couldn't keep up a monologue all evening. It was time to find out why David's summer had been so bad. Matt fervently hoped it wasn't going to be anything to do with Mary; he didn't fancy bearing the brunt of an anguished and deprived father's anger. The official story was that Bryony was two months premature. They hoped that Alex would fall for the story but when they told him, he didn't seem too convinced. Mary wouldn't consider taking him into her confidence so they had to hope that Alex had swallowed it and would pass on the deception to David. David's lack of communication was unnerving Matt: "What's wrong?" he asked, in desperation.

David's eyes showed his surprise, "Nothing."

"You're not saying much."

"I'm listening," he protested.

"I've not a lot more to say."

David smirked, Matt'd never seen him actually smile, but this was a definite start. He grinned back, "Not on Africa, anyway." Matt finished his story. Just before he left Africa, he had spent a day climbing the barren, ashy cone of Longonot. Technically, it was a caldera; an ancient volcano that's centre had collapsed into itself millions of years ago. Matt had expected to find the same ashen environment in the crater but, no. Below him was a mini Eden, an isolated montane rain forest complete with wildlife. The highlight of the story was that he was sitting on the rim surveying this wonderland when an Egyptian vulture, riding on a thermal, hovered only yards in front of him. With a flourish he showed David the photograph of the bird; he was green with envy.

"What about you then?" Matt ventured, "You said you hadn't a great summer."

David looked at Matt; eyes glistening: "You were away. I suppose you didn't hear?"

"What?" he asked.

"One of the men was murdered."

After a decent silent pause Matt asked, "Was he a friend?"

He nodded, ruefully.

Matt put his arm round the sad man: "I'm sorry David. It must have been terrible..... What happened? Do you mind talking about it?"

He slowly shook his head. "He was out on patrol. They came under fire." He put two fingers to the bridge of his nose, "Took it here. Messy, very messy," he nodded slowly.

"Was he a... close friend?"

"Not really. A colleague, I suppose."

"What effect does that sort of thing have on the station?"

He thought for a minute. "Everybody's mad."

"I can imagine," Matt said. "Frightened, too, I should think."

"Not really. More determined to fight the bastards, you know?"

"You must be really scared, though. I would be terrified if it was me"

He smiled sadly, "I am a bit, sometimes. You get used to it."

"Was there much graffiti?"

He nodded with pent up anger.

"That must be more hurtful than the bullets," Matt commented. "Something like that happens and you see vicious gloating on the walls. Remember the Drop In Well?"

He nodded.

"Alex and I used to go there, you know? I remember that morning, after it happened. I was in the kitchen, making breakfast. I had radio four on and I wept. I could imagine it. The packed disco, then mayhem. Bodies, dust, screaming. And then, two days later, someone had painted, PROVOS 7, BRITS 0, HA, HA, HA in huge red letters across the roofs at the end of the shore road."

David nodded wryly. "They send us to clean that sort of filth up," he complained.

"Do they?" Matt asked. "Soldiers cleaned the roofs on the shore road. Big commando raid with buckets of pitch; the residents went mad. They were woken up in the middle of the night by hoards of soldiers swarming over their roofs."

"They didn't object when it was painted!"

"Would you?"

He shook his head, "Probably not."

"Do your lot ever do it?" Matt asked.

"Commando paint-outs?"

"No. Graffiti. Someone does here. It's the soldiers I think, though."

"More than likely. Although some of our boys wouldn't be above suggesting a few choice phrases and some sensitive spots to put them!"

"They had a real splurge here, last winter. They seemed to know exactly who they were going for. Nearly every gable end in the Apostles was done. Have you ever been there?"

David shook his head, looking at Matt as if he'd asked him if he screwed his sister.

Matt explained: "As you go along the Pettigo road there's loads of terraces going off at right angles. They were built for the tannery workers; Matt Street, Mark Street, Luke Street, John Street. The Apostles, you see?"

"Very devout!" he sneered.

Matt smiled. "Every row has a wall painting on its gable end. If you can get over their political content they're quite artistic, really. Folk culture."

"I've seen the sort of thing." He was evidently not as enthusiastic about their artistic merit.

"There was one I loved," Matt smirked. "I wish I'd got a shot of it. A Provo standing against this beautifully painted Irish landscape. All around was an intricate Celtic design border. Adoring little children gazed lovingly at their liberator. It was brilliantly done, almost Jim Fitzpatrick's standard. The Provo's hand was held aloft and from it, dangling by barbed wire locks, was Margaret Thatcher's severed head, dripping with blood. She had this really pissed off look on her face. It says toy ich feller arlach."

"What?"

"T..O..I..C..F..A..I..D..H A..R..L..A," Matt spelt.

"That's chucky our lar," David explained. "Irish for our day will come."

"Oh. Right," Matt said in surprise. "Quite an Irish expert, aren't you?"

David laughed: "No. The corner boys yell it at us all the time. You get to know."

"Anyway" Matt continued. "The soldiers went out one night and defaced every single one of them. Pots of paint everywhere. Quite an operation, really. Then they started painting their own graffiti too. Slanders all over the town." Matt grinned broadly. "The one I remember most was Paddy Rock loves being fucked."

"I see why you remembered that, who is he, anyway?"

"Dunno. Some local hard. Soldiers must think he's a Provo. Maybe he is gay. I doubt it, though. The Brits know how macho the men are round here. They can't stand being called queer, so the Brits try to provoke them. There was an awful bust up the other day. They stopped two boys in a car. Sean and Jimmy; I used to teach them. It was the early hours of the morning and they asked them where they were going. Sean said, his house. The soldier said, you lovers then? 'e your boyfriend? Sean lost the head. He reached for the soldier and got the worst of it."

"If the nationalists would just come to us in situations like that...," David started.

"That was the laugh, wasn't it? Sean's a prod. His dad's in the police! The squaddie went to report he'd been attacked and had defended himself and the officer on duty said, are you calling my son a liar?"

David actually smiled. It wasn't a very pretty smile. He pulled his lips tight against his teeth.

"The soldier was up in court. He got two months for assault."

David wasn't going to admit that the police would commit an unprovoked assault. They weren't angels, but Matt wasn't about to annoy him by suggesting anything. David's ice shell was melting, Matt wondered if it was worth asking him about his love life but he decide to leave it and opened another bottle of Bull's Blood.

"How's Mary?" David asked suddenly.

His heart sank: "Fine, fine."

"She must have had her baby by now."

"Didn't Alex tell you?"

"Why should he?"

"No reason. Except he was here when she had it. It was quite a panic, actually. She went into labour, in the middle of the night. I had to rush her to hospital."

"What did she have?"

"A girl, she's called her Bryony. She a gorgeous little thing, you never hear a peep from her."

"What about the father?"

"Oh!" The pause seemed obvious but he didn't seem to notice, "He's away at the moment."

"He'll be back, then?"

"That's between him and Mary."

"What's......." He was cut off by the doorbell. Saved! thought Matt.

His relief turned sour as he opened the door to Damian's smiling face.

"Hi Matt," he chanted, slapping the palm of his hand in a high five. Before Matt could stop him, he was in the living room leering at David.

Matt drew Damian to him and, under the cover of a fraternal kiss, Matt whispered, "You keep your eyes off him."

That Northern Irish instinct instantly told him that David was a Protestant and, doubtless, David's internal warning lights had activated on seeing the wild young man. Damian was hyper. Matt had never seen him so on edge. Disaster was looming; it was only a matter of who offended whom first. Just my luck! Matt thought. I go to all the trouble of organising a cosy little night together and Damian goes and blows it. Matt had good reason to worry. Robin, a P.E. teacher at Matt's school, who could never be described as a bigot, had stomped out of one of his parties after half an hour of Damian's telling him how he was an oppressor.

Matt tried to deflect Damian, but he couldn't. He was in full flow and within ten minutes he was expounding his own brand of nationalist socialism to the archest conservative Matt knew.

Then Damian had discovered that David was Presbyterian.

"We're on the same side, really, you know," he claimed.

"How do you work that one out?" David replied, with remarkable composure.

He obviously wasn't going to let this uppity little Taig rattle him.

Damian moved closer to explain. "You Presbyterians were just as oppressed by the English ascendancy as we were. They made laws which penalised you lot, too. Derry Presbyterians weren't allowed land to build churches in the city. They had to reclaim it from the sea! Take a look at all the old Presbyterian churches in Derry. They're all down by the sea! If it had been left to the English, Derry would have been surrendered to James; the siege was almost as much in defiance of the English as the French! It was the Presbyterians who kept Irish going, you know. Some of the earliest Home Rulers were Presbyterians too. They were so pissed off by English trade laws. It's only recently that you've been conned into thinking you're better off siding with the Unionists!"

To Matt's amazement, David didn't explode with indignation at these heresies. Instead, a big grin split his hard face. Damian offered his hand. David went to shake it, only to be surprised by Damian's new hand slapping ritual.

Damian was in the middle of a lecture on how the ruling classes had successfully divided the Irish working class by encouraging sectarianism. The true struggle was to free the workers of Ireland from the yoke of capitalist oppression. David had a glazed expression. Damian stopped and sniffed.

"What's that smell?" he demanded.

"What smell?" Matt asked.

"It's him," he squealed, pointing at David.

Matt's eyebrows shot up.

"No, no," Damian giggled. "A nice smell." he turned to David: "Is that your aftershave?"

He darted for David. Matt thought, for a horrible moment, he was going to head-butt him. Instead, he stuck his nose under David's chiselled chin sniffing, like a big, black spaniel.

The look of shock in David's eyes was unpleasantly satisfying; Matt waited for the explosion but it never came. David was as abashed as a teased spinster. Half-heartedly, he tried to push the silky locks away from his throat, "Stop it," he chuckled, "you're tickling!"

Damian withdrew but the room had repolarised. Matt was the outsider and he capitulated to the inevitable, "Look, you two. I've got to get up tomorrow, even if you haven't. I'm going to bed. Make sure everything's locked up, won't you?"

David was up before Matt, the next day.

"Where's Damian?" Matt asked.

David looked surprised: "Went home."

Matt cocked his head, quizzically.

"What?" David demanded sharply.

"A bit slow, weren't you?"

He was embarrassed: "Don't be ridiculous!"

"Don't be so prim! You were in there. Come on, you're not going to tell me you don't fancy him?"

"I thought you and he... "

Matt shook his head slowly; pityingly.

"He wanted to but I said you wouldn't like it."

Matt tried to laugh dismissively. "You twit bonce! Did you tell him that?"

He pursed his lips and shrugged.

Matt rescued the carbonising toast from the grill and David scraped it over the sink. "Don't *you* fancy him?" he asked slowly.

Matt bit his lip, " I do. We did have a thing, a year ago, but it couldn't last."

"I didn't think you worried about that sort of thing."

"Nah, nah. His politics don't worry me. No, look at him. He is too young and beautiful for me. They say that people find lovers who are equally attractive." Matt would have loved to have added, that's why *you* don't fancy *me*! "The only reason he ever went with me was that I was the only gay he knew. I knew I'd lose him as soon as I took him to Derry."

"He *is very* sexy, isn't he," David sighed. "He oozes it. Had I realised..!"

"Look," Matt advised. "I'm not trying to put barriers up, or anything. But you ought to watch out if you do start seeing him." Matt felt an idiot as soon as he said that. Of course David would guess Damian's background. He couldn't be so stupid as to get involved.

"Why?" David demanded.

Matt backtracked, "Well. He's only just twenty, you know. There's the legal thing."

David blushed: "I didn't know he was *that* young."

Matt nodded. "That's why I wasn't too upset when we didn't last."

"He'll be twenty-one soon," the young policeman said seriously. "I've waited this long, I can hang on."

Matt was astounded: "You're talking serious relationships here! I would say Damian's only into a bit of casual sex."

David flushed: "If that's all he wants, I'll soon find out, won't I?"

"You're not into that, then?" Matt said, with evident disappointment.

He shook his head.

David left before Matt went out to work. Almost as soon as he had closed the door behind David the phone rang. It was Damian, and he wanted to know more about David. Matt pondered on the situation. Glad as he was that David and Damian liked each other, he was pessimistic about their future. Even discounting the impossible political and security situation, it was obvious that their expectations of a relationship were at odds. It couldn't possibly work, but they wanted to try, and it looked like Matt was to be their go-between.

CHAPTER 18

AUTUMN 1986, STORM CLOUDS

Robin had been trying to persuade Matt to get involved with the school's outdoor pursuits programme for ages. He had enticed him onto day hikes and Matt had enjoyed the way the kids reacted to him in the more informal environment. Matt didn't feel he was capable of being a group leader, but Robin convinced him that he needed to take more responsibility in the school and prevailed upon him to go on a stage one mountain leadership course.

So, one Friday in September eighty-five, Matt headed for the outdoor education centre at Gortatole. The old Beetle battled against the swell of the long, straight road which dipped and rose over the drumlin country, south of Enniskillen. On the County Cavan border the great bulk of Cuilcagh loomed, ominously, out of a low, grey autumn sky. Gortatole was based in an old Victorian farmhouse which squatted in bleak, marshy grounds between Lough Macnean and the forested, craggy, limestone hem of Cuilcagh. As Matt got out of his little car, a chill wind squirmed up from the grey, reed fringed lake.

The hallway was warm and welcoming and the warden was efficient and friendly. Matt expected the other trainees to be keen, proficient teachers but he was the only teacher there. The rest were youngsters involved in youth clubs and the like; mostly from Derry. They had lots of enthusiasm, but no experience. Suddenly, all his old paranoias welled up. What if they found out? Would they trust him? Would they mind camping with him? But he needn't have worried. The youngsters on the course had all sorts of hang-ups about teachers, but, after a couple of weekends of fairly arduous mountaineering, they began to accept him as a human being. To accept Matt's homosexuality was easy after that. The course did wonders for his self-confidence. The youths were all fitter than Matt but he had an instinct, borne out of years of wandering over the Cumbrian fells and Donegal hills. He was very at home on the hills and the youngsters sensed it.

Bryony didn't drain all Mary's energy. Not only did the Sunflower go from strength to strength but her dream of a women's centre moved one step nearer with her hosting a women's collective in her flat. The close of the year was marked by a series of hopes of finding premises, which were invariably dashed. Years of bombs had put flat and office space in the town at a premium. To Matt, the answer was obvious. "Move in here," he insisted. "Then you could use above the Sunflower as a women's centre!"

"I wouldn't inflict Bryony on you."

"She's as good as gold. I would hardly notice her and I would welcome the company... And the money!" Matt grinned.

"You're very kind, Matt, but I don't think it would be right for me."

Matt loved Donegal. The windswept hills put the problems of urban living into wonderful perspective. Finbar McBarron had been an early convert to hiking. Matt had met him through Elis. If someone had shown Matt a photo of the twenty-two year old before he had met him, he wouldn't have given him a second glance but, in the flesh, he had an extraordinary presence. A keen sportsman with a physique to match, he oozed health and vitality. He was so thoroughly wholesome that Matt was almost afraid of him at first. He couldn't imagine that anyone so 'normal' could accept him. In the back of Matt's mind was an unspoken fear that he could somehow corrupt this 'Boy's Own'-story hero by falling for him. Despite Matt's reticence they soon became firm friends. Striding over Slieve Snaght or Muccish, Matt could chuckle to himself about those early fears. Fin was no schoolboy comic character. His expectations were simple and straightforward; good job, good wife, home and kids. Pedestrian aims compared to Feargal's or Mary's high hopes, but Fin didn't give a hoot. Like his mountain walking, he strode towards them in resolute certainty. He had never had the opportunity to go hiking before he met Matt, they didn't go in for that sort of thing at the Christian Brothers. Now he saw the pastime as a perfect accompaniment to his athletics. With all his training he should have been able to walk Matt off his feet, but that wasn't so. To Matt's delight, Fin seemed genuinely more whacked than Matt at the end of a good day's walk.

It wasn't just the walking that Fin liked. Once into their stride, the two friends would talk for uninterrupted hours on any topic under the sun. Fin's boss took the Irish Times which Fin read avidly when the shop was quiet. Matt kept up with him by listening to Radio Four. Fin's depth of understanding always exceeded Matt's. Fin also helped Matt take the pupils out and Robin was happy to take a back seat, now.

Lough Belshade is a pretty little upland lake nestling between the glowering granite lumps of the Blue Stack Mountains. *Selaginella inundatum*, a rare clubmoss, grows by that lake and bladderworts can be found in the peaty pools which dot the bogs and there was a badger sett by a tiny sandy beach. Matt had only seen the occupant once; like an animated hearth-rug, it was ambling along a path unperturbed by the fact that Matt was following a few paces behind. The chances of seeing it again were remote but Matt always hyped the kids up to be quiet on the campsite, in the hope of having an exciting wild encounter in the gloaming. Nothing could compare with Donegal on a bright summer's day. Vast expanses of clean blue sky, swept with fluffy white clouds provided a backdrop for the patchwork. Vibrant green bog, dun grass and olive heather were punctuated with sheets of mottled grey rock, and dissected by peaty streams which gurgled over boulders. Ring ouzels darted and bobbed up the stream, and an occasional merlin would soar into the blue in search of a pipit or a lark. Matt thought it was perfection, but the kids never seemed to appreciate the beauty. They enjoyed the challenge of the hike and the craic of camping out overnight.

Of his other friends, only David appreciated his passion for Donegal but he wasn't allowed across the border. He shouldn't really be visiting Ballycol, but he risked it more than was wise to see Damian. They were the most unlikely couple but Damian never expressed his Republican ideas when he was with David and the truce was mutual.

"Aren't you afraid that they'll find out?" Matt asked Damian.
"How could they?"
"Don't be so naive! Someone's bound to suss that he's fuzz! Then you're putting both of you in danger. Me too, if it comes to it!"
"You don't want us to come here, then?"
"No... Yes.. I mean, it's not that I don't want you to meet, I'm worried about your safety, that's all."

He looked at Matt with wide eyes: "You're jealous," he chided.

"Don't be ridiculous!" Matt said, but he was right. Matt told them they could stay at number seven but David wasn't comfortable about it; he claimed it was too much like using Matt. Instead he would call for Damian and whisk him off to Portstewart or a hotel somewhere.

A newspaper flopped onto Matt's desk. Robin had dropped it there: "Have you seen this, Matt?"

"The Sunday World! I wouldn't touch that rag with a barge-pole!" he retorted.

Robin turned the lurid sheets until a stark headline leapt from the page; FOSTER'S SHOCK CURE FOR AIDS; DRIVE OUT GAYS!

"Shit!" Matt exclaimed as he read on. "The Bastard!"

The article ran; *Gays in Ulster are in the firing line for a terrifying new campaign of intimidation, a leading churchman warned last night. The Rev. Ivan Foster claimed that God-fearing people would take the law into their own hands to exercise the "ticking time-bomb" of AIDS. He declared: "You don't need an active mind to see what measures people will adopt to prevent the spread of this terrifying disease. If you know your neighbour is a sodomite I'm quite sure you would lift the phone and suggest they move house." And the Rev. Foster, a minister in the Rev. Ian Paisley's Free Presbyterian Church also insisted that homosexual carriers should not be allowed to remain anonymous and that all homosexuals should be isolated.* And it continued in a similar vein, liberally sprinkled with gratuitous insults and dire warnings of danger to children. Matt shook his head: "And that was a message from your friendly neighbourhood Christian. Fuck! I *hate* fuckin' Christians!"

"Listen to yourself! You're as bad as them!" Robin reprimanded.

"I know, I know," Matt said, shaking his head in despair. "It's just that I get so fed up of being constantly told that I'm an inferior being, that I'm evil and I deserve to be dying of a God sent, humiliating disease. You really have to wonder what Christianity is all about. The Moslems are worse. They're actually executing gays in Iran, you know."

"Be careful, Matt," Robin warned, in measured tones. "There are an awful lot of people round here who would agree with Ivan Foster."

"I've already discovered that. Remember the campaign the local yobbos had. Smashing my windows and all that hassle."

"That was amateur stuff compared to the Free Presbyterians. They wouldn't get into a situation where you could accuse them of breaking the law; they'd do it all quite legally. Once they get the bit between their teeth there's no stopping them. Be prepared, Matt, be prepared."

"Well, they can't get me on legal grounds, anyway. I haven't put a step wrong as a teacher."

"I hope you're right but I fear you're being very naïve. You know how easy it is for parents to destroy a teacher. All it needs is for some of them to start chiselling away at the community's confidence and, before you know it, trust is lost and teaching becomes impossible."

Matt couldn't believe that anyone would treat him like that. The parents must trust him. He was about to run his first camp since completing his stage one in mountain leadership. Nine fourth form boys were going to Donegal and Matt was in sole charge. They were to hike from Glencolumbkille to Maghera, camping overnight at Port. Fin drove Matt's car to Maghera then rode in the school minibus to Glencolumbkille. They walked together as far as the Martello tower, then Matt left them in Fin's capable hands and went back for the bus. The road to Port was pretty grim; it started as a pair of rutted tarmac ribbons and degenerated into a dusty, gravel track. He had forgotten how tortuous a road it was, he worried that he wasn't going to get the bus round a couple of hairpin bends where the road dropped into the glen.

Matt experienced a thrill of anticipation as he approached Port. Each bend, each rise in the road, revealed tantalising glimpses of the vista he knew was to come. The sheltered rocky cove was flanked by raw cliffs; art deco strata scoured by centuries of Atlantic storms. Jumbled stacks, chunks of detached cliff, staggered drunkenly away on either side of the bay. The mouth of the glen was littered with the bleached bones of a once thriving community; derelict houses and tumbled walls built from the beach shingle. On the hillside, sheep blared to unsteady lambs on the short turf and, overhead, untidy, argumentative mobs of chough called raucously. The high piping of the oystercatchers and the gentle peet, peeting of the little, grey rock pipits overlaid the soothing roar of the sea. Matt could never see why people flocked to sandy beaches. Rocky shores bustled with life and Port was a gem. Great banks of brown seaweeds, floating like mermaids' hair, fringed the rocky shore. The huge, uneven rocks were freckled with barnacles, peppered with periwinkles and dotted with rock pools of every size. As he approached, darting shapes told him the pool's life had been alerted to his presence. He selected a promising-looking pool and settled down to watch a multi-green-brown, miniature forest of seaweeds separated by pastures, encrusted in pink. Black periwinkles browsed the green fronds and glistening red anemones trailed their deadly tentacles. A movement. It was a transparent shrimp spidering its way across the rock and nervously shovelling invisible food into its invisible mouth. Just as Matt thought he'd seen everything, a blenny flicked out of a crevice, then a slow black shape nosed its way from under a rock. Then Matt watched as an eel, at least a foot in length nudged its way through the weed in the hope of disturbing a tasty tit-bit.

Before Matt knew it an hour was gone and ragged dots on the hillside told him that Fin had navigated them safely to Matt. Soon the tranquillity would be shattered.

"Had a good walk?" Matt smiled as they straggled into camp.

"I'm knackered, sir!"

"You can't be, that was just a wee dander compared with tomorrow!"

"Aw si...r," they chorused.

"You'll have to get a good night's kip tonight then, won't you? What's the matter with Paul?"

"He got a blister, sir."

"Let me have a look. You boys get the tents out of the bus and decide where you're going to camp but DON'T put them up until I've okayed the site, alright?"

"I'll put ours up Matt," Fin offered.

"Hold on. We don't want to be too near the kids. They'll carry on all night and we won't get a wink!"

Paul's blisters plastered, they got the camp set up. As Matt watched them struggling with their Trangias, he reassured himself. This was idyllic, the kids were happy, Robin had to be wrong. Why would anyone want to get rid of him?

CHAPTER 19

AUTUMN 1986, BRUTALITY

Tuesday evenings were reserved for catching up on marking, so Matt was unimpressed when Feargal arrived just after nine. Feargal ushered a young woman into his living room.

"This is Theresa," he explained.

Theresa was indistinguishable from the others in Feargal's endless procession of females. Scantily clad and over made up, she jangled with cheap jewellery. As she entered, a miasma of cheap perfume followed.

"Coffee," Matt asked, as they settled onto the couch, "or tea?"

"I thought you might want to come down to Micky's," Feargal said jovially.

"Can't. I've all this lot to get through," Matt explained, indicating the mass of papers strewn over the floor. "I'll join you later if I get it finished. Want a coffee?"

Feargal looked at his companion, "You want one?"

"Tea please," she smiled at Matt, "if you're making one."

"Feargal?"

"Same please," he replied.

Matt was waiting for the kettle to boil when Feargal sidled into the kitchen and sneaked a conspiratorial arm round Matt's shoulder.

"Matt, old friend," he wheedled.

"Of course you can," Matt grunted.

"You're a mate."

"I'm a soft touch!"

He could use the attic room, he usually did. Matt wondered how many fruitless baby-makings had gone on in that garret; Feargal had probably been responsible for half of them. Matt loved his uncomplicated approach to sex. Why could he not love 'em and leave 'em like Feargal did?

Matt never finished his marking but he did join them later. Everything was going smoothly for Feargal, by midnight he was ensconced with her on Matt's couch. Matt was taking his time over the coffee. I'll give him time to get to work, he thought.

When Matt toed the door open, Theresa was on her feet looking at one of his framed photos. Feargal was hovering behind her.

"Did you take these yourself?" she asked.

Matt nodded, putting the tray down.

"Where is it?"

Feargal leaped in, "Africa."

"I can see that," she said witheringly, "is it East Africa?"

"Yes," Matt confirmed, "Naivasha, Kenya."

"That's the rift valley," she muttered. "Is it one of the soda lakes?"

"No, Nakuru and Elemetitia, which are just to the north are, but Naivasha's sweet water.

"Did you use filters?"

"No. That's how it was. Actually flamingos are difficult to get because the pink usually comes out white. You have to take them at dawn or dusk when there is a cooler light."

She nodded knowledgeably and pointed to some little birds at the water's edge: "What are these?"

"That's a black-winged stilt. There's an avocet and I think that's a greenshank."

Poor Feargal. Theresa was far more interested in Matt and Kenya than in him. When Matt had seen her to the door he returned to his thwarted friend.

"Did I blow it for you?"

"Fuck no," he chuckled. "You win some, you lose some. Had thought I was in, there. Dunno what made her change her mind."

"She didn't know... About me being gay?"

"Nah. But it didn't seem to worry her, did it?"

"I didn't frighten her off, then?"

"Matt, Matt, Matt! You worry too much about what other people think. Most people in this town don't give a toss if you are or if you aren't."

"It doesn't seem like that sometimes. Did you see what the papers did to Michael Ryan?"

"Who?"

"Come on, where have you been? The Hungerford massacre!"

"The clamping down on gun ownership you mean?"

"No. There was a massive headline in the Express, RAMBO WAS GAY CLAIM"

"You read the Express?"

"Do I hell! Mum still gets it, though."

"Was he?"

"I haven't a notion but it's hardly relevant, is it? The bastards are trying to spread the idea that we are dangerous psychopaths now. We don't stand a chance!"

"Nobody believes that sort of crap. Don't get yourself worked up about it. Hey, did I tell you about my new job?"

"What job?"

"Teaching. A couple of days a week in Dublin College of Art."

"Brill! How will you manage? Travelling and that."

"I'll stay up. Get a flat. I start in October."

A hole opened up in Matt's heart: "I'll miss you."

"You'll hardly know I'm gone. I'll be home a lot and you can come down. I bet the Dublin gay scene's better than Ballycol's!"

"Aye. It's better than Belfast too. There's loads of gay pubs and a couple of good clubs too but if I was coming down it would be to see you, not to go whoring!"

He hugged Matt and ruffled his hair. "Come and whore all you like. You'll always be welcome. God, Matt! Might just join you for a night! Try something new!"

Matt knew Feargal was sincere but he had no delusions. Once he was in Dublin, Matt would lose contact with his extraordinary friend. Matt wondered how Feargal would manage on his own on his 'off periods'. Feargal was great fun to be with but he would disappear for weeks on end. If Matt went looking for him Mrs. Collins would say he had a cold or he was busy. Only once did Matt get past his guardian. It was when Matt was going through the break-up with Chris. Matt desperately needed to talk to Feargal and his mother relented and let him in. It was pointless; Feargal remained slumped in the chair, incapable of concentrating on Matt's monologue. Feargal's normally animated face was drawn and slack; his eyes, lacking their usual lustre, were distant. Matt soon realised that Feargal wasn't hearing a word he said and when Matt asked him why he was being so unresponsive he claimed that he was deep in thought about his art. Feargal didn't seem in the least bit interested in Matt, so he gave up and left him to his own devices, making him promise to come and see him when he got better.

Mrs. Collins told Matt not to worry and that Feargal would be perfectly alright in a few days. "He's in one of his funny moods," she said. "At least he got up today. Sometimes the lazy article won't get out of his bed!"

Matt imagined him languishing alone for days on end in a grubby little flat in Dublin. How would he manage? But it was no good worrying about Feargal. He was a big boy. He could look after himself.

The doorbell went when Matt was in that transitional state between dozing thought and slumber. As he stirred, he became aware of the angry throb of stationary Landrover outside. It must be Feargal back again, he thought, what the hell does he want now? Staggering to the window, the sight of an army Landrover parked at his door jolted him into action. Bomb scare, Matt thought, as he dragged his jeans and a tee-shirt on.

"Are you Matt?" the soldier demanded in a broad Manchester accent.

Taken aback, Matt admitted his name.

"We've this bloke in the mobile," he continued. "'e says you'll know what to do."

In his confusion Matt meekly followed the soldier to the waiting van. The heavy doors lay gin-trap wide. The Mancunian indicated the dark interior: "In there," he muttered, needlessly.

A cracked and frightened but familiar voice came from the depths: "Matt?"

"Damian! What's happened?"

"I got a hiding, Matt."

"Did they hurt you? Why did they bring you here?"

"Not them. I've been queer bashed, they found me."

The soldier interjected, "He wouldn't go to the barracks. Asked us to bring him here. I reckon he needs to see an M.O."

"How... I mean, where did you find him?"

"We were coming along Omagh Road. We thought he was pissed until we saw the blood. He told us he was queer-bashed and the cops wouldn't be sympathetic."

"I'm afraid he's probably right," Matt lied, helping Damian climb stiffly out of the Landrover.

"Thank you for looking after him, I'll see to him. He'll be alright now."

"So much for the vicious Brits," Matt chided as he helped him into the living room. Damian's face hardened.

"Sorry," Matt whispered, gently shaking his shoulder. "Are you sure you're O.K.?"

He sniffed and nodded, burying his face in Matt's shoulder. Matt stroked his hair as he sobbed quietly into his shoulder.

When he stopped crying, Matt asked, "Are you sure you're alright? Let me have a look at you."

Matt held him at arms length to examine his face. Other than a bloody nose and a graze on his chin, he didn't look too bad, Matt said so.

"They knew how to hurt without marking," he commented bitterly.

"You'll feel better tomorrow," Matt said softly. "Do you want to stay here?"

He hugged Matt possessively in reply.

Damian slipped under Matt's duvet and winced as Matt drew him to him. Matt was surprised at how much beef he'd put on since he'd last cuddled him. The subtle change from youth to man had wrought pleasing changes on his physique. A hardening of the jaw-line and a stubborn black stubble conspired to angularise his face. No longer could he be described as pretty; strikingly handsome was more apt.

"How did it happen?" Matt whispered.

"I was ambushed, they caught me unawares. I'll be O.K."

"I suppose you'll go to the Provos," Matt paused, "David won't be over-impressed."

"I'm not going to them."

"Police?"

"Just forget it. I don't want to talk about it."

"You can't let the bastards think they can get away with it. You've a duty to the gay community."

"Forget it," he snapped and snuggled up to Matt. "Hold me, Matt," he pleaded. "It's hugs I need, not hassles."

Matt's alarm woke him at seven-thirty. Damian lay heavily along Matt's side. His eyes flicked open when Matt kissed his forehead.

"Thanks," he smiled. "You were exactly what I needed. You're the only one that could have done that for me."

"Nonsense. Any friend would have done the same."

He shook his head slowly, "Wrong! Straights would run a mile and gays would want to screw. There's not many who can just cuddle."

"David?"

"He's not here, is he?"

Matt watched as he struggled painfully into his clothes. The morning light revealed livid bruises all over his body, legs and arms.

"What *did* they *do* to you, Damian," Matt demanded.

Damian looked at Matt as if weighing up how to reply.

"Hurley sticks," he said. "They beat me with hurley sticks." And he was gone.

Matt rang Enniskillen barracks and left a message for David to contact him. He rang back that afternoon at school. He sounded cheery: "Were you trying to contact me?"

"Aye, something's happened. Can you come over?"

"No. I'm on until midnight."

"Do you have a tea break?"

"I've an hour at six but I couldn't get over and back in that time."

"I'll come over," Matt promised.

They met in a little cafe near the barracks. Matt felt horribly conspicuous sitting with a policeman. It was the first time Matt had seen him in uniform. He suited the crisp, bottle green serge.

"Well. What is it?" David asked, tucking into his steak pie and chips.

"It's Damian; he's been beaten up again. He didn't want me to tell you."

He dropped his knife: "Is he alright? Where is he? What happened?"

"He's fine, really. He went to work this morning. He's a bit sore but he's acting strangely. He's won't talk about it. There's something not quite right about it!"

"I'll get off. I'll come and see him. I'll tell them there's a family crisis."

Matt tried to calm him: "Hold your horses. He doesn't know I've come to see you. He made me promise not to but... well... I thought you should know."

David looked stern; perplexed: "Tell him I phoned you and I'm coming over tomorrow evening. Tell him to ring me. He might ring anyway!"

Matt popped into Damian's house on his way home. His little sister answered the door. "He's not been home since yesterday," she said placidly.

"Ask him to call me if he comes in, will you?"

David rang Matt at half-ten. His tinny voice came over the phone: "He's here with me."

"Where are you?"

"Silver Birches in Omagh. He's gone to the toilet."

"Is everything O.K.?" Matt asked.

"I'll tell you later," he said urgently, "He's coming back."

The phone went dead.

It was the weekend before David told Matt the full story. Late on Tuesday, Damian had been walking into town when a car drew up to him. Two big men grabbed him, bundled him into the back seat and sat on him as the car raced out of town. When they stopped, the door was wrenched open and a Balaclava was forced over his head. He was dragged out of the car and tied to a tree. Helpless with fear, all he could think about was how embarrassing it would be when they found his body; he had shit and pissed himself.

The bullets didn't come. He had seen the hurley sticks on the floor of the car and now he felt them. The blows were measured; deliberate. His assailants left time for each stinging blow to sink in before the next was delivered. At last it stopped. Then a cold, cruel voice whispered in his ear, "You know what is going to happen to you if you see your boyfriend again, don't you, Kelly? You little pervert."

Damian nodded.

"We don't like collaborators," another growled.

They untied him and left him sprawling in the quiet lane. The rest, Matt knew.

The tips of Matt's fingers tingled; his cheeks felt cold, his stomach sank: "What will you do?" he asked.

David was remarkably composed: "We'll have to stop seeing each other."

Matt looked sympathetically at him: "Can you? Could you bear to give him up? Could either of you?"

"We'll have to. I love him but what can we do? Our love could be the death of him!"

"You too!" Matt added.

"No. He's the vulnerable one."

Initially Damian wasn't too pleased that David had told Matt, but he needed to talk and, before long, Matt had heard the whole story innumerable times. At first Damian went over the story but, as time went on, he increasingly dwelt on the identity of his assailants. They weren't Ballycol men, he was certain of that and this worried him. Why hadn't the local Provos done the job? Why take him out into the country? Punishments were usually carried out in the maze of back streets in the Apostles and why was it necessary to rough him up like that? He couldn't pin the accent down either. He didn't know what sort of car they drove and he hadn't seen any of their faces.

"I had a dream," he said several days later. "It was fucking awful. So vivid. I lived through it all again."

The poor kid is still torturing himself, Matt thought. He knew Damian had to thoroughly talk it through to get over the experience but it was taking a dreadfully long time.

"The poncey one. You know; the one who sat on my head and stank of aftershave. He had a tattoo on his arm."

"Are you sure? You didn't just dream it?"

"No," he insisted. "I remember the tattoo, I do!"

"What was it of?"

"Can't remember. There was something, though. Something important. Something not right!" But puzzle as he would, Damian could not put his finger on what it was.

Without Damian, David was lost. He never asked Matt how Damian was getting on and Matt didn't like to bring the subject up. If anything, David was becoming more withdrawn than when Matt first knew him and he threw himself wholeheartedly into his job. Damian's traumas were pushed to the back of Matt's mind in the aftermath of the bombing at Enniskillen. Everyone seemed to know someone who was there. David was on duty at the cenotaph that fateful day. Thankfully, he wasn't hurt but the experience had been horrendous.

"Why?" he said, shakily, the following Tuesday. "What do they think they're going to achieve?"

"I suppose they think they'll wear the government down, eventually," Matt reasoned.

"It's times like this when I wonder why I stay here. I used to think I was protecting something good, something worth dying for but what am I doing? I'm putting myself in the firing line for a community that would despise me if they knew what I was! I'm working with astonishingly homophobic men and I'm living in a society that has forced me apart from the one person I have ever loved! I must be mad!"

Damian was going rapidly downhill too. He was becoming obsessed with his attackers' identities. Matt worried that he was descending into a depression. He endured night after night of Damian's self-torture. Sometimes he was so down that Matt wouldn't let him go home, but would take the devastated boy to bed to soothe him to sleep. Nothing happened between them; Damian never showed any interest in sex and Matt didn't feel it would have been right, anyway, despite still being in love with him. In time, Matt thought, he will come round and then, maybe....

On one such night something did happen. Excitedly, Damian was shaking Matt.
"Matt. Wake up. Wake up. I've remembered."
What's the matter?"
"I've remembered the tattoo."
"What are you on about? Have you been dreaming?"
"Yes," he shouted joyfully. "But it's what I dreamed. I remember, Matt. I remember the one who sat on my head, the one with the tattoo on his arm. I remember what it was."
"What was it, then?"
"It was a crest."
"You've told me that before."
"Yeah but I remember where I've seen it before now. It's a regimental crest, of the British army!"
"So you think they were British soldiers, do you? They can't be; you told me they were Northern Irish for a start and why would soldiers beat you up then bring you safely home. It doesn't make sense!"
"Could be U.D.R." he said dubiously, then, "No, it wasn't the U.D.R. It was another regiment, I'm sure of it. Do you have any books with regimental crests in?"
"Are you kidding?"

"Do you?"

"What would I be doing with a book like that? Get to sleep; I'll see if I can find something at school tomorrow."

Matt settled back to sleep. "It's possible, you know," he murmured, "that this guy was in the British army and is now in the Provos. He wouldn't be the first."

"Suppose you're right." Damian paused, then said, "You will look for that book tomorrow won't you?"

"Yes," Matt sighed, and drifted off to sleep.

The crest he identified was the Royal Artillery. Matt carefully introduced this latest development to David; he didn't want David to know the precise circumstances of the disclosure.

David looked agitated.

"What is it?" Matt asked.

"Nah, it's stupid."

"Go on," Matt urged.

"There's a guy on our station, Hackett. He was in the army and he's a tattoo on his arm, left I think."

"You surely don't think..."

"He's hard. He might be capable but I always thought he liked me."

"Maybe that's the answer," Matt declared. "Perhaps he thought he was doing you a favour."

David shook his face violently. "No, no, no. There's no way they'd do that. NO WAY!"

"You're probably right, Matt agreed. "Damian probably dreamed it all. He's been churning it over and over. He's obsessed. Could you have told him about Hackett? He might be confusing memory with imagination. He woke me in the middle of the night ranting that he had remembered."

David's stony stare halted Matt; he flushed.

"Didn't take you long." he said coldly.

"It's not like that."

David simply glared.

"It's not like that," Matt cried. "David, listen to me. He was in my bed but we didn't do anything. He wanted me for company, that's all. It's you he loves, David. "He dropped his voice for an apology: "I'm sorry. I shouldn't remind you. It must hurt."

He nodded. "I love that little twit, Matt. That's why I can't see him again..... Ever."

CHAPTER 20

SPRING 1988, DISASTER

Remembering that one detail seemed to lift a weight off Damian's mind. Never as chirpy again, he was, nevertheless, more at ease with the world. Matt surmised that he was getting over David until one Saturday in February when Matt answered the phone. It was David. Matt hadn't heard much from him since that difficult evening in December. "Hi Matt," he said breezily. "What're you doing tonight?"

"Nowt much. Why? Thinking of coming over?"

"Actually," he started, hesitantly, "I'm meeting Damian this afternoon. We'll probably go for a drive, then head into Omagh for a drink. Fancy joining us in the Royal Arms about nine-thirty?"

Matt was somewhat taken aback: "Dead on, see you then, then. How are you, anyway?"

"Fine, fine but listen. I've got something to tell you about Damian and me but I've got to go now. I'm meeting Damian in an hour so I'll give you the bars tonight."

At that, he rang off.

It was a miserable afternoon, damp and overcast, but not too cold. Matt conceded to necessity and went to get his shopping done. Coming out of Wellworths he spotted Damian with a gang of his mates; they were lounging against the wall of the bank, passing comment on everyone who passed. These were the very boys who would give Matt abuse as he passed; he wondered how Damian managed to mix with them with impunity. Then it struck him that Damian was supposed to be with David. He hesitated to go over; he didn't want to compromise his friend by speaking to him in front of the streetwise lads. On the other hand, Matt was curious and a little concerned as to why he wasn't with David. He crossed to the little group and spoke to Damian. The boys eyed Matt warily but they weren't as hostile as he expected.

"Can I have a word with you, Damian?"

"Aye surely," he replied, and followed Matt down the street.

"What?" he demanded.

"Why aren't you with David?"

"What do you mean?"

"He rang about an hour ago and said he was going to meet you.... about now!" Matt explained.

"Shit! He didn't let me know. What the fuck's he up to?"

"Well that's what he told me. He said that he was meeting you this afternoon and that you would go for a drive, then you were to meet me in the Royal Arms at half-nine."

"That's weird," Damian looked puzzled, his face scrunched up like a little boy's. "We always arrange it really carefully, you know."

Matt was bewildered: "I didn't know you still kept in touch."

"Aye. We couldn't stand not seeing each other so we started meeting secretly. We had to keep it quiet. I'm surprised he told you. I wanted to but he said he didn't want anyone at all to know; even you Matt. I'm sorry."

"It's O.K. I understand. Er... He said that he had something to tell me - about you two."

"Shit!" he grinned, punching the air in celebration. "He's done it! He was trying for a transfer to the Metropolitan Police. Must've come through. Fuckin' great! We're going to live in London."

"How do you do it? I mean..... how do you manage to keep in contact?"

"It's really James Bond stuff," he grinned. "When he gets off, he writes to me giving me a time and place to meet him. We usually find a little hotel room somewhere."

"Thus the Royal Arms!" Matt sniggered. "How does he know you got the letter?"

"He always gives me some sort of instruction like, to ring the station phone three times at four seventeen the day before we meet."

"It works?"

"It has done up to now. I can't see why he should come over without the usual letter." He paused, "Unless he sent a letter and I never got it, it'll probably arrive this afternoon, I'll kill Micky."

"Micky?" Matt asked.

"Aye, Micky Dolan, our postman. He knows more about what's going on in this town from watching what letters you get than the R fuckin' U.C. and the Brits together with all their surveillance."

"Would he come without your reply?" Matt asked.

"He might, on the off-chance that I couldn't get to a phone. I wonder where we were supposed to meet!" Damian shook his head as if inspiration would come.

"I'll tell you what. I'll drive you round some of the usual spots, we might find him and, even if we don't, I can take you up to the Royal Arms tonight."

"Deadly," he grinned.

Matt couldn't believe how many different spots they used. They started by heading over to the Bog Road, the most usual rendezvous, as it was handiest for Damian's house. Then they drove up to Belle Vue and round to the junction of the Omagh and Enniskillen Roads. There was no sign of David. "Is there anywhere else?" Matt queried.

"There's the forest park. We don't go there much in the winter, though. I walk out through the hotel and along the shore. It's dead nice in summer but it's a bit wet at this time of the year."

"Would he have gone there, do you think?"

"Could've. It was the first place we ever had it off," he smirked, "in the back of his car," he chuckled. "If we're headin' off across the water he probably wants to do it there one more time, for old time's sake!"

"O.K." Matt said, "Let's try there, it won't take long to drive round."

The forest park entrance was about a mile along a narrow, winding road. As Matt turned into the gate a motorbike shot out, narrowly missing the car. Matt slammed his foot on the brake and the car slithered to a halt on the gravel. "The bloody maniac," he exclaimed, still shaking. "The stupid bugger could have killed himself." He looked at Damian; he was staring ahead ashen-faced. "Hey, come on." Matt said softly. "It wasn't that bad. Did I frighten you?"

Damian shook his head, curls swishing in slow motion.

"What's wrong?" Matt asked.

"Do you know who that was?" he whispered.

"No."

Damian started into life: "Quick. Get up there and for fuck's sake, get a move on."

"What's up?"

"Just fuckin' move!" he bawled.

The panic in Damian's voice alerted Matt. The blood drained from his face as Matt realised what his terrified friend was saying. He rammed his foot to the floor and the car hurtled along the forest road hitting every bump and rut. The picnic spot was only about one kilometre into the forest but it was the longest k. Matt had ever driven. He could hardly keep the car on the road, once or twice they ricocheted off the banking. The exhaust crashed as the car bottomed and after a particularly violent bump the metallic crashing was replaced by a racing-car roar as they left the exhaust box behind. They were climbing the hill to the car park when Matt was blinded by a livid light. Images of the nuclear holocaust flashed through his mind. The setting sun had broken through the clouds on the horizon bathing everything in an unreal golden light. In normal circumstances Matt would have stopped the car to gaze in awe at the lake of liquid gold spread out before them. The trees were picked out in subtle tones of ochre and pine black. They spiralled up the hill until they could see David's car parked at the view-point. A column of fiery light was arching down as if some celestial being was pointing David out. It was quite unnerving, until Matt realised that it was a rainbow, deprived of the blue end of the spectrum by the setting sun.

At first, Matt couldn't figure out what was on the skyline behind the car, then he realised that there was something on the roof. It was the roof. It looked as if a giant hand had torn it, like the top of a yoghurt carton, its jagged edge pointed, accusingly, to the sky. They raced over to the windowless, de-roofed car and slithered to an appalled standstill. A gross distortion of a human being was at the wheel; headless. David's favourite Arran jumper was clinging to the carcass of a butchered pig. Not a pig. Those gory ribs; that travesty; like a scene from Guernica; was David.

In a dream, they found a phone, then went back to Matt's house where they busied themselves with trivia. When it came, the news item was like countless others. "An off-duty RUC officer has been murdered in County Fermanagh." Then on to an item about the Anglo-Irish agreement. Innumerable times Matt had heard such a headline and ignored it or, at most, said, "Poor man"? But now it was real, it was a friend; a warm, kind person.

David had been killed by a drogue bomb. The motorcyclist had thrown the grenade on the roof. The explosion seared through, delivering the deadly blast into the vehicle. It was so quick that David couldn't have known anything about it.

Even in his shocked state Matt had had the wit not to mention Damian when he called the police. They needed to sort out how much they were going to reveal, but neither of them could think straight.

"Look, you had better go home," Matt said gently, "I have to go to the barracks to make a statement. It's better if you don't get involved."

Damian narrowed his tearful eyes and shook his head.

"You don't want to go home?"

"Can I stay here?"

"Sure. Will you be alright on your own for a while?"

He nodded gently.

Matt wasn't clear in his mind what he would tell the police, he only knew that he mustn't mention Damian or his relationship with David. In almost any situation Matt would trust the police but, for some reason, they had a mental block when it came to homosexuality. The subject turned apparently rational men into vindictive witch-hunters. Going to the police as a gay person was a bit like Russian roulette; you could be dealt with like any member of the public, with courtesy and respect or you could be unlucky and get an officer who considered you as something that has just crawled out from under a stone, and meet with indifference or even obstructiveness. Being gay and, nominally, Unionist, Matt always felt that he was in an odd position. As a member of the Unionist community, he should look on the police as the front-line defenders of his way of life but he knew too many gay people who had suffered at their hands, to be so blindly uncritical. He was not going to risk being treated like a criminal, so he decided to say that he had gone to the forest to do a spot of bird-watching. He would tell them about the motorbike and describe all the subsequent events exactly as they happened, except for Damian's presence. Matt would have loved to have told them about Paddy Rock but, as he hadn't a notion who he was, it would be a bit pointless.

At the heavily fortified gate, Matt explained that it was he who had found the murdered policeman that afternoon and he was admitted. At the desk, he was received with deference, concern even. He was escorted to a room and asked to wait. He was sitting in the uninspiring room for about ten minutes when the door opened, and who should walk in but Damian!

"What?" Matt slowly asked in amazement.

Damian looked awful, worse than when Matt had left him.

"I'm going to tell them everything," he said.

Matt raised his eyebrows and exhaled noisily: "Are you sure that's wise?"

"No, it's not," he said firmly. "But I'm doing it."

Matt put his arm round him and gave him a cuddle. "I suppose you know what you're doing. Best of luck, anyway."

They didn't keep Damian long. Totally drained; he turned up at Matt's an hour or so after him.

"What happened?" Matt asked gently.

"I told them everything and they wrote it down."

"How were they? Did they give you any hassle?"

"No, they were dead on. It's weird, you know. I thought that they would really freak out when I told them about us but they didn't. They were dead kind; I think they were actually sorry for me!"

Matt was relieved: "Thank goodness, what happens next?"

"They want me back tomorrow. Can I stay here tonight? I don't really want to go home," he finished.

"Course you can," Matt smiled, "hungry?"

"Not really, but I suppose I'd better eat."

They turned in early. Damian looked so vulnerable that Matt asked him if he wanted to sleep with him. He accepted with a slight nod, he knew it would be O.K. and slept curled up in Matt's arms like a frightened child.

Next morning he woke Matt with tea and toast and climbed back into bed, warming himself on the sleepy teacher. He looked more self-assured that morning, and confirmed this by his next statement: "I'm leaving." he announced.

"Going home?" Matt murmured.

"No. Leaving Ballycol!"

"I can understand that. Where will you go? Belfast?"

"Dunno," he said and, with that, he clammed up.

Matt watched him slide his jeans on over his lithe hips and regretted that he had lost him to David. Fully dressed, he gave Matt an affectionate kiss and, with a tear in his eye, said good-bye with disturbing finality. Matt was never to see his luxuriant mop again.

CHAPTER 21

WINTER 1988, THE BEGINNING OF THE END

Nineteen eighty-eight was becoming a dreadful year for Matt. The shock of David's death distressed him and with Damian's disappearance, he had been deprived of two of his closest gay friends. Not only that, but Simon's stay in Ballycol had been predictably short before he went to work in Nottingham, Danny hadn't reappeared yet and he hadn't seen Feargal since he went to live in Dublin. Matt felt that he had been drained of all his value. He used to be able to chat to anyone about anything, but now he couldn't find anything interesting to say. Matt became a single issue person. He couldn't talk about Damian and David's relationship, so he compensated by becoming obsessed with how unfair society was to gays. His old friends were disappearing, one by one, and he didn't have the energy to go out and meet new people. Fin was still around but Matt didn't see nearly as much of him as he used to.

Mary watched in concern as Matt became increasingly withdrawn and isolated. He wasn't going out, he wasn't eating properly and he seemed to be losing his zest for life. On the pretext that the Sunflower was too cold for Bryony, she moved back in and Alex made it his duty to be at Ballycol as much as possible.

At school, many of the staff were thoroughly fed up with his diatribes on gay rights. That the kids were, was graphically illustrated when Matt walked into school one morning. Pinned to the notice board in the foyer was a page of a tabloid; *The Sun speaks its mind*, was the by-line. WHEN THE GAYS HAVE TO SHUT UP.

"What the hell...?" Matt muttered as he stalked up to the board; the paper was dated February the tenth. *Homosexuals who say that they are normal and society is perverse are risking a terrible backlash* it started. The murder of a young paperboy had triggered this tirade because the culprit was supposed to be homosexual. The Sun made some astonishing claims; *They believe it is THEY who are normal and the rest of society which is perverse,* was one claim. Another was; *They want grants from local councils for meeting places.* True enough, Matt thought, but the way it was slanted it made it sound somehow dubious. The article said; *They want preference for jobs* and most damning of all; *Above all, some of them want the opportunity to go into schools and make known to children the homosexual way of life.* This sentence was highlighted in orange. The article finished lamely, by claiming that the Sun was sympathetic to gays who kept themselves to themselves but warned that, if they didn't shut up, they were asking for trouble. Matt saw the article as an obvious softener for Clause 28. He ripped the thing off the board and stormed into the headmaster: "Look at this," he fumed.

Matt had caught him unawares: "Mister Woodhead, please!"

"Sorry, sir. I saw this on the announcements board. You can see why I was angry."

"Indeed, yes. I wouldn't worry about it. It was probably some silly little second former trying to upset you. It's best to ignore it. Don't let them see that it works. You, of all people, should have learnt that by now."

Matt nodded apologetically.

"Look, Matthew. I know you've had a terrible experience. Everyone has the greatest sympathy for you but life has to go on, you know. It will be best for everyone if you leave those problems behind you when you come into school and throw yourself into the job in hand. You're a good teacher, Matthew. You have given a lot to the school and a lot of people appreciate you for that, but people have short memories. Don't destroy all you've built up, will you?"

Matt pursed his lips thoughtfully and shook his head: "No sir."

In May, clause 28 became section 28. Matt could hardly believe it was happening; it seemed that they were heading into a new Third Reich. One good thing to come out of it was that a good number of celebrities publicly came out as gay to fight the repression and the B.B.C. seemed keen to point up the inequities of the new mood. The Tories sank to using gays as bogeymen in their party political broadcasts. The propaganda showed a teapot full of tea, representing tax-payers money. There's only so much to go round, it said, then it showed the tea slopping into a series of cups, one of which was prominently labeled as 'gay and lesbian group' or something equally obvious. The message was clear, vote for us and we won't be wasting your nice heterosexual money on those nasty homosexuals. On top of this, school was getting difficult for Matt. It was nothing to do with being gay, though; it was all the changes that had been imposed upon the educational system. Teachers had struggled to bring in the new G.C.S.E. exams for summer that year. With all the new-style teaching and the mountains of continuous assessment, Matt felt like a gibbering wreck by the time the summer holidays came around. Normally, Matt spent those few weeks of peace after the exam classes had left to get his lab tidied up and start his lesson plans for the next year. He was never so glad to walk out of that school for the annual camping trip in the first week of July. The place was a tip, he hadn't even thought about his teaching for the next year and he didn't give one damn! As soon as the camping trip was over, he fled to Holland and spent the first week complaining in Piet's sympathetic arms. Gradually, he wound down and began to enjoy himself and, by August, Matt felt that he could face Ballycol again with a renewed vigour.

On a national level, the outlook for gay people wasn't improving. In the light of section 28 and the government's ban on broadcasts by Sinn Fein, they all chuckled when Kenneth Baker on a visit to Moscow in October, told the Russians that censorship could never work. A national opinion poll in November showed that seventy-five per cent of the population supported the government's anti-gay stance.

By Christmas, Matt was ready for another break. Teachers were being initiated into the pleasures of the new national curriculum and many felt they couldn't cope. Any one of the educational reforms would have been welcomed if they had had the time and resources to implement it but, as soon as they had begun to battle with one, another was thrown at them. They had been struggling with the new G.C.S.E. for two years whilst trying to bring in curriculum development. Now, on top of the new national curriculum, local management of schools was imminent, teacher appraisal was threatened, 'A' level courses were changing and AS levels were coming in; it never seemed to stop. Something had to go and Matt began to hope it would be him. He decided to head to Kendal for Christmas. His cousin Mandy picked him up at Liverpool airport and whisked him up the M6 to the uterine warmth of Birkholm, where she was living with Michael and the kids. At first, Matt's accounts of the events of the last year were guarded, for he feared the reproachful tones that had become the normal response to his tales of woe. He should have known better. They sympathised and rejoiced at exactly the right moments and never once made him feel guilty of his indignation.

On Friday night, they went out for a pint in the local at Crossthwaite but Saturday was New Year's Eve and there was always a big do at Birkholm. Matt was happy. They watched Edinburgh Castle on the telly and heard the chimes of Big Ben. Auld Lang Syne was sung, followed by the pumping of hands and exchanging of kisses. Matt held Mandy to him and wished her all the best.

"What about you?" she asked.

"Nineteen eighty-nine couldn't be worse than eighty-eight," he said morbidly.

"Come on, it wasn't ALL bad, was it now?"

Matt looked at her, trying to impress upon her what he had suffered, that year. "Clause twenty-eight has really frightened me. Thatcher and her minions have put the official seal of approval on the contention that we are less than equal. We are second class citizens, we don't deserve the protection of the law; it's to be used to persecute us. It's bound to affect the way Joe Public sees us!"

"You'll be alright, Matt. No one would want to harm you," she crooned.

"Maybe not me, but think of all those poor bastards out there who haven't been as lucky as me. The frightened kids in the ghettos, the men and women trapped in marriages. There are hundreds of gay people out there whose lives are being made a misery by this new fascism."

She laughed at Matt's long face. "Look forward, not back! Cheer up. This isn't like you. Have you met Colin yet?"

"Colin what's-his-name. Lived near Mike?"

"That's him. He's over there. Recognise him?"

Matt looked over towards a balding man talking to Evan. "Aye, I must have a chat to him later. Can I use the phone?"

This was the first time in years that Matt hadn't been at Willy-John's for New Year. He rang his old friend as soon as he could get near the phone. They were all there. Suddenly, he missed them all.

In the doldrums of the early hours of nineteen eighty-nine, Matt found Colin sitting by the fire in the lounge. They exchanged reminiscences across the glowing embers. They made a fine pair, both fair, thin and single, perched like a pair of garden gnomes on the slate hearth. In the old days, Colin had been Mike and Mandy's constant companion. Always popular, he seemed to be interested in everyone he met. As a youth he was pretty, the girls loved him and he spread himself evenly and fairly between them. In his early thirties he was spare and, at the same time, rugged and gentle. Without either of them realising it, some chemistry came into play and propelled their conversation on towards dawn. Talking about childhood days at Birkholm, they resolved to take a walk around their old haunts. Leaning over the half door of a pig-box, listening to the gentle snuffling of a sow and her sleeping litter, Matt's hand found Colin's shoulder, Colin slipped his arm round Matt's waist and they kissed. In the warmth of the hayloft above the cattle, they let their passions run free.

New Years Day was a lazy day. They popped into Kendal to see Mike's people who lived in the part of the town that creeps up Kendal Fell. Matt decided not to go in with them and, instead, walked up into Serpentine Wood. Oddly enough, Matt had never explored that bit of Kendal before and was surprised to find that the fell was a limestone outcrop topped by a classic beech woodland, complete with yews. Matt had always thought that beech couldn't regenerate, this far north, but there were plenty of saplings springing up to replace any natural wastage. It was a lovely day. The weak sun turned the layer of leaves to a carpet of gold. A bench in a clearing afforded Matt a view of the peaceful scene. Neat little grey stone houses spread from the River Kent in a well ordered jumble. Their smoking chimneys were adding to the slowly writhing mist wreathing the lower reaches of the town. Tendrils of vapour felt their way towards the higher ground. In two days time, Matt would be back in Ballycol and the pressure would be back but, for the moment, he could relax in safe, friendly Kendal.

One of Mike's friends was having a birthday party on New Year's Day. They decided to pop in for an hour or so but to leave in good time to get an early start on Monday morning. Everyone met up in the Dun Horse and they started drifting up to Burnside at closing time. Mike was driving so they got there before most of the foot bound guests.

Colin and Matt had to be a bit circumspect at the party but, when it came time for Matt to leave Colin, threw caution to the wind. As Mike and Mandy walked up to the car, he held Matt back. Matt offered his hand for a fraternal handshake but, once contact had been made, it turned into a hug, then a kiss. Suddenly, as if he had gone too far, Colin shook Matt off, mumbled good-bye and fled inside, slamming the door behind him. Matt turned to go to the car but his way was blocked by a group of youths with carrier bags of cans.

"Are you a queer?" one said, in matter of fact tones.

In a moment of bravado, Matt shot back, "Sure, what if I am?"

The youth's fist connected with Matt's face. The next thing Matt knew, the thug was all over him and, after that, he couldn't remember any details. Matt clutched his assailant to himself, hoping to lessen his blows by restricting his movement, but this seemed to infuriate him even more. The two men crashed to the floor, bouncing off the door as they fell. Then Matt heard his name shouted and it was all over. A sea of willing hands lifted Matt into the house. Colin's distraught face swam in front of him. All Matt could feel was a dull pain all over his head and warm blood wetting his face.

Matt was cleaned up a little, put into Mike's car and whisked up to the Westmorland Hospital where he was dealt with quickly and efficiently. They seemed worried about his head injuries. They took his blood pressure and pulse and peered into his closing eye with an ophthalmoscope. Then Matt was left shivering on the trolley. His friends came to look at him.

"You're going to have a couple of shiners," Mike quipped.

"I'm so sorry; will you ever be able to forgive me?" Colin trembled. "If I'd only thought! I was embarrassed when I saw them coming. That's why I fled inside!"

Matt smiled crookedly at him, "Oh!" he laughed. "That hurts."

"Don't laugh, then," Mandy smiled blearily.

"Why is it so cold in here?" Matt demanded.

"It's not, actually. You're probably suffering from shock."

After an age, Matt was wheeled into a room where a nice-looking young doctor stitched his eyebrow, gave him an anti-tetanus jab and delivered him back to his friends.

Monday heralded the worst hangover Matt had ever had and he hadn't even been drunk! He complained. His head was thumping and sore, his throat was dry, his nose bunged and his chest ached. In the shower, he discovered previously unsuspected grazes and bruises. Judicious applications of cold compresses through the night had brought the swelling down enough for him to see the damage. His face was a mess. Matt hadn't realised just how purple a black eye could be; it was as if a crazed artist had decorated his face with deft strokes of his brush. A neat teardrop shape curled over each eye, finishing at the bridge of his nose. A crisp white stripe separated this from two purple travesties of tiredness bags under his eyes. He looked like a demented panda!

Regardless of how awful he felt, Matt had to get the plane at Speke that morning. He could hardly stand but he was bundled into the car and driven, hell for leather down the M6. The journey passed in a dream, more a nightmare, really. The waking nightmare took Matt across by plane to Belfast, then to Derry by train where his father picked him up. His uncle John had warned Matt's father all about it so Matt didn't have to make any complicated explanations. His mother was suspiciously calm about the whole thing. She ministered to her son's every need but put the foot down when he mentioned going back to Ballycol. She would not contemplate it until he was better.

He managed to brighten up enough on Tuesday for her to let him go back to Ballycol; he would be only one day late back at school. On Wednesday morning, Matt began to doubt the wisdom of his decision. He hadn't slept at all well, his head was still sore all over and aches and new pains were taking up residence all over his body. His eyes had swollen up again, overnight, and one was weeping profusely, but his morning toilette seemed to repair the worst and rendered him marginally human looking for his first day of the new year at school.

As Matt wandered up the main street he conjured with his explanation. He would have loved to tell them what had really happened but he could imagine their response; it serves you right; it's your own fault for flaunting it; if you behave like that what do you expect? They couldn't grasp that, as a human being, Matt had as much right to kiss a man as they had to kiss a member of the opposite sex. To them, Matt's attempt to live his life according to his own principles was an unreasonable provocation!

He had arrived. He stalked through the playground throng of gawping kids.

"What happened sir?" one asked.

"Did you have a fight with your girlfriend, sir?" another giggled.

"Don't be stupid," Matt snapped.

"Boyfriend, more like," another muttered, under his breath.

When he reached the relative sanctuary of the staffroom all eyes turned. "Oh Matthew," Miss Rogers exclaimed. "We'd heard you'd had an accident. Are you alright? What happened?"

"Lager Louts," Matt explained. This term for drunken, urban youths had slipped into the language in eighty-eight. Over the next couple of days Matt refined his account, removing all mention of Colin and emphasising that his assailants were aggrieved gatecrashers. This, much sanitised story, was what the kids got.

By the weekend he was feeling much better. The swelling had gone down and the bruises were merely tender. The livid purple of Matt's eyes had faded to blotchy red and yellow. He still had a dull headache and vague nausea but, worryingly, his weeping eye was rapidly losing focus.

Mike phoned on Sunday. He filled Matt in on some of the details of what had happened and Matt began to appreciate why Mike was more shaken by it than he was. The first thump was all that Matt could really remember; it must have practically knocked him senseless. He discovered that as he lay, pinned to the ground by the first youth, the other three had joined in a frenzy of kicks to his head and body. Mike had leapt out of the car to help but all he could do was throw his body over Matt's face. In doing so he probably saved, if not Matt's life, his sight. Someone in the house had seen what was happening and, as soon as the door opened, the thugs ran off. The police had been unable to find his attackers, so there was no chance of prosecution, but Mike would send Matt a form to claim from the Criminal Injuries Compensation Board.

Until Mike's call, Matt had been sure that he had been a victim of a random attack. It could have happened to anyone, the anti-gay thing was just the excuse they needed to start a fight. It could have been anything else, or so Matt thought, football team, colour of hair, anything. But Mike made Matt realise that those four guys were working out their hatred for homosexuals on him. They were drunk, yes, but their motivation was evident when Matt's attacker called to his mates, "Come on, lets do for this arse bandit."

CHAPTER 22

SPRING 1989, BOZZY AND CON

Matt's first visitors were as unexpected as they were welcome. Matt had hardly got through the door on Tuesday afternoon when the bell rang. Standing at the threshold were two of his fifth form boys. They were clutching disintegrating Adidas bags and their ragged ties looked like knotted string.

Bozzy, as always, spoke for the duo, "We heard you'd had an accident, sir. We've come to see if you're alright."

"That's very nice of you; would you like to come in?"

The two boys sat taking in everything about Matt's sitting room as he fussed about making tea. Their given names were John Boswell and Conor Smyth but they were universally known as Bozzy and Con. Bozzy was a stocky, sandy haired youth, old beyond his years, Wee Con was elfin and dark. Matt's colleagues had little patience with the pair. On his own, Wee Con would have provoked little comment. He was a quiet lad who looked like he belonged in second form, not fifth. However, he had been palling around with Bozzy for about a year and Bozzy was a problem child. In the junior school he had been an enthusiastic pupil, a little too enthusiastic for most teachers' liking; you couldn't keep him down. He simply hadn't understood the concept of putting up his hand and waiting for the teacher to ask him to speak. It was as if having his hand in the air gave him the right to shout over anyone else who happened to be speaking. Every class was a battle to hear what the other kids had to say; it was exhausting. Some staff persevered; other got fed up and bawled him out or put him in detention. His broken home was taken into account, so he wasn't punished as severely as he might otherwise have been, but his behaviour didn't improve. By third year he had decided that school wasn't for him. He descended into a sullen and uncooperative silence that evolved into a pattern of increasingly disruptive behaviour with an unspoken threat of violence. Bozzy's story was far from unique; all too many pupils followed that path to academic disaster.

The turning point came early in eighty-eight when Bozzy was in fourth year. Matt had run into a tear-stained Bozzy in the playground, surrounded by some of the more sympathetic prefects. Technically, they should have all been in class and he should have admonished them. "Hello," Matt said, smiling at the little congregation. "Anything wrong?"

No one spoke for a moment then Helen, a motherly young woman, blustered, "Bozzy's been getting bullied."

That surprised Matt because he always thought of Bozzy as the class bully. However, he tried not to show this. "Who's been bullying you, John?" He asked quietly.

He screwed up his face and contemplated the playground tarmac.

"John, if you've been getting hassle you should tell someone, you know."

"It's nothin' sir," he mumbled.

There was a long silence with Matt willing him to tell him what had been going on. Finally, Richard interjected, "Mr. Allen's been getting at him."

Bozzy looked mutinously at Richard.

"What happened?" Matt pried.

"S'nothin'."

"If you don't want to tell me, that's your business," Matt said. "But it seems to have upset you. I might be able to help."

It seemed unlikely. The most aggressive thug in fifth form and the gay teacher but Matt hoped Bozzy could rise above that. All eyes were on Bozzy. He broke and started to explain. "He's thrown me out of P.E. and he won't let me back until me old man comes up to apologise."

"Apologise for what?"

"Nothin'"

"It must be something. Mr. Allen wouldn't throw you out for nothing." He turned to the gaggle of sixth formers and asked them to go to class. Once they had gone, Matt heard Bozzy's version of the tale. He had been slow coming in from the gym and had changed without having a shower. Jack Allen caught him and told him to strip off and get into the shower. Bozzy refused point blank and Jack had lost the rag with him. Jack could be a bit brittle but he wasn't the ogre he was being made out to be, so Matt was wary of taking Bozzy's account too literally.

"Mr. Allen's only a human being, like you and me, John. You must have done something to upset him, even if you didn't realise it!"

"He's got it in for me," he retorted.

"You really believe that, don't you?"

"It's true!"

"It may seem like that to you but I don't believe he has. I know him, he's a very nice man, really, and he cares a lot about you all."

Bozzy was not shifting: "Well he's got it in for me."

"O.K. Assuming that he has, and I'm not saying he has, what would happen if you didn't apologise?"

"I wouldn't get doin' P.E. no more."

"Aye, and the headmaster would want to know why."

"Hmph," he snorted.

"John. It's a sad fact of life that when you leave this school, you're going to be looking for a job in this town and you know as well as I do that the unemployment situation here is dire. I'm not trying to threaten you but, if some prospective employer rings the head and asks about John Boswell, he's not going to risk his own integrity by lying."

"I don't care."

"O.K. then. Let's think what would happen if you did produce an apology."

"I'm not gettin' me da up."

"I think he'd be very happy if you just said you were sorry."

"I'm not."

"Say you were, for the sake of argument."

"S'pose I'd get doin' P.E."

"Right. And wouldn't that make life easier for all concerned?"

"I'm not apologisin' 'cos I've done nothin'."

"So you say but.... "

"Don't you believe me?"

"I didn't say that. Two people can see the same situation in two different ways. I'm sure you both think you're right. What harm would it do to apologise?"

He didn't reply at all but stared concertedly at Matt's shoes. The bell went.

"Go on. Off you go and, for goodness sake, John, don't make life difficult for yourself over a pointless point of principle."

At break Matt carefully broached the subject with Jack.

"What's John Boswell been up to?"

"Cheeky wee skitter. He's been dodging showers for weeks and when I told him to have one he gave me a mouthful of abuse."

Matt nodded and Jack continued.

"Told him he needn't come back until he had apologised to me in front of his parents."

"That might be difficult," Matt explained. "There's no mother around and his father works."

That seemed to faze Jack a bit and he looked flustered. "Well, he can bring me a letter signed by his father, then."

"Why was he dodging showers?" Matt asked innocently.

"He's a dirty wee skitter."

"He never struck me as dirty. Not like young Marshall, for instance."

"I don't know what he's got about showers but he's a cheeky young pup, and I don't stand for that from anyone." And that was that.

Matt collared Bozzy again at lunch-time and tried to reason with him, to no avail. The stalemate between Bozzy and Jack reigned for the rest of the year but, thereafter, Matt went out of his way to offer a sympathetic ear to Bozzy. He reasoned that, if there was one teacher in the school that the youngster could trust, there was a chance that he might keep on an even keel long enough for him to get the G.C.S.E. grades he was capable of.

Matt took it as a measure of his success when Bozzy and Con asked him if they could come out hiking with him that summer. Until then, the two boys hadn't got involved with any school activity whatsoever. Needless to say, Matt's colleagues warned him of the dire consequences of taking those two trouble-makers up a mountain, but they didn't let him down. In fact, the two lads couldn't help enough. The new, improved Bozzy extended into the classroom too. He could have his off days, when he was impossible, but he always made recompense. Matt extolled Bozzy's virtues in the staff room but his cynical colleagues would not concede that he had changed in any way. They accused Matt of having the wool pulled over his eyes: "The little thug's only buttering you up so he can get away on your camping trips," Jack sneered.

Returning to the living room with the tea, Matt gave the two boys the first of his modified versions of how he got beaten up. They sat, entranced, as he unfolded the events. It was the intensity of Bozzy's concern that sent a flutter of unease through Matt's mind.

"If I'd been there I wouldn't have let 'em get away," he declared vehemently.

"My friends did their best."

"You're too nice, sir. Bet your mates are too. Bet they don't know how to handle hard men."

"And you do, do you, John?" Tough nut as he was, Matt could hardly imagine him tackling four thugs.

"No prob."

"He could, sir," Con chipped in. "I was being hassled by Ade's gang and he dealt with them, didn't you, Bozzy?"

Bozzy smiled, slyly.

"What did you do, John?"

"Nothin'! I told 'em 'e was my friend and they were to leave 'im alone. They knew what would happen if they laid one finger on him."

Matt looked at his pugnacious face and bony fists at the end of thick-set arms and decided that he wouldn't like to tangle with Bozzy.

The two boys spent a lot of time in the park, so passed his house at all hours. After they had broken the ice, their visits became more frequent. Matt came to realise that Wee Con wasn't as dozy as he had thought. He heard more about what was going on in the school from those two than he had ever heard before. Their stories were always amusing although Matt realised that, once the bare framework of fact had been established, there was a lot of embellishment that owed more to their corporate imagination than to actual events. The two boys fed off each other. One would make an outrageous statement and the other would top it; Matt was even drawn into the game himself on occasions. Sometimes, their gossip alerted Matt to situations that needed addressing. For example, when Jenny Lyttle disappeared for no apparent reason, it was they who alerted Matt to her pregnancy. Her parents hadn't a notion she even had an older boyfriend but Matt's spies knew his address, and Matt was able to track her down and broker a reunion between her and her distraught family.

Jim Cassidy was a notoriously flamboyant gay man who frequented Micky's. Matt didn't have a lot to do with him but, as Matt was the only other openly gay person to drink there, Jim took it that they had a common interest. Alex was getting the drinks in one night, when Jim sidled up to Matt: "We don't see you in here any more," he said slyly. "I suppose you don't need to. I hear you've your own private supply of chicken these days."

"I don't know what you're talking about," Matt replied crossly.

"Come off it, Matt. Who do you think *you're* fooling? We all know about those two little queens."

"I haven't a notion what you're on about."

"It's alright for some," Jim sneered, before melting back into the crowd.

Alex came back from the bar to find Matt looking agitated.

"What's wrong with you?"

"Nothing. Well, something," Matt said, irritatedly. "Oh, that silly queen, Jim Cassidy, has just said something. It's nothing. It's really stupid. Forget it!"

Later Matt found Jim in his usual perch next to the toilet door.
"Jim, can I have a word with you, please."

They went into the bog together. That'll look great, Matt thought. It didn't take long to get the gist of Jim's story. Matt cursed himself for being so blind, he should have guessed really; both boys had been cruising the park for over a year. They made quite a tidy sum, according to Jim. Con, in particular, was popular with the regulars and Bozzy looked after him. Jim assumed that they had some sort of relationship as well.

Matt convinced him that there was nothing going on; he hadn't really believed it, anyway. Matt realised he had to keep the boys at arms length in future, but he worried for their safety too. He had a difficult task ahead of him.

It was harder than he had expected. Bozzy was sitting alone in Matt's lounge expecting relaxing conversation and Matt was about to deliver him a body blow. Bozzy was happily chomping biscuits and sipping tea to the strains of Erasure when Matt said: "I've got to say something to you."

Bozzy watched Matt pacing up and down with a bemused look on his face.

"You know I'm gay, don't you?"

A fleeting alarmed expression crossed his face, then he assumed a matter of fact appearance: "Course. So what?"

"Well. I've been hearing stories about you and Con from other gay people in Ballycol and, well, to be honest, I'm worried about you." Matt was blushing violently. "I hear that you two have been... Well, not to put it in too polite a term, you've been on the game in the park."

Bozzy didn't move. He stared at Matt, grinding his jaw. Matt thought the little tough was about to leap up and hit him.

"I'm worried about you, Bozzy. I'm always going on about A.I.D.S. and that at school. If you're not careful... It's you I'm worried for but it's me too. I know there's nothing but. Well, people might think... I don't think you should visit me any more. It would be better for all of us." Matt ended lamely. He couldn't believe how crass he was sounding.

"So, you're telling me to piss off, then. Is that it?"

"Not exactly. It really would be better for all of us if you didn't call here so often."

"O.K." he said jumping up. "If you don't like me, that's fine." He yelled. "You can just fuck off, yourself!"

"Bozzy!" Matt called, but it was too late. He had stormed out of the room and slammed the door without even finishing his tea.

Bozzy became impossible in class. He wouldn't answer questions, he wouldn't do what he was told and he stopped handing homework in. The other kids must have begun to wonder what was going on; any other pupil behaving like that would have been with the boss like a shot, but Matt simply accepted it. Matt consoled himself with the thought that it was only a few weeks until May, when they got off to do their G.C.S.E.

About three weeks later, Matt was summoned to the head's study. He looked very uncomfortable; the vice principal was there, too. He asked Matt to sit.

"I find this rather embarrassing," he started. "I'm sure it's all silly tittle-tattle, but I'm afraid I have to ask you about it."

Matt's heart sank; he had a rough idea what was coming.

"John Boswell seems to have been saying some extraordinary things."

Matt's eyes narrowed and looked at the headmaster seriously.

"Boswell appears to have been telling his friends that he and Conor Smyth have been having… a… em… a sexual… liaison with you."

Matt's face drained of colour. His throat dried: "You don't believe him, do you?"

"Of course not. But I had to tell you that. You understand, don't you."

"No. I don't actually. Kids are always saying things like that. You know John as well as I do. He fantasises."

The head and the V.P. looked at each other then Mr. Wright said, "Someone has been to see me."

"Who?"

"I can't tell you that. Suffice to say that the story made the transition from schoolboy tittle-tattle to general gossip and came to the ears of a very *influential* parent. Now, I'm sure you can assure me that there is nothing at all in this story."

"Of course. The boys started visiting me after my accident but I asked them to stop doing so for fear of that very sort of gossip."

"Good. Now this unpleasant interview is over, I hope I can lay this whole business to rest."

Matt didn't know at whom he was angrier; the person who had spoken to the head or the headmaster himself for listening. He was thankful, too. If the parent had made an official complaint he would have been suspended immediately, pending a full enquiry and even if they discovered the truth, the allegation would forever be on his record. He was cross with Bozzy, but guilty too. He had abandoned the boy when he needed him most. He would have to try to re-establish some sort of contact with him.

At four a.m. on Thursday, June the eighth Matt was awoken by an almighty crash, followed by the sound of splintering wood. Startled, he leapt out of bed and made for the stairs. As he wrenched his bedroom door open, the sound of heavy feet pounding up the stairs stopped his heart. His blood froze. This is it, he thought. A Provo assassination. Why me? He stood, transfixed, as shadowy figures appeared on the landing. "What do you want?" Matt heard himself saying shakily. In the ghostly light of morning he could see a hand-gun pointing at him.

A controlled voice said, "Matthew Woodhead?"

"Yes," he replied weakly.

"Would you switch the light on?"

He did, and after a moment of dazzle he was confronted by an extraordinary sight. There, on his landing, were three policemen; each wearing a surgical mask and plastic gloves.

Matt breathed a sigh of relief. "Police! What's going on?"

One of the constables came over and reeled off a caution, "Matthew Woodhead, I'm arresting you on two charges of indecent assault against Conor Smyth and John Boswell. You have the right to remain silent but anything you say may be taken down and used in evidence."

Matt looked at him in amazement. "Are you serious?"

He was. "You have to accompany us to the police station where you will be formally charged."

"May I put some clothes on first?" Matt asked sarcastically, "or would you prefer to drag me through the streets of Ballycol naked?"

"That won't be necessary, sir." The policeman turned to the youngest: "Keith. You go with him."

Constable Keith shot him a mutinous look and followed Matt gingerly into his bedroom.

Matt's heart was in his throat as he dressed. He turned to the nervous constable. "Look. What's all this about?"

"I couldn't say, sir."

"What's with the masks and gloves?"

He wavered. "Precautions, sir."

"Precautions against what?" As if Matt didn't know.

"A.I.D.S."

"MY GOD!" Matt exploded. "Just because I'm gay you think I'm some sort of leper! Even if I had H.I.V., which I haven't, there's no way you could catch it. Unless you habitually screw every man you arrest!" The young constable looked appalled and Matt realised how offensive he'd been: "I'm sorry. I didn't mean it to sound like that."

Fully dressed, Matt was escorted past his shattered door. He turned to the arresting officer. "Do they not teach you about doorbells at the R.U.C. training school?"

"Standard operational procedure," he said dryly.

"You can't leave it lying open like that! My lodger is away, fortunately. Do you realise a nursing mother lives in this house!"

"We'll see to that. Now, just get into the mobile," he insisted.

On the short drive to the barracks, Matt tried to make conversation but they all resolutely ignored him. He was escorted into the station and put into a poky little room that was then locked. The walls were painted hospital green and cream. He sat at a big wooden table scored by years of disgruntled customers. I'll have to get my act together, he decided. There has to be a mistake but how do I deal with it? Willy-John would know what to do. I wonder, would they let me phone him? After what seemed like an age, Matt heard the voices of two young men, obviously enjoying life. One laughed, said, "Keep your arse to the wall," and laughed again. The door opened and Constable Keith edged his way in. He stood with his back a little too obviously to the wall. Shortly, a more senior policeman entered and sat opposite Matt. He introduced himself as Detective Sergeant Boyd. With obvious distaste, he checked that Matt had been cautioned and then read out the charge. In essence, it was that Matt had indecently assaulted Bozzy and Con on a number of specified dates at his house.

Matt wanted to find out exactly what he was supposed to have done, so he asked him what he meant by indecent assault.

"You know what I'm talking about."

"I don't actually," Matt said, as innocently as he could muster.

"You indulged in sexual activity with a non-consenting person," he said as if every word was poison.

"Well, I certainly haven't done that," Matt replied cheerfully."

"Those boys were minors. They may have let you have your filthy way with them but they were under twenty-one so they couldn't consent."

"Look!" Matt objected. "I've done nothing. My God, I'm a teacher, they're my pupils. Have you never heard of professional conduct?"

"Yes and you don't seem to have any!"

"Look. It's all untrue. I think I had better have someone here who can advise me. Can I contact someone?"

"We can get you a solicitor but you'll have to wait until he comes. You could be here a long time."

"I know someone. Can I ring him?"

Willy-John's phone rang and rang. Matt wondered what he would do if Willy-John was away. At last Louise's sleepy voice answered.

"Louise? It's Matt. I'm really sorry to wake you but it's urgent. Is Willy-John there?"

"Just a minute."

Matt could hear a muffled conversation, then his friend came on the line: "Matt?" he barked.

"Willy-John?"

"Who else did you expect to be in bed with my wife?" he quipped. "What the hell are you doing ringing me at... Jesus, Matt, it's quarter to bloody five!"

"I'm in bother. I've been arrested. I'm in the barracks."

"What have you done?"

"Nothing. It's all a horrible mistake but I don't know what to do."

"Where are you? Ballycol?"

"Aye."

"Say nothing. I'll be with you in.... An hour and a half. Hold tight Matt. Don't worry, I'll sort you out."

His old school-friend was as good as his word. Once Matt saw his confident, if hurriedly shaven, face he felt everything would be O.K. Before long he had been charged and released on bail. Sitting in Willy-John's car, it all seemed like a horrible dream.

"How did it happen? What made them think that you had done it?"

Matt told him the story. He assumed that the police had heard the same rumours as the person who complained to the head.

"They would have had to have more evidence than that," Willy-John explained, as Matt made coffee. "Someone must have made a statement. They had dates and everything. That's not just rumour Matt."

"Who, though? Whoever it was, they lied."

"That's up to your barrister to prove."

"What happens now?"

"You will be summoned to appear in front of a magistrate. If you plead guilty, that will be the end of it but I don't think the resident magistrate will want to try you."

"Why not?"

"Too controversial. Local school teacher accused of seducing his pupils. No, he will almost certainly send you to the crown court in Enniskillen."

By the time Willy-John left, Matt felt worse. He wished that Mary and Alex weren't away, although he was glad they hadn't suffered the indignity of being there when the house was raided. He dreaded going to school that day but staying off would feel like an admission of guilt, it would only fuel gossip. He needed to be there to support his case.

The headmaster was shocked by Matt's story but he seemed supportive enough. However, an hour later, Matt was called to his office. Mr. Wright looked grim: "I'm sorry Matthew. As of this moment you are suspended on full pay."

Matt was flabbergasted. "But... But why? Surely I'm innocent until proven guilty."

"In the eyes of the law I'm sure you are but the board has a policy. If any staff member is accused of any such crime they are suspended."

Mary and Alex got home to find Matt moping in his room. "What happened to the door?" Alex demanded.

"Your friends," Matt grunted.

"Hey?"

"The Royal Ulster Constabulary! They took it into their heads that I was shagging Bozzy and Con so they smashed my door down at four-o-clock this morning and dragged me off to charge me."

Mary flung her arms round Matt and hugged him: "Oh Matthew. You poor thing. There, there."

Matt breathed deeply, drawing in the wonderful smell of herbs and spices from her warm body.

"Matt," Alex said sharply. "Tell me exactly what happened."

When Alex had heard Matt's full story, he limped off to the Barracks, determined to find out more.

He returned, looking worried. "I know some guys there; it wasn't too difficult to get what I wanted. They've a signed statement."

"Who by?"

"One John Boswell!"

CHAPTER 23
SUMMER 1989, BRIEF RESPITE

Alex's information made Matt worry more. It was their word against his but why, oh why, Matt puzzled, had Bozzy said such a thing? Matt knew how upset Bozzy was but what made him do this?

Reading Gay Times offered Matt no comfort. The Clause twenty-eight backlash was hitting hard and gay people didn't seem to stand a chance in the courts. He could envisage the cogs of justice drawing him in and grinding him to a pulp.

Alex tried in vain to cheer him up: "I hate seeing you like this," Alex complained. "You're supposed to be the strong one, the one everyone else leans on."

"I wish I knew when my case was going to come up. It's the waiting I can't stand. I want to get it over with."

"It'll all be a formality," Alex tried to reassure him. "You'll be in there and you'll come out a free man. I wish you would realise that and be yourself. I wish everything was like it was before."

Matt was puzzled: "Before when?"

"Before everything. Before all this, before David, before the crash."

Matt smiled at him.

"That's better!" Alex beamed, dropping his big hand on Matt's head.

Matt gazed into his gentle face. Age and experience had been kind to it.

"I have happy memories of that time, Alex. I was really in love with you." Matt drew a breath and let it out slowly. "You love Mary, don't you?"

Alex smiled beatifically: "I am very fond of her."

"And Bryony!" Matt added.

"Aye."

"Has she ever told you whose she is?"

"Do you know?"

"Do you?"

Alex nodded.

"Sad, isn't it?" Matt said.

"If he had only known. He would have loved a child."

"And you?"

"I've no chance of that now," Alex lamented.

"Why? You're much better now. The accident," Matt hesitated. "It didn't.... did it?"

Alex shook his head. He stood up and crossed to the window where he stood and stared at the setting sun across the lake. "It's not that."

Matt sidled up to Alex, slipped his arms around his waist and buried his head in Alex's big neck. Once the sun had disappeared Alex spoke, but so quietly that Matt had to strain to hear: "Mary always falls for the wrong ones. I love her but I can't give her what she needs."

"Let her be the judge of that."

"You don't understand, Matt, I'm some sort of weirdo. I love her but I love you as well." He dropped to a whisper, "You… You turn me on. I could make babies with you but I don't love you like I love her!"

Matt hugged him tighter. Alex turned and they kissed, sending Matt spiralling back to those luscious nights lost in his huge embrace. At that moment, all his resolve evaporated and Alex could have done what he liked with him.

Alex withdrew his gentle lips: "I'm no good for you, Matt. I can never give you what you need. I'm the eternal one night stand."

Before Matt had time to rebut this, Mary walked in. He tried to pull away but Alex was gripping his arms.

"You've told him?" she said.

"What?" Alex asked, letting Matt go.

"That you love him."

"I love you," he objected.

"And him. That's beautiful," she smiled. "And I love both of you."

Alex's piece de resistance arrived on Matt's doorstep late in July. "Piet! What...? Oh God, I'm glad to see you. Why didn't you say you were coming?"

"Alexander telephoned me. He told me what has happened. He said you needed moral support from another gay person," Piet explained, "or is it immoral support?" he chuckled

"Amoral," Matt said.

Not only had Alex contacted Piet but he had paid for his ticket. Almost simultaneously, the summons arrived.

Jim Cassidy flounced into Matt's house ten days before his court appearance in August. "Would you give a parched queen a cup of tea?" he flapped.

Matt hurried him in before anyone could see him. He wasn't the sort of person Matt encouraged at number seven. Tea made, Matt settled down to make polite conversation. Since his demise, there had been a stream of the most unlikely well-wishers and Matt supposed this to be another.

"Well now," Jim said in excited campery, "have I bars for you?"

"Go on."

"You'll never guess who *I* had in the park last night?"

Matt had heard that line so many times. It usually prefaced some revelation about one of the most macho men in the town or a local worthy. "No. Never," Matt shook his head.

"Your little friend, Bozzy Boswell," Jim said, pouting coyly.

"Watch him," Matt said cynically. "He's probably with the police now giving them a blow by blow account."

Piet wandered in and plonked himself next to Matt. He instantly weighed Jim up and draped himself over Matt.

Jim looked at Piet appreciatively. "How wrong you are," he simpered. "At this moment she is sitting in my house chewing her pretty little nails." He produced a sheet of paper with a flourish: "This is for you."

Dear Sir,

Ime dead sorry for everything. Billy McKnight got me to say all that stuff about you when I were still mad at you. I never knew he would tell the cops. Ime dead sorry sir.

Yours sinserly John Boswell

"Fucking McKnight!" Matt exploded. "I might have known he was behind it all. He's had it in for me ever since Simon gave his bastard son a hiding." He turned to Jim, "How did you get him to write this?"

He smiled primly, "Pillow talk, dear, pillow talk!"

"Tell me more."

"Well," he smacked his lips. "I hadn't seen her on the park since before your little.... you know."

"My arrest."

"Yes. Well, I saw her last night and I watched her for at least twenty minutes. Well, dear. You might have thought she had the *plague*!" Jim rolled his eyeballs. "The regulars wouldn't go *near* her. Very different from her usual form I'm telling you! She looked terrible, the poor dear. Well. I was only being charitable."

I bet, Matt thought.

"Fortunately for you, dear, my sister's away this week so we adjourned to my place for the evening. Then it all came out. In more ways than one," he smirked. "If you didn't have her you missed something; hung like a stallion. Rides like one, too!"

"Please Jim," Matt objected. "This is one of my pupils you're talking about!"

"Lucky you! Well she didn't want to go, did she? Said that she had no friends any more."

"What about Wee Con?"

"Gone. Parents sent her off to some Christian Brothers boarding school in Galway. The brothers will soon bash every last ounce of spirit out of her, poor girl. She'll come out of there a eunuch!"

Matt gripped Piet. "God! This is awful. The poor things. What about Bozzy?"

"None of her old friends will have anything to do with her. The straights because they say she's a whoring poof and the sisterhood because she's dropped you in it. She said that she and Con made all that up about you because the ones at school were getting on at them about why you and them had fallen out."

"I suppose they couldn't very well tell their friends that I was hassling them about being on the game."

"Exactly. She said she wanted to make it alright but she was too scared to come and see you, so, Jim beamed jubilantly, "I got her to write this. She's waiting to see how you take it."

"Jim, you're great! I don't know how to thank you."

"Well," he said archly, "Next time you see me you might try not treating me as if I'd just crawled out from under a pile of dog shit!"

Matt was floored; he went scarlet: "I don't do that, do I?"

"Yes you *do*, dear but so does *everyone* else in this town, so don't worry about it. I'll go and tell her it's alright, shall I."

"Yes, no.. I don't know. Will he talk to me?"

"She would love nothing more."

Bozzy stood sheepishly at the front door. "I'm really sorry, sir!" he burst out, as soon as Matt opened it. "I'm sorry," he repeated through floods of tears, as Matt ushered him into the living room.

Matt looked helplessly at Mary and she sat next to the boy and put her arm round his shoulders: "Come on Bozzy," she said gently. "Tell us all about it."

Bozzy started from the very beginning. He had evidently been a precocious developer; even at primary school he had preferred doctors to nurses. Everything was fine until about second year at the High School when, one by one, the boys he used to mess with deserted him. Bozzy knew that he wasn't in the least bit attracted to girls but he was terrified of the others finding out, so he played along with them and made all the usual remarks about girls. The fact that he was the best fighter in the class made it easy for him to cover up; none of his mates suspected a thing. Then, one magical day in third year, one of the boys was telling the others about the queers in the park.

This was news to Bozzy; he was intrigued but he couldn't show it. "What do they do?" he asked, as innocently as he could.

Tall, sturdy and blonde, Ade was the class know-all. He was also the one who Bozzy had most fun with at primary school and Bozzy would have given anything to relive those days with him. "Stick it up each other!" Ade said, with such disgust that Bozzy shuddered. "Filthy bastards. I wouldn't go there at night, Bozzy. Or you'll get something nasty up your arse!"

Bozzy made the appropriate sounds of scorn but, that night, he lay in bed fantasising about being with Ade in the park as he wanked himself silly.

Inevitably, Bozzy found his way to the park, one night. He was dizzy with anticipation as he walked along the blustery promenade in front of Matt's house. At the gate, he hesitated for a moment before pushing through the creaking wrought iron and into the gloom.

Quite what he expected to find, he wasn't sure, but the place was apparently deserted. For almost an hour he wandered through the shrubbery, disturbing nothing more than a group of roosting mallards. He was leaving the park when a deep voice said, "Any action tonight?"

"What?" he said, peering into the gloom cast by the high wall.

A tall man stepped into the light cast by the streetlamps in Richmond Terrace. Bozzy couldn't make out his face, lined as it was with the shadow of the gate's bars.

"Any action?" the man repeated. "Or have you finished for the night?"

"No," he said, sounding perkier than he felt. "What about you?"

"How much?"

"Fiver."

The man made a noise in his throat, it could have been a laugh, "This way."

Bozzy followed him into the darkness.

"Can I suck you for that?"

"No, that's a tenner," he ventured.

"How much to do me?"

Bozzy clutched the four fivers in his pocket as he swaggered home through the deserted streets of Ballycol. He couldn't believe it. That man had actually paid him to do it! O.K., he wasn't that nice, but he'd closed his eyes and pretended that it was Ade he was sucking. One day it would be Ade; he was determined.

Bozzy was only fourteen, but he had the physique of a boy two years older and could look after himself. He soon learned to work the punters on the park. If anyone got heavy with him, he could turn into a frightening ball of aggression – no one messed with Bozzy. He usually enjoyed the sex and they almost always paid him, but he never found a man to fall in love with.

Conor was a slight, timid boy with a feminine grace and a slightly effeminate voice. This had led to merciless bullying at the Christian Brothers' so his parents had transferred him to the High School in his third year. Bozzy didn't take much notice of him at first, but the other boys soon found Con's Achilles' heel and the bullying he'd fled from, recommenced. It became received wisdom that Con was queer, and the boys never missed an opportunity to let him know what they felt about that. Before long, Con was absent almost as often as he was present, and Bozzy wondered why the teachers didn't seem to do anything about it. It didn't stop Bozzy joining in the bullying, however, until one day during a tussle he made contact with Con's exquisite blue eyes. It was as if the world around him had stopped and all that existed were two pools of intense blue. A shock went through Bozzy's system as he realised that what he actually wanted to do was hold and protect the elfin creature for ever.

The opportunity didn't come immediately. The crucial incident was just before the summer holiday in fourth form. There was a gang of boys hanging around in the cloakrooms on a wet lunchtime and Con was, as usual, on the fringe of the crowd. Ade was telling a story about some girl he'd scored with and Bozzy was bantering along with him, secretly envying that girl. Suddenly, the focus shifted to Con, and Ade made some banal quip about Con never getting a shag with any woman, unless she was a lesbian. Con exploded and flew at Ade with such fury that Ade was taken by surprise but he soon recovered and punched Con in the body and face, screaming, 'you disgusting little queer' with a fury that scared even Bozzy.

A teacher soon intervened, and the next thing Ade and Con knew was that they were in front of the headmaster in his office. Ade was still white with fury and all he could stammer was that Con had attacked him and he'd defended himself. Con, bloodied and bruised, simply shivered and snivelled.

Ade was back in school the next day but Con didn't reappear, so Bozzy went round to his house. He wasn't exactly sure why he was going but, somewhere in the back of his mind, was the idea that they had something in common and he needed to care for him.

Con was sitting in his bedroom watching a video, when his mother showed Bozzy in. Con looked surprised to see him; after all, this guy was one of Ade's best friends.

"Are you alright?" he asked lamely.

Con nodded.

Bozzy produced a bag of grapes: "I brought you these."

Con nodded. Bozzy hoped he wouldn't ask how he'd got the money to buy them.

"Ade's alright really, you know," Bozzy said uncertainly. "He's just a bit thick sometimes, that's all."

Con didn't look convinced.

"He is!"

The two boys watched the video in silence for a while.

"When are you coming back to school?"

"I'm not."

"Where are you going?"

"Don't know."

"You should come back. I'll look after you."

Con looked at him as if to say 'why' and Bozzy kneeled on the floor and took Con's little hands in his rough paws: "Please come back Con. The school won't be the same without you there."

Con was frightened: "What are you talking about?"

Bozzy looked confused, he was still holding Con's hands: "I don't know. I just know I'm not like the others, but I think I'm like you. If you go, I'll be the only one again and I couldn't bear that, hey!"

Con's eyes were filling but he said nothing.

"Con? Do you ever look at boys?"

"What do you mean?"

"Look at them. You know. Like they look at girls."

"No!" he lied.

"I do. Ade is really sexy. I think he knows that. We used to do stuff, you know, and now and he's trying to prove he's a man or something. That's why he hit you. He had to prove something to me. I think he'd still like to do it with me and I could show him a thing or two!" Bozzy grinned. "So you see it's my fault he hit you. He hit you to tell me he hates queers because he's queer… and so am I. Are you?"

Con nodded tearfully, and sat in stunned silence as Bozzy moved next to him and put his arm around the trembling boy. They sat for an age, as if Bozzy's strong arms could shield them both from the cruel world they lived in.

From then on Bozzy and Con were always there for each other. Bozzy informed Ade and the others that Con was O.K. and if anyone wanted to have a go at him they would have to go through him first. No one was going to risk that. Con, on the other hand was Bozzy's confidant. For the first time in his life he could tell someone about his feelings and fantasies. He could talk about his encounters in the park and he could discuss the merits of their male class-mates as they blossomed into young men. Strangely, Bozzy never thought of Con in a sexual way. Con resisted the draw of the park for a while, but, by the end of the summer, he too was a regular, and a formidable team they made.

Bozzy had heard the others saying that Mr. Woodhead was a poof but he didn't connect that with him and Con until that incident with

Mr. Allen. Bozzy was finding showering with the other boys increasingly difficult. Firstly they teased him about the size of his cock. They called him donkey-dick, but that didn't worry him too much as he was quite proud of it, and he knew how much his punters liked it. However, one day Ade brushed against him in the shower and his donkey-dick took on a life of its own. He managed to get out of the shower with a concealing towel before anyone noticed but, thereafter, he was terrified of going into the shower in case his rampant member gave him away.

Matt's sympathy for him made him realise that Matt had something he and Con needed, although he wasn't sure what it was, yet. Matt's getting beaten up it was the perfect excuse to go and see him. For the first time, the boys had found someone who wasn't likely to criticise them for being gay. They had found a safe haven.

Bozzy hesitated in his narration. He didn't want to tell Matt what he really felt about him. How could he tell this man he'd nearly destroyed that he was gorgeous? How could he say that he wanted to hold his hand? That he wanted to push his tongue into Matt's mouth and that the little swathe of chest hair at his open neck sent him crazy? He couldn't tell Matt that now, when he was on the park, he closed his eyes and pretended that his punters were Matt.

"So," he continued. "When you told me an' Con not to come here I was really, really mad with you an' when they asked me why I was being ignorant with you at school, I said what I did. I didn't mean to hurt you, sir! I was just mad at you for stopping me coming here. And then Billy McKnight got to hear about it an'e came to see me dad. He went mad, hey, and made me tell 'im what happened. I couldn't tell him I was gay. He would've killed me, I'm not just sayin' that. I would be dead – *really* dead! So I said you'd 'ad me and Con when we came to see you."

"Why did they believe that?" Matt asked. "I mean, you're a tough lad. I could never force you to do something you didn't want to do. It's ridiculous."

"I don't know. They just did. I couldn't believe it myself, but they just lapped it all up and I was happy 'cos I thought I was off the hook."

Mary interrupted: "They believed it because they wanted to believe it."

"Yah," Piet added. "The heterosexual majority wish to belief that we homosexuals can corrupt younk people. This is why they haf this clause 28 in your country."

"Billy McKnight had a tape recorder goin' when we was talking' an'e played it back and asked me if I would sign that it were true an' I had to say yes in front of me da'! I'm really, really sorry sir." His eyes filled with tears again. "I've ruined everythin'. Con's gone and you won't want to see me and no one on the park wants to 'ave anything to do with me and Ade won't come near me. I'll do anything in the world to make it right but please don't stop me coming to see you! *Please*."

Matt looked at Mary. "Jesus!" he exclaimed. "I hadn't a notion what was going on. I hadn't even realised you two were gay until Jim spoke to me! I'm so sorry, Bozzy. I've really let you down haven't I?"

Bozzy looked outraged: "No sir! It's me's let you down and now I'm suffering for being such a pillock."

"Look Bozzy. I'll promise you this. If I'm still free after this court case you will be welcome here any time."

"Thank you, sir! I'll do anything I can to help, sir. Anything."

CHAPTER 24

AUTUMN 1989, BIGOTS TRIUMPHANT

Bozzy had never written anything down but McKnight had recorded his fantasies about Matt, and the basis of the police evidence was a transcript of the tape. Bozzy amazed Matt. On his own initiative, he contacted the police and admitted that he and Con had made the whole thing up. He said that McKnight had encouraged him to make stuff up. Bozzy even managed to make the police believe that the DUP man had somehow promised to reward them for incriminating their teacher. The case was dropped like a hot potato and Matt didn't even have to appear in court. He believed he could go back to work in September and put the whole sordid saga behind him.

But that wasn't the end of the matter, for rumours were buzzing round the staffroom. None of Matt's colleagues said anything to him directly, at least at first, but he would overhear the ends of conversations or, worse still, they would abruptly stop as Matt walked in. Eventually, Robin took him to one side: "Matt," he started. "This probably isn't any of my business. But... people are saying things about you and I think you ought to know."

"What sort of things?"

He faltered. It was evident that he hated what he was saying. "You know what people here are like. You've lived here long enough."

Matt nodded.

"Some of the parents aren't very happy. They've some funny ideas about you. I presume.... no. I'm sure they're not right but, unless they're scotched, I think you could run into problems."

"They've tried that before," Matt replied.

"Last time it was a few hard-liners. Most folk here don't pay much attention to them. But now it's the influential ones. I don't need to mention any names. You know who I mean."

Matt had a good idea. They were the prominent businessmen, the clergy and their wives. They dominated every committee in town, including the school management committee. They couldn't get Matt the sack for being gay but they could make life in Ballycol uncomfortable.

"What do you think I should do?"

"I'm not sure. You have to convince them that you are trustworthy."

"How can I do that? I don't even know for sure what they're saying about me!"

"I really don't know," he admitted.

Gradually, a plan materialised in Matt's head. He had to lay his cards on the table. If they all knew what he stood for, what he was, their sense of fair play would do the rest. However Machiavellian they might seem, Matt reasoned, they were fundamentally good people. If he could show them he wasn't a threat, things might get back to normal. His first idea was to write a letter to the local paper, but it belonged to the anti-Matt faction and he suspected that his letter would never see the light of day. He briefly, toyed, with the idea of sending a letter to every parent but dismissed it as expensive and unlikely to succeed. He would have to involve the headmaster; perhaps he would think of something.

Mr. Wright was perfectly aware of what was being said: "One or two parents have come to see me. They have some vague idea that you try to 'recruit' youngsters. I have assured them that you wouldn't do any such thing. I would suggest you leave it alone. It'll soon blow over," he reassured Matt.

"I have to get it cleared up," Matt said. "I'm not so sure they'll let it drop. I have to put them straight. I can't do my job properly if I don't have their trust."

"Yes, yes, Matthew. I see that, but I don't see what you can do about it."

"I could go public," Matt suggested. "If they see what I am really like, they might stop gossiping."

"That would be most unwise. I do appreciate why you feel the need to get the issue out of the way and I respect that. But you are an employee of the school and it would be in the best interests of all concerned if you would forget any ideas you have in that direction."

Matt left; temporarily relieved.

Talking to Mary and Alex, made him feel like a real wimp; he had let his boss talk him out of clearing his reputation because it was the easiest course. Alex was dubious that it would have done any good, but Mary disagreed.

"I'll go in tomorrow," Matt vowed, "And I'll tell him that I want to go through with it!"

The headmaster was reluctant, but he conceded. "Would you help me set up a meeting, then?" Matt asked.

"If we have a one issue meeting the only people who will attend will be those with an axe to grind. No. What you want, if I have the correct impression, is to convince the silent majority."

Matt nodded.

"There's a parents' association meeting at the end of the month. I'll put it to the management committee that you should be allowed to address the meeting, if you really insist. Would that suffice?"

"That should do the trick. Thank you very much, sir." He was on his way out when he paused and said: "I don't relish the idea, you know. It's something I have to do."

All was settled. Matt would be put on the agenda. Good vibes came back. It seemed that the management committee were quite happy at the opportunity to get Matt on the spot. Possibly they thought they could crucify him in public. Strangely enough, Matt wasn't at all nervous about the forthcoming ordeal. About three days beforehand, he started jotting some ideas down but he thought it sounded too contrived; he didn't want it to look like he was reading a prepared statement.

Matt had seen the agenda being typed in the office. He was down as, 'Extraordinary business (Mr. Woodhead)'.

The meeting was in the school assembly hall. There were nearly two hundred there; less than a fifth of the parents. Not a very good turn out, Matt thought, but all the important people were in attendance. Mr. Houston was chairing the meeting from a desk on the stage. He called the meeting to order: "We have a lot of business to get through tonight, so we had better start...... Ladies and gentlemen, fellow parents, members of staff. Welcome to this meeting of the Ballycol High School Parents' Association. On the agenda tonight we have fund raising, as always," he joked. "Mr. Wilson is here from the Western Education and Library Board to tell us about the new national curriculum and we have to elect the parent representatives for the management committee. But first, we have a very serious matter to deal with." He paused and fidgeted. "Mr. Woodhead has been with us for ten years and in that time, he has proved to be a dedicated, if unconventional teacher. You will be aware of the unfortunate events surrounding him this year. I'm sure you also know that the accusations against him were dropped as being groundless. However, rumours have persisted so Mr. Woodhead has requested that he be given the opportunity to put his case. Mr. Woodhead is being very courageous in doing this and he deserves a hearing." Mr. Houston turned to Matt, "Mr. Woodhead."

Nervous for the first time, Matt made his way up onto the stage. "Thank you," he said, shakily, to Mr. Houston.

There they all were, spread out in front of him in their neat suits or twin-sets. Mary winked at him, Alex smiled.

"I'm going to find this very hard," Matt started. "I'm going to explain about something that most people don't like to think about, but I've been forced to face up to it. From when I was very young, I have known that I was different. It took me a long time to discover a name for the difference; it was homosexuality. I know that to many of you, it is a sin to give in to homosexual feelings. It's easy to think like that when you're not directly involved but, when you find that that's what you are, you have to come to terms with it. It took me a long time to realise that being gay didn't diminish me as a person. I have spent much of my life trying to carve out a life which I can live with the self respect that every human being deserves.

I discovered that being gay isn't something to be ashamed of; I shouldn't have to hide it.

I know certain of you have objected to having an openly homosexual man teaching your children but I have continued because I know that it can do them no harm. Like any teacher, I have professional standards. The welfare of my pupils is my prime consideration. I hope I'm not inflating my own significance when I say that I believe that their understanding and tolerance of minorities is enhanced through contact with me.

I had expected complications through being open but the nature of those complications has been a great shock to me. The most troublesome people have been those with their own sexual confusion. They seem to be drawn to me and, often, they end up by making life difficult for me. Unfortunately, I can never turn away someone who seems to be in trouble; this was nearly my downfall. I am not going to speculate on why those boys made up stories. Suffice to say, they were troubled youngsters and they needed help. My mistake was to think I could help without being dragged into their problem. It's not fair to say anything more about them but, if the same thing happened again, I'm sure I would try to get them the support they need. So there you have it. I am gay, I'm not ashamed of it and I care deeply about people."

Matt stood, surveying the silent crowd. "If you want to ask me any questions, I'll try to answer them as best I can," Matt said.

No one spoke up for a while and Matt thought he was going to get away with it, when Simon's mother stood up.

"Matthew," she started. "You and Simon were very good friends when he was at the school."

Matt nodded.

"I hope you don't mind me saying this. At first, we were worried about him. We did wonder... Well, I think you can understand why. I would just like to say that we had nothing to worry about. Matthew has been a good friend to our son. He has been a stabilising influence on him." She looked a little embarrassed, said, "That's all I wanted to say," and sat down.

Hands started going up all over the hall.

The first difficult one came from Mr. Catterson; he had several sons in the school: "What worries me is our children. I don't want my sons being influenced. I mean I don't want them turning queer. Having people like Woodhead there, teaching them. Well I mean, they have to be at risk, don't they? It's not right, it shouldn't be allowed," he shook his head, "that's what I think!"

"I do understand your worries," Matt started. "I think it stems from a misunderstanding of the nature of homosexuality. No one knows why someone is homosexual. All that is known is that a person is gay or they are not gay. It can't be prevented or caused by things that happen to us as we are growing up. Look at myself. All the influences that were on me were trying to push me into the heterosexual way of life. All it did was tear me between what I was and what I was being told to be. If every person I ever came into contact with couldn't turn me, a natural born homosexual into a heterosexual, how could being taught by one homosexual turn a heterosexual into a homosexual?"

Mr. Catterson wasn't letting Matt get away that easily. "Trouble is, it's fashionable to be queer nowadays. Youngsters are going to be attracted to it because it's different..., like drugs."

"Honestly Mr. Catterson. I don't think any youngster that knows anything about the sort of things that have happened to me could possibly be drawn to being gay as an attractive alternative to the usual life style."

"Why have the government passed that law then?" he demanded. Some parents mumbled in agreement.

"You're referring to clause twenty-eight of the local government act, I imagine. It was introduced in May last year in England and Wales. It says that no local authority can do anything that could promote homosexual relationships as a preferable alternative to heterosexual relationships. The law is based on the mistaken belief that, by telling someone about homosexuality, you can turn them into homosexuals. When drafting the bill they never consulted experts in the field to see what the professional point of view was; the vast majority of professionals would have told them that the whole premise of the law was wrong. Papers like the Sun and the Star have spent the last ten years whipping up hatred against us to sell more newspapers. Many people are afraid of us and they love to read how dreadful we are. Section twenty-eight, as it was, was a government ploy to gain easy popularity by appealing to the prejudices of tabloids' readers!"

Mr. Catterson was not impressed: "That's an exaggeration! They wouldn't waste time passing a law if it wasn't needed! There's a reason for it. It's there to stop people like you!"

"With respect. That law was hastily cobbled together. It's so badly worded that it's practically impossible to prove that someone has breached it. It's an embarrassment in a so-called civilised country and the government knows it. I don't think they would let anyone use it!"

"Mr. Wilson," another man said. "You are the local authority representative here. Surely by employing this man you are breaking this law."

The man from the board looked taken aback. "I can't answer that at present. I would have to look into it."

"I can answer that very simply," Matt said. "Number one, the law does not apply to Northern Ireland and, number two, I am not promoting homosexuality in the way the law proscribes. Yes, I talk about it honestly to some of the senior classes, but since when has it been against the law to tell students facts?"

"What if a youngster thinks he might be homosexual? Not that any of mine would," Mr. Catterson hastily assured the hall. "Having you talking about it might make them decide to try it. They would never know about it if it wasn't for you and they would grow up normal."

"You mean you would prefer it if a gay child spent his or her life in the misery of having to pretend they were heterosexual just to satisfy your desire for them to be socially acceptable?" Matt's gore was rising and tears were getting dangerously close. "If that is loving your children I pity them, I really do. I thank goodness that my parents are not like that. All they ever wanted for me is that I was happy and I have had nothing but love and support from them."

That actually got a little round of applause and Mr. Catterson shut up. An elderly lady in a neat red dress stood up, Matt recognised her as one of the workers in the Oxfam shop. "A man's moral behaviour," she started haltingly, "does affect his ability to do his work. The bible says, As a man thinketh in his heart so is he. His moral behaviour affects his whole outlook. Teachers should be the cream of morality, particularly when teaching young children. The word of God states; If a man also lie with mankind as to lie with womankind both of them have committed an abomination. They shall surely be put to death. And their blood shall be upon them. Leviticus, Chapter 20 Verse 13," she concluded, triumphantly.

"That's the Old Testament!" Matt complained. He was on shaky ground. Matt did not want to get bogged down in theology. "It was written for a nomadic people, thousands of years ago. What relevance has that to today?"

"We are all accountable to God. It's what He says is right. If we hadn't got the bible and we couldn't hear his word we wouldn't know we were doing wrong."

Someone, from another part of the hall, shouted. "If you take it literally, you should be stoned! According to the same chapter, we should treat women in red dresses the same way!" That got a brief chuckle from some quarters.

A skeletal man stood up. He spoke slowly, sepulchrally, "It's against God's law and it's against the human nature. It's a slow suicide of the human race. The more homosexuals, gays they like to call themselves, there are around, the sooner will be the end of the Human race!" He paused to let his message of doom sink in.

Mary spoke up, "How are gays going to destroy the world?"

Matt knew the answer; it was going to be A.I.D.S. Though why the disease God sent to punish gays was going to miss the target, so to speak, and wipe humankind out, Matt was interested to hear.

"If they are not practising normal, intermarriage, sex. They are not producing mankind!" he explained.

Matt was flabbergasted. "But everyone knows that this world has an appalling problem of overpopulation. If your theory was even partially true, gays would be doing the world a favour by reducing the rate at which the population was growing!"

"I think you will find that, very soon, homosexuality is spreading quicker than the increase in the Human race. And once the turn around comes and mankind is on the decline, we will not be able to stop it! The sooner we take heed to the wellbeing of our spiritual side, with our ways of life, the better the country will be and there will be less disease. This gay practice has to be stamped out the same as the A.I.D.S. has to be stamped out." The horrid man looked round the room as if he was expecting rapturous applause but all he heard was a few calls of, 'Here! Here!' and some solitary claps.

Mrs. Hamilton, the Church of Ireland minister's wife, was next to speak. She commanded great respect in Ballycol society and they waited in a hushed awe for her to pronounce on the issue. She spoke slowly and clearly, enunciating all her words like a nineteen fifties, B.B.C. announcer: "It isn't intolerant to uphold Christian values. What's wrong with this country at the moment is that we have a very sad society with sloppy standards." She paused for her words to sink in. "Anyone in a position of responsibility; a teacher, a minister, a doctor, a politician or whatever, should be like Caesar's wife; above suspicion. The sadness at the end of all this is AIDS. I'm very compassionate. If a person is born homosexual or lesbian or whatever, that's a great sadness. But I was in the army and I suffered greatly under people who were lesbians; physically and mentally. It was a real torture and I was glad to get out!"

"Do you think that to just be homosexual is, by definition, to have sloppy standards?" Mary asked.

"If they are practising it's worse than sloppy," she smiled smugly. "I'm trying not to be too intolerant. But, you know, the Greek Periclean Government fell due to sloppy morals, the Roman Empire fell for the same reason and the kind of moral society that we have in Britain today is fast going the same way."

"But The Church of England embraces homosexuals as a group." Mary objected. "It doesn't say that they are exercising sloppy standards by being practising homosexuals."

Mrs. Hamilton didn't think much of that suggestion. "There are two lots of views. As a Christian, I am saying that we should stand firm on principles. Sloppy discipline, sloppy standards. Look at the kind of society we are creating! Example, not precept we were taught."

"So you say we should go back to Victorian standards, then?" Matt asked

"The Victorians pushed everything under the carpet; I don't think we should get back to that sort of society."

"Surely that's exactly what you seem to be suggesting we should do!" he tried to say

"We learn the hard way," she continued, in full flow now, "A.I.D.S. is one of the terrible hard ways that we're learning."

Matt didn't know which prong to refute: "Surely it would be swept under the carpet if you create the repressive environment you seem to want by making it totally socially unacceptable to be homosexual," he managed to say, at last.

"No." she insisted. "I said practising homosexual. A person can't help being born homosexual or, possibly, lesbian although what I saw in the army was that it bred lesbianism. Whether that would continue when they were out of the army, I don't know. I only think that practising homosexuality is wrong. You can't help the way you were born but you can have the moral strength not to give in to it!"

Matt faced her square on: "I have the moral strength to live my life as a gay man. I resent the assumption that, just because someone happens to follow one particular religious doctrine, they have the moral high ground. My morality is humanistic. I value everyone as an individual. I don't think less of someone because they happen not to share my viewpoint. A society can only thrive if different points of view are given fresh air to grow and develop. That's what democracy is supposed to be about. Isn't it?"

Mrs. Hamilton looked smug, but didn't bother to reply.

Another lady stood up and craved the chairman's attention. She was probably a parent too although Matt didn't recognise her. He braced himself for another onslaught of cruel Christianity.

"Mrs. Hamilton," she started, respectfully. "I read my bible." Mrs. Hamilton smiled condescendingly. "Canon Hamilton gave us a wonderful sermon a few weeks ago when he asked us to think what Christ would do if he came here amongst us now. He told us that Christ wouldn't be in the great houses of Ballycol."

Matt smiled inwardly; the Manse was a beautiful big Victorian mansion.

"The Bible was written hundreds of years ago and the language then was very different but, if Jesus were here, on earth today, I feel that he would go along with the gay people just as he did at the time when the Bible was written. And the New Testament, as far as I am concerned, is a book of love. And Jesus was a man of love. He would have gone along with the homosexuals, the prostitutes and the poor souls who have caught A.I.D.S."

She turned to Mrs. Hamilton. "A.I.D.S. isn't a curse on the gay people any more than cancer was a curse sent to punish my dear husband. It doesn't matter if they are this, as long as they do their job properly. Mr. Woodhead taught my daughter to respect all sorts of people and she's nursing the A.I.D.S. people in London now. A lot of those are the gays. She says that it's the most worthwhile and fulfilling thing she has ever done. She would never have thought of applying for that job if he hadn't taught her."

It dawned on Matt that the daughter must be Sophie Walker. He remembered her father dying; she was emotionally fragile for a long time afterwards. She got very involved with the Scripture Union and became quite evangelical on the quiet. She did 'A' level biology, and Matt and she wasted hours of his teaching time arguing over moral issues. Matt had thought that she had left school thinking he was a hopeless soul bound for eternal damnation.

"What about this A.I.D.S then," a young man asked. "What if he gives it to our kids? What then?"

Matt smiled indulgently. He had been expecting this one. "For a start, I'm as certain as I can be that I'm not carrying the virus and...."

"How do you know that." the young man demanded. "It seems to me that it's the homosexuals who are spreading it."

An alarming mutter of approval rumbled round the hall.

"I know how it is caught," Matt insisted. "And I know I haven't done anything to catch it."

"That's not what I heard!" the man scoffed.

Matt couldn't believe what he was hearing. He glared at his accuser, "I assure you it's true. But, even if I did carry the virus, the pupils would be in no danger, isn't that so Doctor Henderson?"

Doctor Henderson had been sitting, listening, in the corner, now he stood up and spoke: "Medically, you can't say there would be no chance but the likelihood is small of an infected person passing the virus on through normal social contact. Yes."

"And the chance is so small as not to be worth worrying about, isn't it?" Matt added.

"Well." the doctor said slowly. "It's very small but it is there!"

"So if he has it, there is a chance that our children could get it!" the young man shouted.

"A small chance. Yes," the doctor admitted.

Matt could have killed him. Why did he not tell them that no-one had ever got HIV from normal social contact, as far as anyone knew?

"Have you been tested?" the young man challenged.

"That's my business."

"He's afraid to tell us!" he sneered. "Perhaps he has something to hide!"

Another unpleasant ripple ran through the audience; it was getting nasty.

"I've nothing to hide!" he blurted out. "I'll take the test to prove it, if you like!"

Matt's thoughts were cut short by a strident voice, "MATTHEW WOODHEAD. You have become a tool of the dark power himself!"

To his amazement, his former school friend, Aaron was standing at the back of the room. He had embraced the Reverend Ian Paisley's politics and religion at university but, until now, Matt had heard nothing of him. He wore a big black gabardine, which flapped behind him like the tattered wings of some avenging angel, as he strode towards the front: "In Paul's second letter to the Corinthians, chapter eleven, he warns that Satan himself masquerades as an angel. How much easier is it, then, for his agents to pull the wool over the eyes of the Godly? But Paul tells us that they will reap their just deserts in the fires of Hell! And in One Corinthians, chapter six, he says, Nor abusers of themselves with Mankind shall inherit the kingdom of God. The sodomist is against the law of God."

Matt's erstwhile friend pointed accusingly at him. "I came here tonight to tell you about this man" he bellowed. "I had the misfortune to attend school with this degenerate. It may be hard for you to believe this now, but he was a good and innocent youth. But the school we attended was a Godless institution and I watched as his innocent mind was corrupted by the agents of the devil. Don't think that he is the only one. This school is like any other in this corrupt nation of ours," he boomed. "It is a nest of sinners, a breeding ground for every vice Satan has dreamed of. To stop the same fate befalling your children, if you don't want them to end up wandering hell, in torment like this lost soul, get your children out of this cesspool of sin. The Free Presbyterian church of Ulster has a school in Annaghry. There, children are taught in a God fearing institution where you can be sure that there are no sodomites or any other sinners dedicated to the corruption of your children." At this, Aaron gently bowed his head to indicate that his sermon was over. A murmur went round the room, whether of approval or disapproval Matt couldn't know.

Mr. Houston called the meeting to order. "It is very nearly nine o'clock. Unless anyone has anything else to say, I think we should move onto the next item on the agenda. I think we should thank Mr. Woodhead for coming here tonight and being so frank with us. As I said earlier, he had no obligation to come here and I think you would agree with me that he has helped by allowing some, er, very diverse points of view to be aired."

Matt realised that to stay any longer would be to get caught up in the tedium of coffee mornings and a lecture about the new national curriculum. "I need a pint," he said to his friends.

"So do I!" Mary grinned, so they sneaked out and headed for Micky's.

"Well, how do you think it went?" she asked as they settled down to their drinks.

"Don't know. There were some pretty intransigent points of view, weren't there? It's quite frightening to discover that people think about you like that. What about that grubby little man with his extraordinary views on the world population problem?"

"I thought he was going to demand the final solution for gays!" Alex said.

"If he'd had a few minutes more he would have had a lynching mob out for me. I couldn't believe Aaron turning up."

"Who was he?" Mary asked.

"A guy we were at school with," Alex explained. "Used to be one of our mates. I'm telling you, he never gave us any notion he was like that when he was out boozing and screwing with the rest of the gang."

"Guilty conscience," she grinned. "Probably regrets all the hell raising he did as a youngster and is trying to make life hell for other people to make amends. But what I don't understand is, that if he isn't connected with this school, how did he come to be there?"

"The D.U.P. Mafia, I suppose. There are plenty of them in this school. I suppose it went through the grapevine and he heard it."

"You don't suppose it could have been the other way round, do you?" she asked.

"What are you getting at?"

"Could he have been stirring it for you here. It could suit them very well to have the school's morality questioned. They're trying to get that Free Presbyterian School going in Annaghry. They might think this is just the sort of issue to get iffy parents to switch!"

"Well, to be quite honest, I'm happy to see them go!"

"I'm not," she cautioned. "How can we ever hope to have any tolerance if parents only allow their kids to mix with other bigots of the same type? You are the first one to rejoice at the increased proportion of Catholics at the High School. It's a bit hypocritical to say you don't want a particular Protestant minority in the school, isn't it?" she beamed.

"I suppose you're right, but there ain't a lot we can do about it, they're determined."

"There is, actually," she assured Matt. "If the school makes an effort not to isolate the Free Presby. kids, make sure they feel happy in the school, they won't want to be moved. Think about it!"

Matt nodded, thoughtfully. "Anyway, how do you think Aaron went down with the parents?"

"If they already share his views, they probably thought he was wonderful. I don't think there was that much support for him, though. They didn't show much favour for any point of view, really, but I think most listened to the arguments. Any of them with an ounce of fair play would see that the religious cranks were just that."

"I don't know," Matt worried. "Mrs. Hamilton probably said what a lot of them were thinking. We'll just have to wait and see what happens. I wonder, will the kids know all about it at school tomorrow?"

One or two more of the staff drifted in to Micky's. Matt could tell that they weren't over-impressed by the whole episode, but they made all the right noises and, by the time they left, Matt was feeling quite encouraged.

He couldn't bring himself to walk up the hill with the pupils next morning so he took the car. He was acutely self-conscious crossing the playground but, as none of the youngsters reacted unusually, he presumed they hadn't heard anything. In the staffroom, Matt huddled with his supporters not daring to sneak a look at the puritan faction.

Mrs. Hammond came over: "The Headmaster would like a word with you, dear," she informed Matt.

"Now?"

"If you can," she confirmed.

"Ah! Come in, sit down," he smiled.

"Well?" Matt asked, "What did you think?"

"As you know I was not in favour of the whole project and I'm not sure even now if it was a profitable exercise. However I have to concede that you did make a good impression on some of the parents. You probably made converts, in both directions. You have certainly succeeded in polarising opinion."

Matt grimaced.

"You heard about the attempted coup, later?"

"No."

"There were elections to the management committee and Mr. McKnight stood."

"Oh!"

"His platform was essentially that, if elected, he would ensure that you, and any other subversives, would be rooted out of the school.

He also assured them that he would work towards the eventual re-Protestantisation of the school."

"How did that go down?"

"Strangely, his anti-Catholic rhetoric was your salvation. By linking the two, he probably lost the support of many who would like to have seen you removed. When it came to the vote his defeat was overwhelming and, as a result, the message has gone out that most of the parents were in your favour. That *is not*, I am afraid, the case."

"How do you know?"

"When they said you spoke well, they meant dangerously well. You had better not say anything controversial for a while and hope that the whole affair blows over."

Matt nodded.

"There's one other thing, Matthew."

"What's that?"

"Just to put people's minds at rest, Doctor Henderson has offered to do an A.I.D.S. test for you. You say you don't have it. Why not prove it to them?"

Matt did not want to take an antibody test but, to keep the committee happy, he agreed.

If the headmaster was unimpressed by Matt's performance, the kids weren't. The junior forms were restless, but Matt wouldn't let them start discussing what they evidently wanted to. With upper sixth he had no such restraints. They were dying to discuss the last evening's events. Those who spoke up were supportive of what Matt had done; any who disapproved wouldn't risk saying so. He was under no illusion that their support was representative of the wider pupil opinion.

"The trouble is," Matt complained to his class. "I completely miscalculated. I thought that if your parents could see that I was a reasonable and responsible person, they would find it easier to accept me. What I hadn't taken into account was the depth of pure ignorance and prejudice I was plumbing. A lot of them genuinely see being gay as a choice, a moral perversion or a psychiatric disorder. Some even look on it as the work of the devil. You just cannot argue with those points of view. All I have succeeded in doing is making them think that I am dangerous. What I am doing now is exactly what they fear. They view my voice of reason as a dangerous influence which could corrupt young minds. I think I'm in bother, kids."

"They can't sack you, sir."
"There's more than one way to skin a rabbit!"
"What can they do?"
"I don't know. Doubtless, I will find out in the fullness of time."

CHAPTER 25
SPRING 1990, BETRAYAL

Easter was rapidly approaching when the head approached him: "I'm sorry to ask you Matthew, but there was a management committee meeting last night and Billy McKnight asked Doctor Henderson if you'd been for the test, yet." He had almost forgotten his rash promise at the meeting and didn't suppose that anyone had taken him seriously. His immediate reaction was to refuse but it *had* been his own suggestion. A few years previously, Matt wouldn't have contemplated taking the test; there were problems with confidentiality and he reckoned that you were better off not knowing anyway. However, the situation had changed; they were developing treatments and hospital records were tighter.

Had he not been so sure he was negative, he would have gone to the G.U.M. clinic in the Erne hospital, where he would have been counselled but he hadn't wanted the hassle of going into Enniskillen so, when Doctor Henderson offered to take a blood sample and send it for testing, he agreed. With hardly an unnecessary word, Matt's skin was clinically pierced and the scarlet sample was extracted.

Matt hadn't contemplated what to do with his negative result when it came as, it inevitably would. It was supposed to be used to allay the parents' fears of his infecting their children, but it wasn't exactly the sort of thing that you put in the Ballycol Advertiser. The headmaster would be the person to inform; it really was all very silly.

Barely a week after the test, he was asked to go to the head's office and Mrs. Hammond's demeanour warned him that all wasn't well.

Matt had never seen the head looking so terrible. His immediate thought was that he was ill: "Are you alright, Mr. Wright?"

The head shook himself out of a reverie: "Yes Matthew. I've just had some rather distressing news. Sit down... please. I'm afraid it's serious, Matthew."

He sat; silently waiting for the hammer blow.

"I've just had a visit from Doctor Henderson. He asked me to speak to you. He thought it would be better coming from me." He paused, took a breath and said, "The test. It was positive, I'm afraid."

It took a few seconds for what the head had said to sink in. He hadn't even considered this eventuality; he was indignant: "There must be a mistake. I... I mean it... it can't be. It's not possible."

Mr. Wright handed Matt a manila envelope. The formal confirmation was there in black and white. Matt hardly heard the head saying, "Doctor Henderson said that they double checked. You should contact the Erne for advice."

Matt stood up to leave.

"Are you alright, Matthew?"

"Yes, yes," he said, sounding more confident than he was.

"I'm dreadfully sorry, Matthew," Mrs. Hammond said as he distractedly passed her.

"I'll be fine," he smiled, wandering out into the bustling corridor.

How he taught that afternoon he never knew; all he could think of was how he had picked up the virus. Five o'clock found Matt muddy-footed, perched on a rock in the forest park. Grey water lapped desultorily at his seat; behind him, the black pines were steadily defeating the gloaming. Pin-pricks of light from the far side of the cove only served to make Ballycol more remote. Over and over, he puzzled, Who had given it him? Who had he given it to? Chris? Damian? Alex? Luc, that French soldier? It couldn't be Piet; he had always been scrupulous about safer sex. There was that guy he had screwed in Ballycol one night, could he have been the weak link? What if it *was* Luc? He was in the army and Matt could only guess how many women he'd screwed and 'le SIDA' was far more common in French heterosexuals. But that was back in seventy-seven; Matt didn't imagine it had got to France that early. His heart sank; it could have been Luc. Just because it wasn't identified, then doesn't mean it wasn't there. Jesus! He thought, I've probably given it to Chris, Alex and Damian; half the people I care about. He shivered; and not in response to the chill, damp wind which crept up from the lake.

Alex had the fire going in the living room and was glued to the six o'clock news. The smell of boiling lentils told Matt that Mary was busy in the kitchen.

"I'm sorry," Matt said, listlessly, as he entered the steamy room, "it was my turn tonight, wasn't it?"

"Yes Matthew, it was. But it's alright," she chirped, "I've a meeting tomorrow so you can do mine then." She smiled in a 'gotcha' fashion. "Where were you anyway? Working late?"

Matt shook his head: "I... went for a walk... needed space."

Hearing the quaver in his voice, she turned and put the clove of garlic down: "What's wrong, Matthew?"

"The test's positive."

"Ah!"

He shook his bowed head: "I don't know what to do," he whimpered.

"You look after yourself," she whispered. "You eat good food, you steer clear of booze and dope, you keep fit and you live until you're a hundred."

"I don't want to live to a hundred," Matt said, tearfully.

"Ninety-nine then."

Matt sniffed.

"You'll be fine, Matt, fine."

"But what about Alex?"

If she was alarmed, she didn't show it.

"He'll say the same as me, you know he will."

"He might not...... " he hesitated. "If I've given it to him."

"I'll have two of you to keep healthy then, won't I? I've been trying for years to get you both onto a healthy diet!"

"But Mary, what if you... "

She shook her head: "Can't have."

"I thought... "

"No."

"If I've given it to him he'll never forgive me; I'll never forgive myself."

"It could be the other way round, you know. Alex wasn't exactly a virgin before his accident and, who knows?"

"How will I tell him?"

"You'll think of a way."

Alex took it amazingly calmly. His concerns were entirely selfless.

"I'm worried for you, Alex."

"I'm not exactly overjoyed, myself, but it's a risk we took.
"Will you have the test?"

He nodded, tight-lipped: "I don't know if this is the right time to be telling you this, but here goes. I'm going to ask Mary to marry me."

Matt felt terrible.

Alex saw his reaction: "I'm sorry, Matty. I didn't think you would take it so badly. You know my feelings."

"No, of course I know," Matt insisted. "But this makes it worse! If you've got it, well..... how can you ever have kids?"

"I'm perfectly aware of the problem. That's why I'll have the test. She's got to know one way or the other when I ask her."

Once over the trauma of telling Alex and Mary, Matt had time to dwell on himself. He knew that lots of people lived for years with HIV without any ill effects but the spectre of weakened and emaciated men in the last stages of AIDS stalked his subconscious. He thought he could cope with the physical pain, that could be dulled by drugs, and he was surprisingly untroubled by the possibility of an early death. The waking nightmare was that of premature dementia. The fear would sneak up on him unexpectedly, freezing his blood, putting lead in his stomach and drawing a frosty veil of black hopelessness over him. He was in great danger of spiralling into a severe depression.

Matt would never have got through those first testing weeks without Mary and Alex. Mary knew what to say and when. She let Matt agonise so long, then pushed him on some positive point or forced him to analyse, then rationalize, his fear. Thanks to Mary the presence of the virus in Matt's blood was kept as just that. It wasn't a thunderbolt from God, it wasn't a certain death sentence and he hadn't suddenly become a pariah. It was there and Matt had to roll with it.

Alex was more sensible about getting a test than Matt had been. He did it the proper way and, when he returned from his second visit to the Erne, his relief was palpable. For a few brief days, Matt forgot his own problems and celebrated the engagement of his two dearest friends.

In the intervening weeks, he hadn't done anything about his other contacts. The next person to contact was Damian but a visit to his parents ruled that out. Not only did they not know where he was but, they frostily informed Matt, they didn't want to know where he was and, as far as they were concerned, he was no son of theirs.

The McDaid house in Rosemount hadn't changed one jot, nor had Mrs. McDaid. As always, Matt was made welcome: "Christopher's in Belfast now," she said, "He's married. Didn't you know?"

"No. We sort of lost touch. Has he a phone?"

Whilst she scurried off to find the number, Matt scanned the familiar parlour cluttered with the usual religious paraphernalia. Some things never change, Matt thought. A baby cried in another part of the house and Mrs. McDaid returned clutching a tiny baby and a page off a note block.

"Who's this," Matt smiled, poking at the baby.

"Danny and Sandra's," she beamed.

Matt peered at the tiny face framed with wisps of red hair: "Is it a boy?"

"Yes, Patrick Daniel."

Patrick Daniel let out a strangled 'whaaa'.

"I'll leave you to it, Mrs. McDaid. I'll let myself out."

Chris was not pleased to hear Matt's voice and it took him some time to persuade him to meet. The drive down to Belfast gave Matt ample opportunity to practice his approach but, when it came to the crunch and Chris was sitting there in front of Matt in a neat, modern flat just off the Falls Road, Matt dried up.

"Well. What is it that's so important," Chris demanded.

"I've had some bad news," Matt started. "I had an AIDS test and I'm positive."

Chris glared at the pale, nervous teacher with barely disguised contempt: "Well, I'm sorry, but I can't say I'm surprised. You've only yourself to blame. Why are you telling me, anyway?"

Matt couldn't look him in the eye. "I think," Matt stammered, "I might have caught it before I met you."

"Oh, that's fucking great!" he roared. "Fucking lovely, that. You dirty bastard!"

"That's not fair!" Matt shouted. "You know that Alex and Luc were the only ones before you."

"And your bloody Dutch poufter. And how many others that you didn't tell me about? You sicken me, you do. It was the worst thing I ever did, getting mixed up with you and now, when I thought I had shaken you off, this happens."

He was pacing like a caged lion gripping his forehead. He swung round stamped his foot and yelled, "Shit, shit, shiiiit!"

"It wasn't like that, it wasn't. I promise you. Alex and Luc *were* the only ones and Alex's clear so it must have been Luc. He was a soldier and he raped me. Remember?"

"I shouldn't have let you," Chris raged. "You seduced me. If I had just listened to what common sense told me I would have known."

"Come off it, Chris. You can't put it all onto me! I seem to remember that you had something to do with it!"

"I was young. I hadn't sorted myself out. If my kid has got AIDS I swear I'll do for you."

"What kid?"

"We've just had a wee boy."

"Congratulations."

"Phah! From you, that sounds a bit hollow."

"There's one thing, anyway. If she had had it they would have found out at the hospital and I'm sure they'd have told her by now, so she must be O.K. and, if she is, you probably are."

Chris towered menacingly over Matt: "For your sake, it better be. I don't want to see you again. *Ever*. Now fuck off."

It was only a short drive down the Falls Road but every menacing yard seemed like a mile. Chris said he would do for Matt. Perhaps Paddy wasn't the only one involved in terrorism.

"Mr. Wright was looking for you," Alex said.

"He came here?"

"Aye. He said to ring him when you got back. I've got his number somewhere."

"It's alright, I know it. What did he want?"

"Search me."

Matt always liked the school in the holidays. The corridors and classrooms looked so much tidier without the kids.

"I'll come straight to the point, Matthew. The management committee are not happy about you teaching. They are worried that you could infect the kids."

"That's ludicrous! Didn't Doctor Henderson tell them that there was no way that I could?"

"Well no. Actually he said you could if you cut yourself or something and in science or when you are mountaineering that's a definite possibility. This isn't a very pleasant thing to say but Doctor Henderson explained that it can affect the brain, and he said that you were increasingly likely to have little accidents. They're concerned, Matthew... and so am I."

"But I'm perfectly well! I've never felt better in my life! I've stopped drinking and I'm exercising regularly. Look at me. Do I look sick?"

"It isn't as simple as that. If this gets out, the parents won't listen to reason. They're not going to expose their children to a risk, however small it may be; and there's the rest of the staff to think of. The caretaking staff have already said they don't want to clean your room."

"How the hell do *they* know about it? This is supposed to be confidential, isn't it?"

"I'm sorry Matthew. I don't know how they got wind of it and I didn't confirm their suspicions but they sounded pretty certain."

"Basically, you're saying that it's only a matter of time before the whole town knows."

He nodded.

"O.K. You win. What do you want me to do?"

"Matthew. It's not like that. I don't want to lose you this way but I *have* to think of the children. Doctor Henderson can get you released on health grounds. You'll get an invalidity pension and you'll be free to get another, non-teaching job if you want one."

Matt flopped back into the chair: "They've won, haven't they."

"Nobody's won, Matthew. I think you're better out of teaching, anyway. Doctor Henderson says that stress is one of the things that can bring it on and you can't deny that teaching's become a highly stressful profession."

It was true, Matt had to admit that. With all the changes, GCSE, the new national curriculum, local management of schools, internal assessment, new 'A' level syllabuses and on, and on, teaching had ceased to be a pleasure. You simply couldn't do everything and you ended up feeling that you had done nothing properly. Perhaps he would be better off! He would miss the kids, though.

"Not with a bang but with a whimper," Matt said, strolling into The Sunflower.

"What was it?" Mary asked.

"I'm out."

"We know that, dear. You never were very closeted."

"Seriously. They've given me the heave-ho."

"They can't. What for?"

"The rabbit is skinned."

"Matthew! You're talking in riddles."

Matt explained.

"You're not going to take it lying down, are you?"

Matt stretched out on the floor in reply: "I am now a man of leisure. Want another hand in the shop?"

CHAPTER 26
SPRING 1990, DERRYLAGHAN

Fin was Matt's one tenuous link with "normal" life in Ballycol. He seemed to have accepted Matt's story about being made redundant, and tried hard to integrate him into Ballycol society. It was difficult, because everything seemed to revolve about the Catholic Church. They went to discos at the local community centre, which were a far cry from the Orange hall *dances* of Matt's youth! For a start, there was a bar and, secondly, the crowd was young and urban. Fin and his friends seemed to know every girl in the place and it was never long before they were up, dancing. Fin usually got off, so Matt was invariably left nursing his coke. It was frustrating for him; there were so many gorgeous-looking fellers but they were terribly young and they all seemed aggressively straight.

Being fairly typical of Ballycol's youth, Fin didn't consider a night out complete unless he got a shag. After a particularly sordid encounter with a girl behind the community hall, Matt expressed his fears: "I hope you don't think I'm prying but, you do worry me."

Fin looked confused: "Why?"

"Well, did you use a condom last night?"

Fin shook his head: "She was on the pill."

"That's not the point."

"I know, I know but, you know…, in the heat of the moment... I'll be alright. There's nothing around here."

"How do you know?"

"Fuck! You'd hear if there was," he replied. "Anyway, didn't you tell me that most of the AIDS cases in Northern Ireland were gay?"

"Yes, but there are straights with it, you know, and I don't think you would hear about them."

"Come on Matt! This *is* Ballycol! *Someone* would know and soon *everyone* would."

Matt heard his retort with a shudder and wondered just how many people in Ballycol knew about him.

Fin used to go to the leisure centre for circuit training every day after work and, most evenings, he could be found pounding round the running track preparing for the innumerable athletics meetings he seemed to attend. Saturday nights would find him at a disco, but he would be up on Sunday, without fail, for mass followed by soccer. Now he wasn't drinking, Matt didn't like going to Micky's but Fin made him come, pointing out that half the regulars in Micky's were on the dole and he didn't want to see Matt sinking into the doldrums. They were to meet one Tuesday evening in June but Fin's athletics were reaching fever pitch and he was late. There were a few of the old faithfuls at the bar when Matt arrived. A couple of lads, friends of Fin's whom Matt half knew, were leaning at the bar. Matt sauntered over to them and tried to strike up a conversation as he got served, but they moved over to a table. Matt sat in splendid isolation until Fin buzzed in apologetically: "Sorry, had to get something sorted out."

"Pint?" Matt asked.

"I'd love a gallon of orange juice."

"Might manage a pint," Matt chuckled. "How did the meeting go, this weekend?"

"Blew it. Came second. I just didn't pace myself. I'll get it right next time. Liam and Jim are over there." Fin turned and nodded to his mates. "Should we join 'em?" he asked.

"I don't know. They weren't very friendly earlier."

"Mister hypersensitivity," Fin chided. "Come on."

They joined the couple, but they soon made an excuse and left. "See what I mean," Matt scowled. "They obviously don't want to be in my company."

"So it seems. Odd though; I thought they were O.K."

"I have lived here long enough to know that hardly anyone is O.K. when it comes to me."

Micky's had changed. It wasn't the bustling lively place of old and Micky wasn't his jolly self. "Where does everyone go, these days?" he asked Fin.

"Isn't one, really. Elis says Maguire's is good."

"Let's try there, then. See what the craic is." They drank up.

"Look at that!" Matt said, brandishing his empty glass.

"What?"

"I always get the same glass. See. It's got a chip out of the base."

Maguire's was a new pub in mock Victorian style. It had taken the younger crowd from Micky's when it opened but Matt hadn't complained; he thought Micky's was getting too much like a kindergarten anyway. Nevertheless, he was surprised to see how many of Micky's regulars were drinking in Maguire's. Fin pushed to the bar as Matt nodded acquaintance to a few familiar faces, but he was ignored. It was at that point Matt realised what was happening.

Fin returned from the bar: "What's up? You look like you've seen a ghost."

"Nothing," Matt replied distractedly. "I don't like the atmosphere in here, a bit heavy."

"It was you that wanted somewhere a bit livelier. I like it here; they do good lunches too."

A group of lads were watching Matt and talking animatedly. When Fin went to the toilet, it didn't surprise Matt when they approached en masse.

"Why don't you fuck off, you AIDS bastard," a burly youth challenged.

"Yeah," added another. "Fucking arse bandit. Spreading fucking AIDS all round this town. It was clean until you came. Filthy pervert."

"What are you on about? Just because I'm gay, it doesn't mean that I have AIDS."

Matt thought the thug was going to hit him but he seemed to think better of it. He squared up to Matt: "You walk out now or you get carried."

Fin was at Matt's shoulder. "We were going anyway," he said.

"And don't come back," the thug shouted at their retreating back.

Matt stalked out with as much dignity as he could muster but outside he shook.

"What brought that on?" Fin demanded.

"They think I have AIDS."

"Ah!"

Fin paused to consider his next statement: "There has been talk, you know."

"What sort of talk?"

"They're saying you lost your job because you've got AIDS."

"Do I look sick?"

"No, but you can't always tell. Look, Matt, there's a girl who works in the education in Omagh; she says it's all round the office."

"It's nonsense, it's all rumours, and you know what places like that are like."

"I know you, Matt. You're the worst liar I've ever met."

Matt cringed, "Oh fuck!" He stared at the ground for a moment, then looked at Fin and said, "Want a cup of coffee?"

The rumours had prepared Fin for the news but he was still shocked by the reality, and upset with Matt for not trusting him enough to tell him sooner. He took Matt's calmness as bravado and Matt found himself in the extraordinary situation of having to console Fin in his distress.

July was a scorcher and Matt's hair was getting bushy, so he popped into his usual hairdresser. Young Gail had Matt sitting in the chair when Trudy, the owner, bustled over and told Gail to see to Mrs. McCrea.

"I'm sorry," Trudy said. "We can't cut your hair."

"You don't look very busy."

"We're booked up all day," she assured Matt. "I'm sorry, Gail made a mistake."

"I'll pop in again, then."

Bitch! Matt sneered to himself as he walked out. He needed a drink. "A large Gin and Tonic, please, Micky," He called to his host's back.

Micky wavered, "I don't think that's a very good idea, do you Matt?"

"What?" Matt exclaimed. "Not you as well!"

"I'm sorry, Matt. I have to think about my other customers."

"O.K. I get the message," Matt sighed. "GOOD BYE!"

Matt needed space and Ballycol was closing in around him. He couldn't go home, he still hadn't told his folks; that would take time and preparation. He drove far west into remote Donegal. He didn't know where he was going until the Beetle chugged down Kilcar's steep main street. If he could cope with the hoards of Germans who invariably dominated the place, the hostel at Derrylaghan would make the perfect bolt hole for him.

The little cottage slumbered at the end of its leafy lane. A rank of racing bikes against the white-washed wall meant it was as busy as usual. As the Beetle growled to a halt the elderly owner puffed out to greet his new arrival: "Oh Matt. Welcome, welcome," he wheezed. "Come in and have a cup of tea."

"Have you room for a small one, Patrick?" Matt asked

"Yes," he lilted. "There's a bed upstairs. Two French went this morning so that left two spare and a Dutch boy has one of them, so there'll be room for you in the big room."

He ushered Matt into his cosy kitchen. Even in mid-summer, the range was lit.

"Sit down, sit down. I'll get you some tea." At that, he shuffled out leaving Matt to nod a greeting to a young woman reading a novel by the range and a tall, spare Nordic type studying a map.

Usually, Matt enjoyed the craic with Patrick and he loved trying to chat up the foreign boys but, today, he wasn't feeling very communicative. He hoped that Patrick didn't think he was being rude when, binoculars at his neck, he sidled out of the kitchen to stride off down the narrow lanes, where he revelled in the tranquillity of that summer evening. Tiny stone-fenced fields dotted the crumpled countryside. In some, contented cows stared placidly as Matt passed. He stopped to watch a frisky calf tupping its unflinching mother's udder. Uncut hay fields sparkled with dog daisies, clover and buttercups. Those already scythed were roasting to gold in the Donegal sun and, in one, a strapping young man was turning the hay by hand. Nineteen-ninety, Matt thought, and they're still doing that! The lane's walls were busy with tangles of flowers; heavy scented honeysuckle; mats of fragrant, purple thyme; sky blue buttons of scabious and glistening, pink stonecrops. Across the estuary, Slieve League's shattered ridge marched to its rounded summit. Tomorrow, Matt decided, he would go up. He would honour Piet.

The lane led down to a little sandy cove where gentle little waves ran up the beach. A few gulls cried in the distance and, just offshore, a pair of black guillemots bobbed. Everything is so simple and pure here, he thought, me and my contagion don't belong. Pierce me and I'll contaminate the whole fucking landscape. He closed his eyes and tears trickled down his sun-warmed face. The road to that point in his life stretched back in his imagination. It was dotted with disasters but, somehow, the triumphs were brighter. The faces of supportive friends outshone the scowls of the miserable, small-minded people he'd run across. Mary, Alex, Piet and all the rest were there but one beautiful face dominated them all; Damian; how he missed him. Matt owed it to him to let him know, but how?

It was a long walk from Derrylaghan to Slieve League but it was still and hot, he had all day and he loved those drowsy lanes. At Piet's cliff he recalled Piet's glorious nakedness dancing with the Atlantic breeze and then Matt was there, naked too, with Piet in spirit. The gentle wind stripped Matt's soul, layer by layer. He knew what he had to do.

CHAPTER 27

SUMMER 1990, AMSTERDAM

"I've made a mess of everything!" Matt moaned. "Getting near me is like the kiss of death!"

He was sitting in Lisa's flat in London. She had been Danny's girlfriend at college and she and Matt had become very close through Danny's decline into alcoholism.

"Now you're being melodramatic!" she reprimanded.

"It was for David! And look at the rest! There's hardly one of my close friends that hasn't suffered as a result of knowing me; look at Danny!"

She softened: "You really are feeling sorry for yourself, aren't you? Should I tell you something about Danny?"

"What?"

"Danny was the most self-centred bastard you could meet. Oh, he was great when you were with him, but he didn't give a tuppenny cuss for anyone but himself. His mammy had waited on him hand and foot and all he was looking for was someone else to do the same. I wouldn't play the meek Irish wife, mother and slave role, so he left me. He saw you in the same light. You worshipped him, so he could twist you round his little finger and, when he found he couldn't any more, he dropped you. He's too scared to face you now, because he knows he's been a shit and he doesn't want that poor girl he's conned into wedlock to find out how much of a shit he is."

"What about Chris? He never tried to use me but I seem to have blighted his existence."

"It was him that blew it, not you. If he was anything like his brother, he was lost before you started."

"There are people who have gay feelings when they are younger but who sort of settle into heterosexuality, you know. Even Tom Robinson is having a relationship with a woman at the moment."

"How old is Chris? Twenty-five, twenty-six?" she asked.

Matt thought about it and was shocked: "God, he'll be thirty-two now!"

"And do you think he's settled down into middle-aged heterosexuality?"

He shook his head sadly: "Poor guy. But Damian," Matt lamented. "I loved him so much and then I rejected him. I couldn't cope with a teenage lover. Jesus, some of the things he used to do really freaked me. He got high on listening to heavy metal at a million decibels. When his hair flailed away from his face you could see he was completely consumed by the music; the concentration was total. Once he leapt on the bed, knees astride me with his cock thrashing my face as he writhed to a riff. He actually *came* to the music; would you believe that?"

"He sounds amazing!" she giggled.

"He was. But I wanted Mozart and roses. I drove him to David and they were both destroyed. That's why I've got to warn him. I owe him that much."

"But how will you find him?"

"He sent me a Christmas card the year after he disappeared. There was a letter in it. He said I had to destroy it in case the Provos got hold of it, but he said that if there was ever a real emergency, a life and death matter, I should ring this guy in London."

"Well, what are you waiting for?" she grinned.

After a short ring, a man answered and Matt asked for Alan Harding.

"Sorry man," he drawled. "No dude of that name here."

"It was quite a long time ago. Maybe he's moved. Have you been there long?"

"Listen man, I don't know this guy."

"Is there anyone there who might remember him?"

"Maybe."

"Could you ask them?"

"Yeah, O.K. then," he said and hung up.

Matt dialled again and a Brummie replied. This guy seemed more together: "Hi. You the goy was talkin' to Carl?"

"Yes, he didn't seem to understand me."

"He's spiced. Who you lookin' for?"

"Alan Harding."

"Nope. I dunno 'im. Sure you got the right number?"

"Pretty certain. Look this is very important. I've got to find him. I'm not exaggerating when I say it's.... well... it's life and death. Can't you help me find him?"

"Tell you what, mate. You gimme your number an' if any of the goys know 'im, we'll ring ya. Awe right?"

"Thanks very much. That's very kind of you... Em... Where exactly are you?"

"Kilburn."

Great, Matt thought. Find an Irish man in Kilburn; needle in a haystack job.

"What now?" Lisa asked.

"Haven't a clue. I've got to find him, though."

"What about his parents?"

"They've disowned him. It was bad enough being a queer but, going with a policeman, then touting! Do you know that his mum got a priest in to say prayers in his bedroom because she found some gay porn after he'd gone?"

Lisa shook her head in disgust.

"I could look for him. I could go round all the gay bars."

"Have you any idea how many gay bars there *are* in London?"

"A lot, I know, but I have to start somewhere."

A quick glance at the London listing in Gay Times showed Matt the enormity of the task.

"You wouldn't get round them all in a week!" she exclaimed. "Look Matt. I don't want to be pessimistic but you must have considered the possibility that he's already... well... "

"Don't think I've not thought of that."

"That wouldn't be too difficult to check, there aren't that many that specialise in..." She was interrupted by the phone. "Always at the wrong moment," she grimaced, making a fist at the hall door.

Shortly, she bobbed round the door: "It's for you-hoo."

A thickly accented voice came over the hand set: "Matthew Woot-het?"

"Speaking."

"Goot. I am Joop; I am a friend of Piet Vondel."

"Can you come to Holland to visit him?"

Matt's heart sank, "What's wrong? Why didn't he ring me, himself? Is he alright?"

"No. I am sorry to tell you that he is not goot. Is it possible for you to come soon?"
"What's wrong?"
"He is very sick."
Matt was silent for a moment: "Yes, I'll come."
"Can you come on Thursday?"
"Yeah, that'll be O.K."
"You haff his new address?"
"In Delft?"
"No, this is in Amsterdam. Fifty-nine Singelstraat, it is at the south of the city. Come at twelf, pleese."
"Just one thing," Matt gasped, before he had chance to hang up.
"Yes?"
"How did you know I was here?"
"I made a telephone to your home in Ireland."

His old friend Henk, picked, Matt up at Rotterdam Centraal on Wednesday evening, Matt was to stay with him and Katelijne. "This is most strange," Henk puzzled. "Only three weeks ago I saw Piet in Delft. He said nothing of moving to Amsterdam and he looked very fine to me!"

"It can hit you very suddenly. The pneumonia can take hold in days. I wish he'd....."

"What?"

"Sorry, Nothing. Well, it's not nothing really. I was going to say I wish he'd told me he had it, but... I haven't told him I have."

Matt waited for the news to sink in but Henk took it in his usually phlegmatic way: "You are not sick at the moment?"

"Never felt better. But it's like that. I could be struck by something at any moment but, in the meantime, I get on with living life to its full."

"This is the correct attitude to this, Matt, I think."

At Henk's flat, his two kids swarmed all over Matt. He looked to see if Henk objected but he was smiling indulgently at the youngsters. Katelijne let them chatter to Matt for a few more minutes, then told them to say goodnight, which they did in giggled English before she hoisted them off to bed.

Fifty-nine Singelstraat was an undistinguished Amsterdam town house; small brown bricks and tall windows curtained with plants. A thin, bespectacled guy answered the door; he wore faded jeans and a shabby tee-shirt with an anti-nuclear slogan peeling off it.

"Hello," Matt smiled. "Er... I'm Matthew." Matt proffered his hand but the man acted as if he didn't notice it.

"Come," he instructed and, without a word of introduction turned and prowled into the depths of the house.

"How's Piet? Where is he?" Matt asked as he followed him down the dark passageway.

He pointed to the front room: "Wait, pleese."

Matt sat alone; green light dappled the bare wooden floor and minimalist furniture. Surly sort, Matt thought, I suppose he doesn't speak English very well. He could be upset; perhaps Piet's in a bad state and he's too preoccupied to be civil.

When the door opened, Matt stood up to see a striking young man with blond, spiked hair. "Matt!" he cried, flinging his arms around him. He kissed Matt full on his lips. Only one mouth in the world kissed like that!

"Damian! What are YOU doing here? Where's Piet? What's going on?"

"Piet's probably in Rotterdam. I'm sorry I had to lead you on like that but I had to be sure it was really you. I'm not Damian, by the way, I'm David, David Martins."

"I suppose the R.U.C. got you out."

"Did they fuck? I couldn't tell them anything they didn't already know." His face took on a disturbingly serious expression. "Matt, some fucker in the R.U.C. must have stitched David up."

Matt could hardly respond, his mouth flapped limply as he mouthed, "What?"

"Just what I said. I'm certain that someone in the R.U.C. tipped the Provos off."

"I don't believe it. Why should they?"

"You don't know the half of it, Matt. You wouldn't believe some of the things David told me. The depth of anti-gay paranoia in the police is sick! Some twisted bastard would do that. Being queer's worse than being a Fenian to some of them fundamentalists!"

"What did the police say?"

"I didn't tell them."

"But why not? That's exactly the sort of thing the Stevens enquiry was all about but worse, much worse!"

"Come off it Matt. If David wasn't safe, neither was I. No! I was getting out and quick."

"How did you do it? Disappear, I mean."

"Remember Stevie?"

Matt nodded.

"He was in London; I went there until I could find somewhere. Stevie's Alan Harding, by the way. He rang me as soon as he heard you'd been trying to find me."

"He lives there? That's a bit risky isn't it? Anyone could go there they would find him and you'd both be in danger then!"

He nodded his head solemnly: "He's been a good mate. Anyway, you're the only one I gave the number to."

"So how did you end up here?"

"Cut and dyed my hair, got a visitor's passport in Stevie's name and headed over with Joop, the guy who opened the door; this is his place."

"Is he your partner?"

Damian smiled mischievously, "Sort of." He chuckled at the way Matt's face fell, then squeezed his arm: "Don't be jealous, Matt. It's nothing serious."

Matt shook his head sadly: "That's not what I'm worried about." He drew his strands of courage together with a deep breath and embarked upon his catastrophic news. "I've got to tell you something really important."

Damian's face became serious: "It had to be bad to bring you looking for me. What's happened?"

"I had the test."

"Oh."

Matt nodded.

"But you're alright, aren't you?"

"At the moment, are you?"

"Aye," Damian said casually but with a questioning note.

"I was worried about you."

"I'm O.K., I told you. I'm fine."

Matt sat down heavily, rubbing his brow in an attempt to marshal his thoughts. "You know me, Damian. You, Alex and Chris are the only ones I've had unsafe sex with and the other two are clear."

At last, it dawned on him what Matt was saying. "No. No way! What about that French guy who had you? And the guy you told me about in Ballycol!"

"It couldn't be Luc. That was in seventy-seven! It just wasn't around then! And a straight guy in Ballycol in nineteen eighty-two was hardly likely to have had it, was he? I'm sorry. It has to be you."

"You're wrong, Matt."

"I'm not blaming you. I just want to warn you to be careful. You've got to look after yourself... and those you love."

"You're not reading me, Matt. I've had the test; I'm O.K. Thanks to you always goin' on at me, I've been dead careful. Well, I was. Then I got pissed and, well... you know...; I got a dose of something. I was shittin' myself, so I was; so I went for the test. They were dead on. It was only twenty-five Guilders, that's about eight quid, and I had the all clear in ten days."

Matt's face betrayed him.

"Matt!" exclaimed Damian. "You wanted it to be me."

"No! I'm really pleased."

"That's not what it looked like to me! Exactly why did you come looking for me? Did you want to *punish* me givin' you it?"

Matt was horrified: "No," he pleaded, tears welling up in his eyes as he collapsed onto a settee. "I didn't, I didn't. How could you think that?"

Damian sat next to Matt, cuddled him and gently kissed his forehead. "I'm sorry, Matt. I'm not being very kind am I? You must feel so shite."

Matt nodded and sniffed. "Mary and Alex have been great but they are very involved with each other, and they can't really know what it's like."

"So you wanted to find a fellow sufferer?"

Matt's head movement confirmed his suggestion, but the words stuck in his throat.

As they mulled over the events that had so dramatically shaped both their lives, two years of separation evaporated. Matt wanted to get Alex to intercede on Damian's behalf. He was sure that the police would want to root out whoever it was who betrayed David, but Damian was adamant that there was no way he would go back to the police.

"How is Alex, anyway?" he asked.

"Great. Still has difficulty walking but his speech is almost back to normal and he seems to have got his head together. In fact, he's more together now than he ever was."

"Has he decided, yet?"

"What?"

"Is he straight or gay?"

"He getting married to Mary!"

"So he's pretending to be straight, then," Damian sneered

Matt was defensive: "Don't be so cynical. He's bisexual."

"I see. The worst of both worlds. And maximum emotional trauma for you!"

Matt shook his head: "No, I've got over that now. I'm still very fond of him, of course, but I know he needs a relationship with a woman. I always knew that, you know. That's why I never really let myself fall in love with him."

They spent a relaxing afternoon strolling along the canals and lanes of the city and catching up on each other's news. They reached a triangular platform in pink stone which jutted out into the canal. Damian led Matt down to it.

"Do you know what this is?"

Matt didn't.

"It's the homomonument; it was built to commemorate the lives of all the gay people killed by the Nazis."

Matt surveyed the simple structure, and the limp roses strewn over it made sense to him.

"They don't need the Nazis, when I'm around," Matt mourned. "I'm a one-man exterminator. Look at what happens to gay people who come near me! Alex crippled; Con banished; Chris married; Bozzy destroyed; you exiled and David…."

Damian flung his arms round Matt and clung to him. "Shut up. Shut up!" he sobbed.

"I'm sorry. I didn't mean to upset you."

"I'm all right, honestly. But, Matt! None of it was your fault. Yes, we've all been damaged but not by you, Matt; not by you."

"Of course it was me! If none of you had ever met me you would be all alright."

Damian hugged him harder: "No, Matt. No. If we had never met you we would be all be safe, but fucked up in our respective closets. It wasn't you who damaged them; it was that fucked up society! Stop blaming yourself. Please, Matt, *please*!"

They stood in silence on the triangle, holding each other as if the world was trying to tear them apart. Damian sobbed gently as what he said sunk in through Matt's pain and guilt. He found it profoundly moving to hold the wonderful man in his arms in full view of the public, without the slightest fear of harassment.

Damian dried his tears and stroked Matt's hair, before running his hand gently down his cheek: "Don't go back, Matt. Stay here. I'll look after you and you'll be fine. You don't just have to keep physically fit, you know. Stress fucks your immune system and if you go back you'll have nothing but hassle! Just *being* in that fucking place could make you ill! Stay here with me."

"I can't. I've friends there, and commitments. I can't just walk out."

"Henk here, and Piet.... and me," he finished, quietly.

Matt gave him a wan smile.

"Come on," Damian whispered, "let's go home. I want to take you to my bed."

Matt looked at him in disbelief.

"What's up? Don't you want to?"

"I can't!"

"Of course you can! We'll be safe."

"I can't, Damian. It wouldn't feel right."

"Don't you like me any more?"

"I do but.... You've got to understand. I can't."

Damian looked at him with those beautiful, big, brown eyes: "I still get a kick remembering what it was like with you. Shit, Matt! I could lie awake all night just touching you. I've never met anyone like you since! You were always dead gentle with me! I loved David, but he was crap in bed! I was working on him, though, teaching him what I learned from you. I've missed you, Matt. That's why I tricked you into coming here." He slipped his hand inside Matt's shirt and kissed him again. "Come on Matt. Please."

Matt pulled away from him: "But that was before you knew I was positive!"

"For fuck's sake, Matt! It was you who gave me all the stuff on low risk sex! Don't you practice what you preach?"

"I did but, it hasn't done any good. I mustn't hurt you any more. I'm sorry."

He looked at Matt long and hard as if deciding whether or not to accept his refusal. "Sleep with me, then. Like the old days; just a cuddle and no sex? We'll be totally safe! *Please*."

So that night, for the first time in months, Matt slept wrapped in loving arms.

CHAPTER 28

SUMMER 1990, THE END?

In the drowsy, dappled light of morning Matt luxuriated in the warmth of Damian's body. All too soon he stirred, smiled at Matt and kissed his shoulder.

"Don't you have work to go to?" Matt remarked.

"Not today. I rang in last night."

"Presumptuous!" Matt mumbled, as he kissed him.

Damian's hand slid down Matt's side until he found his penis.

"Damian!" he pleaded. "Please, don't make it hard for me."

"That's just what I want to do."

Matt giggled: "You know what I mean. I can't, I'm scared for you."

"It's my responsibility. My decision. We can be safe."

"Give me time, my love. I'll come round, but, I'm sorry, I can't; not yet."

They lay together in silence for several minutes before Damian excused himself and slipped away to make breakfast.

When Matt came out of the shower, the aroma of fresh coffee was drifting up the stairs. On the table was fresh bread and Gouda cheese with caraway; Matt's favourite.

"There's one thing that puzzles me," Damian said. "If I didn't give you H.I.V., and none of the others have it, how the hell did you get it?"

"It must have been Luc; the French soldier."

"But you said yourself, that was in '77; it just wasn't around then, was it? And if it was him, surely me or Chris or Alex would have got it, wouldn't we? Are you sure there isn't anyone else it could have been?"

"There was the guy in Ballycol. I suppose it could have been him but I fucked him once and I don't think he had had gay sex before so it's pretty unlikely."

Damian fixed Matt with his soft, brown eyes. "He could have got it from a woman, you know."

"Suppose," Matt conceded.
"Exactly where *were* you tested?"

Two weeks later, Matt was on a train to Amsterdam. He would have stayed on with Damian but he had to go to Brussels for a two week computer course. Piet was on holiday in Greece, so Matt had ended up staying at Henk's for the last week. He was nearly there. The train stopped just short of Amsterdam Centraal and Matt could see the city bustling below him; yellow trams gliding in and out of the station square, tourist barges churning the canal, and thousands of people thronging the pavements. They were moving again; slowly slotting into the platform. Most people were up and ready to get off. With a hiss of pneumatics, the doors were open and the passengers were pouring out onto the platform. Matt didn't know which way to go so he followed the crowd down into an underpass. He didn't bother to look for signboards as everyone seemed to know where they were going. Soon, he was being swept along a dim, tiled passage. At a door was a bottleneck; one exit was blocked. A tall man dropped something, a wallet; Matt retrieved it and handed it to him.

"Austubleif!" he replied, and hurried on.

"That's alright," Matt smiled, but the man had rushed off.

That's city life, he reflected. No one notices you, here; you can live any lifestyle you want. Matt hadn't a clue which tram to get so he checked the route map. "Nieuwe Achtergracht, Nieuwe Achtergracht," he said to himself, "there it is. A one, a two or a five to Leidesplein."

It was a lovely, sunny day. He should have been sitting in a Leidesplein cafe sipping pils, not changing trams. He had to take a seven from there.

"Matt, Matt!" someone shouted, as he pondered the map.

He turned to the voice as loving arms wrapped round him and a strawberry-sweet mouth connected with his.

Matt smiled at Damian: "I thought you were in Brussels!"

His liquid eyes were reproving: "You didn't think I'd leave you to face this alone, did you?"

A tram rattled in. Damian punched Matt's arm: "Come on, it's this one."

They boarded, the machine pling'd as Damian punched his national strippenkaart for the two of them, and they found an empty seat. Matt sat by the window, Damian slid in after him and his warm, reassuring hand found Matt's clammy one.

"Henk used to call them crowling snakes," Matt said.

"What?"

"Trams. Rotterdam ones, anyway. He said they were a nuisance in the city. He called them crowling snakes; he meant crawling."

The tram was crowling up Leidesstraat; a narrow shopping street crammed with pedestrians, with a single track up the centre. Cyclists charged up and down, dodging the trams. Glad to get Matt's mind off the impending encounter, Damian said: "I saw an accident here last week. A cyclist was a bit slow getting off the tracks, his bike was mangled and he didn't look so good."

But Matt acted as if he hadn't heard: "Is it far, now?"

He squeezed Matt's hand: "You're going to be alright, Matt."

Matt pressed his forehead against the window and looked at the teeming people beyond. He felt a soft warmth on his neck and realised, with a shock, that Damian was kissing it.

"I can feel it in my bones," Damian murmured, "it's going to be alright. I'm with you, whatever happens." And he added quietly, "If you'll let me, I'll always be with you."

Matt couldn't look at him, he didn't want him to see the tears in his eyes, but he squeezed his hand to say thank-you.

Damian jerked him out of his reveries: "Come on, this is ours."

The next ride was short and they were there. How many male couples must have gone through these doors, reassuring hand in reassuring hand? Matt thought.

They were ushered into the office with courteous Dutch efficiency. A relaxed young woman smiled at them as they sat down nervously.

The result was imparted; swift, no frills. "Mr. Woodhead," she said gently. "Do you understand what I'm saying?"

Matt nodded a dazed head.

"A false result is possible but the chances are very low indeed," she explained. "If you require it, we can run another test but I would be satisfied that this is correct."

Now they are outside, blinking in the sun. "Come on, let's get back to my place," Damian says. "You've no excuses now, and we don't have to worry about safer sex any more!"

The End

The story continues in Book 3, 'Ulster Queens'.